STUDIES IN HISTORY, ECONOMICS AND
PUBLIC LAW

Edited by the

FACULTY OF POLITICAL SCIENCE
OF COLUMBIA UNIVERSITY

Number 537

AMERICAN INTEREST IN CUBA: 1848-1855

BY

BASIL RAUCH

AMERICAN INTEREST
IN CUBA: 1848-1855

BY

BASIL RAUCH, Ph.D.

Assistant Professor of History
Barnard College, Columbia University

NEW YORK
COLUMBIA UNIVERSITY PRESS
1948

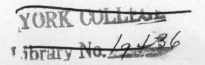

To

MY MOTHER

AND

FATHER

CONTENTS

ACKNOWLEDGMENTS

THIS book originated in a paper written for the seminar of Professor Allan Nevins at Columbia University. The author is deeply indebted to Professor Nevins for his constant encouragement and advice, and also to Professors John A. Krout and Dwight C. Miner for their helpful suggestions. The staffs of the following were particularly generous and efficient in helping with research problems: Columbia University Libraries, Harvard University Library, University of North Carolina Library, Boston Public Library, Boston Athenaeum, Duke University Library, Library of Congress, New York Public Library, New York Historical Society, National Archives. Special thanks are due Mrs. Natalia Summers, whose charm and learning made work in the Department of State Archives a distinct pleasure, and Miss Jean F. Macalister of the Reference Department, Columbia University Library. Professor Samuel Eliot Morison of Harvard University has kindly granted permission to use the John A. Quitman Papers.

B. R.

CHAPTER 1

CUBA: THE "TRANSATLANTIC TURKEY"

AMERICAN interest in Cuba originated in the relationships created by geography and economic, social, and political institutions. Long before the American people became independent, the imperial rivalries of Great Britain and Spain revealed the importance of Cuba as a key to strategic control of the Caribbean Sea, the Gulf of Mexico, the rivers that flow into them, and the lands whose shores they wash. Cuba became the most important producer of semi-tropical staples in the neighborhood of the English colonies in America. Those colonies became the nearest source of manufactured goods for Cuba, and of foods native to the temperate zone. The exchange of these complementary productions was frustrated by mercantilist policies that forced the trade of colonies into channels thought to be more beneficial to their mother countries.

During the later half of the eighteenth century, mercantilist control of American colonial trade weakened. First to overthrow the rule of their mother country were the British colonies, motivated in part by the desire to develop trade with non-British areas. Cuba on three occasions enjoyed temporary freedom from Spanish mercantilism. Britain captured Havana during the Seven Years' War, and an unprecedented prosperity resulted from the opening of trade with the British colonies. In 1763 Britain returned the island to Spain in exchange for the Floridas, but trade channels were kept partially open in spite of efforts by both powers to restore their monopolies.

The Spanish government in 1778 allowed its interest in humbling Great Britain to weaken its economic hold on Cuba. Open trade was permitted between the island and the new-born United States. Agents of American merchants established branch houses in Havana and traded flour, meal, salt fish and

meat for sugar and coffee. One of the leaders in the trade was
Robert Morris. Philadelphia became its chief North American
port. When Spain declared war on Great Britain in 1779, it
hoped to avoid direct aid to the American revolutionaries for
fear that the example would be disastrous to its own empire.
But the British Navy weakened Spanish sea communications,
food from the United States became a necessity of life for the
Cubans, and Spain allowed the island authorities to import food
and give hospitality to United States warships and privateers.
Thus the strategic value of Cuba to the United States was dem-
onstrated.

Congress attempted to strengthen these ties by appointing
Robert Smith, Morris' agent in Havana, commercial agent of
the United States, but the Spanish authorities refused to recognize him. They required that all business transactions take
place through the Royal Hacienda and insisted that the existing
trade relations with the United States were purely temporary.

After Yorktown, Rendón, Spain's agent in the United States,
discussed with Secretary of Foreign Affairs Livingston the
future commercial relations of the two countries. Livingston
proposed trade reciprocity between the United States and Cuba.
He pointed out that their productions were complementary and
that low duties and governmental support on both sides would
assure a very advantageous trade.[1] But Spain did not seriously
consider the proposal because it was apparent that reciprociaty
would make Cuba economically dependent upon the United
States and subvert the mercantile system by which Spain used
its political control of Cuba to exploit its economic life.

The Spanish government turned rather to restore Cuba to its
strict dependence on the mother country. It considered the
Floridas, which it had seized in 1782 and retained under the
Treaty of Versailles of 1783, essential buffers between the

1 Rendón to Galvez, Philadelphia, April 20, 1782. Quoted in Herminio
Portell Vilá, *Historia de Cuba: En Sus Relaciones con los Estados Unidos
y España* (Havana, 1938), I, 96.

United States and Cuba, and tried to extend their boundary northward beyond the thirty-first parallel. In 1784, Cuban importation of foreign flour and meal was forbidden by a Royal Order, a blow at the most important export of the United States to Cuba. The death in 1788 of the " enlightened despot " ·Charles III was followed by a severe reaction against all concessions to a freer economic and political life. When Congress named Oliver Pollock, long a resident of Cuba, commercial agent in Havana to succeed Robert Smith, the Spanish authorities not only refused to recognize him but then imprisoned and expelled him.

Yet it was impossible for Spain to break completely the ties that had developed between its colony and the North American republic. Pollock wrote that necessity obliged the authorities in Cuba to admit provisions from the United States.[2] Sugar production in the island had expanded and become dependent on refining machinery imported from the United States. Consequently, Spain allowed the machines to be imported free of duty, although only in Spanish vessels. In 1794, revolution in Haiti, which had been the chief source of the world's sugar, opened new markets to the Cuban planters. They demanded greater supplies of Negro slaves, and Spain allowed foreign vessels to bring the victims from Africa. American shipowners became leaders in this business.

The European wars that began in 1793 forced Spain further to relax the restrictions on colonial trade. Food again found a ready market in Cuba as American merchants were permitted to take advantage of Spain's weakness. Cuba bought American textiles in increasing quantities. Spain was forced to permit foreign ships, chiefly American, to carry Cuban exports to Europe and European and American cargoes to Cuba. The traffic was heavily taxed by Spain but nevertheless flourished under the stimuli of inflation and shortages.

2 Pollock to Livingston, Havana, December 14, 1783. Department of State, *Consular Despatches: Havana*, I.

This lively trade depended on the whim of the Spanish authorities in Cuba and was not protected by the Pinckney Treaty of 1795 in which Spain made important concessions on other questions. Spain established consulates in the major cities of the United States to facilitate the trade, but when President Adams tried to reciprocate by appointing Daniel Hawley in Havana and Josiah Blakely in Santiago as consuls, the Spanish authorities refused to recognize them and protested, although they did not expel them. Piracy, smuggling, and injuries to Americans were common. American warships cruised in Cuban waters to protect United States merchantmen. The undeclared war with France threatened to involve the United States with Spain, France's ally. John Morton, sent by Adams in 1799 to replace Hawley, was received cordially by the Captain-General who governed the island, but was not officially recognized as consul.

A Royal Order in the same year forbade the trade between the United States and Cuba. Spanish officials, including the Minister to the United States, protested that the Order could not be enforced, and the Captain-General informed the Spanish government that he did not intend to enforce it. Cubans and Spaniards in the island united in demanding trade with the United States to preserve the life and prosperity of the colony. The trade worked a great change in many phases of Cuban life. George C. Morton, temporary agent of the United States, wrote to Secretary of State Madison in 1801:

The wealth and importance of this colony, has increased during the few years that it has been open to the American trade, in a most astonishing degree, with regards to the habits of industry, knowledge of commerce, general civilization, and comforts of life, and for the continuance of which trade, after Peace shall take place, many petitions have gone forward to Court.[3]

3 George C. Morton to Madison, Havana, April 21, 1801. Department of State, *Consular Despatches: Havana*, I.

But after the Peace of Amiens Spain again tried to cut the ties between her colony and the United States.[4] Restrictions were revived, Blakely was imprisoned for smuggling, and American traders and shippers received harsh treatment. Spain admitted Cuba's continuing need of foreign flour, but granted the exclusive privilege of importing it from the United States to the Count de Mopox y de Jaruco. Other trade continued by resort to illegal methods and by payment of exorbitant charges.

Thomas Jefferson was the first President of the United States to contemplate annexation of Cuba as a solution of the strategic and commercial problems it presented. His purchase of Louisiana offended Spain, but it could do nothing about it except invite Spaniards from New Orleans to settle in Cuba. These, together with emigrés from Haiti and the later revolutions on the Spanish mainland, considerably strengthened the pro-Spanish party in Cuba. James Monroe, United States Minister in Madrid, tried to obtain Spanish agreement that West Florida was included in the Louisiana Purchase. Failing in that, he advised Jefferson to take it by force and embargo all the Spanish colonies in America. Jefferson submitted the question to his cabinet. Gallatin opposed a policy that might involve war with Spain. But Jefferson was not frightened by the prospect. He told Anthony Merry, the British Minister to the United States:

> in the Event of Hostilities he considered that East and West Florida and successively the Island of Cuba, the possession of which was necessary to the Defense of Louisiana and Florida, ... would be an easy conquest ....[5]

The administration sent Henry Hill to Havana to take the place of Vincent Gray as agent, because the latter had been imprisoned, and secretly to learn what military and naval forces

4 John Morton to Madison, Havana, December 25, 1801. *Ibid.*

5 Merry to Mulgrave, November 3, 1805. Quoted in J. F. Rippy, *Rivalry of the United States and Great Britain over Latin America: 1808-1830* (Baltimore, 1929), 72.

Spain commanded in Cuba.[6] When Spain complained that Miranda's filibuster expedition had been organized on American soil in defiance of the warnings of the Spanish Chargé d' Affaires, Jefferson wrote to Madison that if the United States went to war with England, he would rather have war with Spain than not, because the Floridas, the " rich pabulum " offered by Spanish commerce to privateers, and Cuba would all be available for the taking.[7]

War with the United States became out of the question for Spain when Napoleon invaded the peninsula. The collapse of the home government gave Spanish-Americans the chance to seize control of the colonial administrations. They were quick to grasp it everywhere except in Cuba. A mass meeting in Havana passed a resolution to create a governmental junta, but success was prevented by the opposition of Spaniards and wealthy Creole planters who feared the consequences of revolution to their own position. The new situation led the Jefferson administration to formulate a policy towards Cuba that was pursued by the United States government throughout the nineteenth century. The cabinet adopted a resolution that influential personages in Cuba and Mexico should be told:

> If you remain under the dominion of the kingdom and family of Spain, we are contented; but we should be extremely unwilling to see you pass under the domination or ascendance of France or England. In the latter case, should you choose to declare independence, we cannot now commit ourselves by saying that we would make common cause with you, but must reserve ourselves to act according to the then existing circumstances; but in our proceedings we shall be influenced by friendship to you, by a firm feeling that our interests are intimately connected, and by the strongest repugnance to see

6 Hill to Madison, Havana, September 18, 1805. Department of State, *Consular Despatches: Havana*, I.

7 Jefferson to Madison, Monticello, August 16, 1807. Jefferson Papers.

you under subordination to either France or England, either politically or commercially.[8]

The Embargo Act of 1807 weakened Jefferson's Cuban policy. The Spanish authorities in the island took advantage of the American prohibition of exports to lower duties on imports from other countries and to raise discriminatory rates on ships and cargoes from the United States. Britain thereupon assumed leadership in trade with Cuba. But Jefferson's chief interest was in Cuba's strategic value. When war with England approached, he advised President Madison that the United States might well pay Spain the price of not aiding revolution in the rest of Spanish America in exchange for Cuba and then:

> I would immediately erect a column on the southernmost limit of Cuba and inscribe on it a ne plus ultra as to us in that direction . . . . Cuba can be defended by us without a navy, and this develops the principle which ought to limit our views.[9]

President Madison appointed as consul in Havana William Shaler, whose Cuban friends in the United States assured him that revolution was imminent in the island.[10] Shaler found that two revolutionary groups were active. The Creole planters were fearful that violence would give their slaves a chance to revolt. For a time, they considered a scheme to make Cuba a province under a Mexican monarchy with Britain as protector. But in the Cortes at Cadiz, British influence was on the side of abolitionist measures which the Cuban delegates and the Havana Cabildo opposed. The latter organization, representing chiefly wealthy planters, authorized José de Arangó, Treasurer

8 Quoted in Henry Adams, *History of the United States during the Second Administration of Thomas Jefferson* (New York, 1890), II, 340-1.

9 Quoted in J. H. Latané, *Diplomacy of the United States in Regard to Cuba.* American Historical Association Annual Report, 1897 (Washington, 1898), 220.

10 Shaler to Smith, New York, June 5, 1810. Department of State, *Consular Despatches: Havana,* II.

of the Royal Hacienda, to oppose British influence and abolition. Arangó told Shaler that the Creoles preferred annexation
to the United States, whose institutions promised them a great
future of freedom and prosperity with slavery. Another revolutionary group was devoted to independence for the island
and abolition of slavery. Some of its members were free
Negroes.[11]

The aims of the two groups were irreconcilable and the
situation was unpromising for the Madison administration.
The timidity of the Creoles was apparent in a written expression of their views which they handed Shaler in December,
1811. This document expressed opposition to Britain, especially
because it desired to ruin " our trade with Africa," but also fear
that in a crisis the United States would not act decisively to
prevent British occupation. A Cuban revolt could easily be
subdued by a blockade. The statement was in effect a demand
for guaranties by the United States before the Creoles would
act.[12] No response was made to this demand, and Britain used
Havana as a base during the War of 1812.

When Havana was recovered and Ferdinand VII resumed
the throne of Spain, Royal Orders were issued to stop foreign
ships from going to Cuba. Captain-General Apodaca counter-
manded the Orders because privateers of the revolted colonies
prevented Spanish vessels from carrying on the island's commerce. Trade with the United States boomed. Apodaca was
relieved by Cienfuegos as Captain-General. The latter was
friendly towards the United States and freed American prisoners who had been taken in Florida, but he used the depredations
of pirates from the mouth of the Mississippi River as an excuse
to raise discriminatory charges against American ships and
trade.

11 Shaler to Smith, Havana, October 24, 1810 and June 14, 1811. *Ibid*.

12 Shaler to Monroe, Havana, December 6, 1811 and enclosed " *Nota* ",
December 1, 1811. *Ibid*.

Contrary to its policy in Spain, the government of Ferdinand VII made concessions to liberalism in Cuba. In 1818 a Royal Order opened the island's ports to the ships of the world. This finally destroyed the Spanish monopoly. Another Order suppressed the monopolies of particular products. In a treaty with Great Britain, Spain promised to abolish the slave trade in 1820, gave Britain the right of search and agreed to establish Courts of Mixed Commission in Africa and Havana to adjudicate prizes. Cuban liberals had supported the measure, and plans were made to replenish the planters' labor supply by encouraging white immigration. Stimulated by tax concessions and the opening of royal lands, considerable immigration developed from Latin America, Spain and the United States. Planters found the newcomers no substitute for slaves and the trade from Africa was not effectively stopped.[13] But for a time, as agriculture was diversified, new towns were founded, and new classes of small proprietors and businessmen developed, Cuba showed promise of freeing itself from dependence on slave labor and the production of staples.

Trade increased rapidly, especially with the United States, which took the lead away from Britain in Cuba alone of all the Spanish-American countries. Relations between the two peoples became closer as many wealthy Cuban families sent their sons to the United States to be educated and American institutions won the admiration of a new generation of young intellectuals. Felix Varela, José Antonio Saco, José de la Luz Caballero and many others wrote and taught in praise of liberalism. Cuba's relations with the United States brought her the products of industrialism sooner than they arrived in any comparable region. In 1819, the Cuban Juan O'Farrill put one of the first steamships known outside the United States, where it had been built, in the coasting trade between Matanzas and Havana. The first steam-powered sugar machinery was brought from the

13 William L. Mathieson, *Great Britain and the Slave Trade: 1839-1865* (London, 1929), 13-14.

United States at the same time and installed in the *ingenio* of Pedro Diago.[14]

Cuban liberals in 1820 induced the Captain-General to restore the Constitution of 1812 under which the island was not a colony but a province of Spain. Three deputies were elected to the Cortes at Madrid. They tried to obtain concessions in favor of the trade of the United States with Cuba, which now amounted to over half the trade of the island. Plans were drawn up for the abolition of slavery, the development of food production by small landowners, and liberal self-government. But the restoration of absolutism in Spain put an end to these dreams.

The possibility that the Cuban deputies would succeed in their plans, or that liberals might even make the island independent, frightened the Creole planters and made them turn again to the United States. Vincent Gray, an American merchant long resident in the island and several times the consul of the United States, wrote to the State Department in 1821:

> If any Nation would come forward and offer them protection, with a competent Naval Force, the Island would be declared Independent in one month or less .... Many wealthy men are selling off their property, for the purpose of leaving the Country, fearing that it will be declared Independent in the present year.[15]

In 1822, as France prepared to invade Spain, the fate of Cuba became of momentous interest to the Monroe administration. Cuban leaders sent an agent to lay before the cabinet a plan for annexation. James Biddle, commander of the *Macedonia,* had made contacts during a visit to Cuba which led him to assure the President that the agent was trustworthy, and he

14 Vilá, *Historia de Cuba,* I, 199-200.

15 Gray to Daniel Brent, Havana, October 31, 1821. Department of State, *Consular Despatches: Havana,* III.

described the fears of the Creoles that a revolution would result in the ascendancy of the Negroes.[16]

When the agent Sanchez arrived, Monroe called a cabinet meeting to consider his plan. Secretary of State John Quincy Adams noted in his diary that Calhoun had a " most ardent desire " to annex the island, and added:

> There are two dangers to be averted by that event: one, that the island should fall into the hands of Great Britain; the other, that it should be revolutionized by the negroes. Calhoun says Mr. Jefferson told him two years ago that we ought, at the first possible opportunity, to take Cuba, though at the cost of a war with England; but as we are not now prepared for this, and as our great object must be to gain time, he thought we should answer this overture by dissuading them from their present purpose, and urging them to adhere at present to their connection with Spain.[17]

The subject was discussed at another meeting. On October 1, 1822, Monroe had answers ready for Sanchez. The official response rejected the offer of annexation on grounds formulated by Adams that the Executive was powerless to promise Cuba admission to the Union and, in any case, amity with Spain forbade the United States government to countenance the proposal. But another more secret answer requested more information concerning the agent's authority, the maturity of the revolutionary movement, and its resources and chances of success.[18]

Rumors now became common that Mexico or Colombia would annex Cuba, that France would invade it, that Spain would cede it to Britain in return for loans, and that the Cubans themselves would precipitate a revolution. Joel R. Poinsett, a

16 Biddle to Monroe, Chesapeake Bay, August 3, 1822. Monroe Papers.

17 *Memoirs of John Quincy Adams Comprising Portions of His Diary from 1795 to 1848*, edited by Charles Francis Adams (Philadelphia, 1874-1877), VI, 70.

18 *Ibid.*, 73-4.

secret agent sent to the island by Monroe, reported that the largest group of revolutionists wanted annexation to the United States. Diplomatic means of blocking threats by third powers were considered. John Forsyth, United States Minister to Spain, told a commission of the Cortes that if Spain would recognize the independence of Mexico and Colombia and liberalize its commercial regulations, the United States would make a joint guaranty with Colombia and Mexico of Spanish possession of Cuba.[19] But Adams hoped for stronger support against Britain which should at the same time end the threat of French invasion of the island. He instructed Forsyth to offer Spain a joint guaranty with France.[20]

Nothing came of these projects to abandon the isolationist policy of the United States. The administration turned to pursue a unilateral course. The "no-transfer" corollary of the Monroe Doctrine was asserted to prevent Britain or France from taking Cuba. Jefferson wanted to join this principle with Canning's proposed engagement that neither the United States nor Britain would take the island. He thought that "future chances" might nevertheless make possible Cuban annexation to the United States.[21] Adams agreed with the "no-transfer" policy, and he was certain that the "laws. . . of political gravitation" would inevitably bring Cuba into the Union,[22] but he was unwilling to join in Canning's self-denying declaration, because, as he wrote in his diary, the inhabitants of either Cuba or Texas

> may exercise their primitive rights, and solicit a union with us
> .... we should ... keep ourselves free to act as emergencies

19 Forsyth to Adams, Madrid, November 20, 1822. Department of State, *Diplomatic Despatches: Spain*, XXI.

20 Adams to Forsyth, Washington, December 17, 1822. Department of State, *Instructions: United States Ministers*, IX.

21 Jefferson to Monroe, Monticello, October 24, 1823. Jefferson Papers.

22 Adams to Hugh Nelson, Washington, April 28, 1823. Department of State, *Instructions: United States Ministers*, IX.

may arise, and not tie ourselves down to any principle which might immediately afterwards be brought to bear against ourselves.[23]

The desire to leave the way open to future annexation of Cuba was a factor in the rejection of Canning's proposal by the Monroe administration. Strangely enough, the "no-transfer" principle was not enunciated in Monroe's famous Message to Congress of December, 1823, but in the future it became identified with the Monroe Doctrine in the popular mind and in official statements, despite the fact that it was asserted against American as well as European powers.[24] Cuba now became, in the words of the *London Courier,* the

> Turkey of transatlantic politics, tottering to its fall, and kept from falling only by the struggles of those who contend for the right of catching her in her descent.[25]

Depite the emergence of the Cuban slavery problem during the several years prior to the announcement of the Monroe Doctrine, the chief motives for American interest in Cuba remained strategic and commercial. They were best summed up by Adams:

> Cuba, almost in sight of our shores, from a multitude of considerations has become an object of transcendent importance to the political and commercial interests of our Union. Its commanding position, with reference to the Gulph of Mexico, and the West India seas; the character of its population; its situation midway between our Southern Coast, and the Island of St. Domingo; its safe and capacious harbor of Havanna fronting a long line of our shores destitute of the same advantage; the nature of its productions, and of its wants fur-

23 *Memoirs of J. Q. Adams,* ed. C. F. Adams, VI, 178.

24 Dexter Perkins, *The Monroe Doctrine: 1823-1826* (Cambridge, 1932), 202-4.

25 Quoted in J. M. Callahan, *Cuba and Anglo-American Relations.* Annual Report of the American Historical Association, 1897 (Washington, 1898), 202.

nishing the supplies and needing the returns of a commerce immensely profitable, and mutually beneficial, give it an importance in the sum of our national interests with which that of no other foreign Territory can be compared, and little inferior to that which binds the different members of this Union together.

Such indeed are, between the interests of that Island and of this country, the geographical, commercial, moral, and political relations formed by nature, gathering in the process of time, and even now verging to maturity that in looking forward to the probable course of events for the short period of half a century, it is scarcely possible to resist the conviction, that the annexation of Cuba to our federal Republic will be indispensable to the continuance and integrity of the Union itself.[26]

Monroe stressed the relation of Cuba to the security of the river communications of the West in which he was deeply interested. He wrote to Jefferson:

I consider Cape Florida, & Cuba, as forming the mouth of the Mississippi, & other rivers, emptying into the Gulph of Mexico, within our limits, as of the Gulph itself, & in consequence that the acquisition of it to our union was of the highest importance to our internal tranquility, as well as to our prosperity and aggrandizement.[27]

Jefferson amplified Monroe's conception:

The control which, with Florida point, [Cuba] would give us over the Gulph of Mexico, and the countries, and the isthmus bordering on it, as well as those whose waters flow into it, would fill up the measure of our political well-being.[28]

If the purpose uppermost in the minds of the authors of the Monroe Doctrine in their Cuban policy was strategic security,

26 Adams to Nelson, Washington, April 28, 1823. Department of State, *Instructions: United States Ministers*, IX.

27 Monroe to Jefferson, Washington, June 30, 1823. Jefferson Papers.

28 Jefferson to Monroe, Monticello, October 24, 1823. *Ibid.*

to Cuban revolutionaries it meant the end of hope for American aid in achieving independence or annexation. The blow came when the restoration of absolutism in Spain under French patronage inaugurated a desperate effort to stamp out all revolutionary activity in Cuba. In 1825, Captain-General Vives was given unlimited dictatorial powers, and the Permanent Executive Military Commission was established to supersede the courts. Many revolutionary leaders, including members of the wealthy Creole families of Betancourt, Sanchez, and Agüero, were executed. Vives sent an assassin to Philadelphia to kill Varela, one of the Cuban deputies to the Spanish Cortes, who was publishing in exile the revolutionary paper *La Habañero*. Forty thousand veteran Spanish troops terrorized the island. Cubans were not allowed to hold office in the army, the treasury and customs, or the judicial departments. Informers penetrated all ranks of society and reported suspected persons and those who refused to pay blackmail. Accused persons were often condemned to solitary confinement in dungeons for life without hearings or knowledge by relatives of their whereabouts. These measures were added to routine features of Spanish colonial rule. The wealth of the island was drained by taxes on all documents, property and activities from Papal Bulls and crucifixes to cockfighting and entertaining friends in the home. All crops except sugar were taxed. It was estimated that taxes amounted to $38 for every person in Cuba in 1850 when the per capita revenue in the United States was $2. The personal incomes of officials, including most of the captains-general, were augmented by collusion in the slave trade. The latter steadily increased the " gratification " they demanded for each illegally imported slave until it reached forty-eight dollars in 1848. The captain-general who did not acquire a million dollars in four years in office, although he received no salary, was said to be a poor manager. After 1823 the press was again completely censored and possession of liberal literature, political tracts, and the Bible was forbidden. Under Vives not only was tyranny formalized by a complete military dictatorship, but the mitigations which came by virtue of the inefficiency of traditional Spanish colonial rule were to a considerable extent eliminated.[29]

President Adams viewed with complacency the rigors of Vives' regime because it put an end to the threat of revolution in Cuba. He had known Vives as Spanish Minister to the United States, and wrote that:

> He was precisely the man to tranquillize and conciliate the submission of the people of the island to their old government, and he so effectually accomplished that purpose that the government of the United States heard nothing further of intended insurrection is Cuba during the remainder of Mr. Monroe's administration, and the whole of mine.[30]

The activity of Cuban revolutionists was actually intensified after the refusal of support by the Monroe administration. The American policy discouraged the annexationist planters and their property made them timid in the face of Vives, but liberals who favored independence redoubled their efforts. The successive conspiracies of the *Soles y Rayos de Bolívar* and *Gran Legión del Aguila Negra* were discovered and violently suppressed by Vives. Masonic lodges, which had been prohibited by a Royal Order of 1824, were clandestinely active in the independence movements. Earlier, the Cuban lodges had formed ties with American Masons.[31] and Philadelphia Masons had been accused by Spain of promoting revolution in Cuba through related lodges in the island.[32] But now the Cuban

29 W. F. Johnson, *The History of Cuba* (New York, 1920), III, 1-17. Vilá, *Historia de Cuba*, I, *passim.* R. B. Kimball, *Cuba, and the Cubans* (New York, 1850), 165-86. Mathieson, *op. cit.*, 141.

30 Quoted in Vilá, *Historia de Cuba*, I, 244.

31 L. O. Pulgarón, *Apuntes Históricos Sobre la Masonería Cubana* (Guanabacoa, Cuba, 1933), 12 ff.

32 Forsyth to Adams, Madrid, November 20, 1822. Department of State, *Diplomatic Despatches: Spain*, XXI.

Masons turned to lodges in Mexico and Colombia for aid, and when the *Junta Promotora de la Libertad de Cuba* was organized in Mexico under the patronage of leading officials of the new republic and its neighbor, Colombia, the administration of President Adams became alarmed.

Shortly after he became Secretary of State, Henry Clay took strong ground against the independence of Cuba and Puerto Rico in a letter to Alexander H. Everett, Minister to Spain:

> The population itself, of the Islands, is incompetent, at present, from its composition and its amount, to maintain self government. The maritime force of the neighbouring Republics of Mexico and Colombia is not now, nor is it likely shortly to be, adequate to the protection of those Islands, if the conquest of them were effected. The United States would entertain constant apprehensions of their passing from their possession to that of some less friendly sovereignty. And of all the European Powers, this country prefers that Cuba and Porto Rico should remain dependent on Spain.[33]

Later he wrote to James Brown, Minister to France, that the United States " could not see with indifference " the islands of Cuba and Puerto Rico pass into the hands of any other power. Dexter Perkins, the foremost authority on the Monroe Doctrine, has interpreted Clay's policy as a call for European aid against Mexico and Colombia. The light this absolute " no-transfer " policy threw on the Monroe Doctrine, Perkins adds, revealed to Latin America the selfish purpose of the United States.[34] When the report came that General Santa Anna was organizing an expedition in Mexico to free Cuba and complete the expulsion of Spain from the Western Hemisphere, Clay campaigned to induce Russia, Great Britain and France to press the Spanish government to make peace with its revolted colonies and thereby prevent Mexico from making war on the

33 Clay to Everett, Washington, April 27, 1825. Department of State, *Instructions: United States Ministers*, X.

34 Perkins, *Monroe Doctrine: 1823-1826*, 202-7.

Spanish power in Cuba.[35] Everett was instructed to tell the Spanish government that its best guaranty of security in Cuba and Puerto Rico was to recognize the independence of the other colonies.[36]

The campaign was a failure. James Brown found that the French government had no hope of inducing the " exalted or fanatical " governors of Spain to make peace or face reality.[37] Russia made an ineffective gesture towards influencing Spain after the " staggering " proposal had been approved by Prince Metternich of Austria.[38] Canning told Minister King that the effort to bring Spain to make peace was hopeless, particularly as the Emperor of Russia was secretly urging Spain to renew military action against the colonies.[39] The American proposal was countered by Canning with a plan for the United States, France and Britain to make a joint guaranty of Spain's possession of Cuba.[40] This and the fact that France was convoying Spanish troops to Cuba, giving weight to suspicions that it had designs on the island, put Clay on the defensive. He warned France that the President could imagine no circumstances in which France or Britain would feel justified in occupying Cuba.[41] Canning's counter-proposal was rejected with an as-

35 Clay to Henry Middleton, Minister to Russia, Washington, May 10, 1825; Clay to Rufus King, Minister to Great Britain, Washington, May 11, 1825; Clay to James Brown, Minister to France, Washington, May 13, 1825. Department of State, *Instructions: United States Ministers*, X.

36 Clay to Everett, Washington, April 27, 1825. *Ibid.*

37 Brown to Clay, Paris, March 12, 1826. Department of State, *Diplomatic Despatches: France*, XXIII.

38 Middleton to Clay, St. Petersburgh, September 8, 1825. Department of State, *Diplomatic Despatches: Russia*, X. Clay to Anderson and Sergeant, Washington, May 8, 1826. Department of State, *Panama Congress*, I.

39 Canning to King, Wortley Hall, August 7, 1825. Department of State, *Diplomatic Despatches: Great Britain*, XXXII.

40 Canning to King, Storrs, August 21, 1825. *Ibid.*

41 Clay to Brown, Washington, October 25, 1825. Department of State, *Instructions: United States Ministers*, X.

surance to Spain that the situation was "almost equivalent to an actual guaranty." [42]

United States opposition to the Mexican-Colombian expedition nevertheless had effect. The Panama Congress of 1826 was intended to discuss the project of freeing Cuba. The Senate Foreign Relations Committee rejected President Adams' proposal that delegates be sent to the Congress. The Committee argued that the interest of the United States in Cuba and Puerto Rico forbade discussion of their destiny with countries planning to invade them. But in Congress that very interest was urged as the reason why envoys should represent American views, and the vote in both Houses was favorable. In his instructions to the delegates, Clay expressed opposition to the independence of Cuba, to its annexation by a Spanish-American republic, and to a guaranty by other countries of Spain's possession of Cuba. The delegates were told to secure the suspension of any military or naval expedition by holding out the possibility that the United States would side with the European powers against Colombia and Mexico.[43] The accepted view is that the policy of the United States had no effect because its delegates did not arrive at the Congress and in any case the Congress did not officially deliberate on Cuba.[44] But Bolívar believed that the opposition of the United States to the expedition had been made so clear as to have been, coupled with the opposition of Great Britain, "little less than insuperable," and the plan was abandoned.[45] Martin Van Buren, Clay's successor as Secretary of State, instructed Minister Van Ness to

[42] Clay to Everett, Washington, April 13, 1826. *Ibid.*, XI.

[43] Clay to Anderson and Sergeant, Washington, May 8, 1826, Department of State, *Panama Congress*, I.

[44] T. E. Burton, "Henry Clay," *The American Secretaries of State and Their Diplomacy*, edited by S. F. Bemis (New York, 1928), IV, 148-9.

[45] Vidal Morales y Morales, *Iniciadores y Primeros Martires de La Revolucion Cubana* (Havana, 1931), I, 97.

explain to the Spanish government that the United States was chiefly responsible for preserving Cuba and Puerto Rico from attack by Colombia and Mexico.[46]

It was perhaps in gratitude and with new-found confidence in the United States that Spain in 1830 granted an exequatur to the current American agent in Havana, William Shaler, and made him the first officially recognized Consul of the United States in the island. For a time, Americans enjoyed advantages in Cuba commensurate with the position of the United States as the island's economic mother country and the unofficial protector of Spanish rule. Immigrants from the United States were exempt from many taxes, and they became so numerous in Cardenas that it was called "the American city". The *Mercantile Weekly Report* was published in Havana for the American colony. More sugar and coffee were exported to the United States than to Spain. American vessels numbered 783 of the 964 that came into Havana in 1826. One of the first railroads outside Britain and the United States was built in 1832 by American engineers with American equipment. By 1837 the route from Güines to Havana was completed, and others were being built. American planters in the vicinities of Cardenas and Matanzas led in the application of steam power to the sugar industry.[47]

Spain disrupted the improved situation by initiating a tariff war in 1832 against the United States. New discriminatory rates were laid on imports. Congress retaliated by raising the tonnage duties on Spanish vessels coming from Cuba and Puerto Rico. In 1834 Spain raised the duty on American flour brought to Cuba in American vessels to $9.50 a barrel and $8.50 when imported in Spanish ships. Congress then raised the tonnage duties on Spanish vessels from the islands still

46 Van Buren to Van Ness, Washington, October 2, 1829. Department of State, *Instructions: United States Ministers*, XIII.

47 Leland H. Jenks, *Our Cuban Colony* (New York, 1928), 19 *et passim*. R. R. Madden, *The Island of Cuba* (London, 1853), 83-4.

higher and laid a special duty on Cuban coffee. Trade between Cuba and the United States was seriously injured.[48] But Spain was lapsing into the chaos of the Carlist Wars and hardly benefited from the demonstration of Cuba's dependence on the United States. The sentiments of Cubans turned against their neighbor. They supported a movement that was presently strengthened by a law against sending young men to the United States to be educated. At the same time, they lost all hope of aid from Mexico and Colombia as Spain in 1836 recognized the independence of its revolted colonies.

Nicholas P. Trist, appointed United States Consul in 1833, further alienated Cuban liberals by his intimate co-operation with the brutally reactionary Captain-General Miguel Tacón. Cubans tried to take advantage of the Spanish constitutional regime of 1834. They elected the exiled abolitionist Saco their deputy to the Cortes, but Tacón twice annulled the elections, whereupon Saco was elected a third time. Then the Cortes refused to seat him or any of the Cuban deputies. Tacón was instructed by Spain to make no changes in the island's administration but to govern it by " special laws." When the Governor of the Eastern Department proclaimed the re-establishment of the Constitution of 1812, Tacón organized a military expedition to put down the revolt. Americans owned plantations, *ingenios,* and the Juragua Iron Company's mines in the neighborhood of Santiago, the center of the uprising. English companies owned copper mines. Consular officers of the United States, Britain and France called for warships of their respective flags to go to Santiago in support of Tacón. Captain Jones of the British *Vestal* was most active in aid of the Captain-General, while Commodore Dallas of the United States Navy and the French lent him their friendly presence. This remarkable co-operation among the rival powers when they were faced by an internal threat to Spanish rule in Cuba was described by

---

48 *Senate Reports* (32nd Cong., 1st Sess.), 318, pp. 1-13. *Senate Executive Documents* (32: 1), 53.

Trist in a letter to Forsyth. He praised Tacón's vigorous suppression of the revolt.[49]

Trist was reputed to take part in the slave trade in collusion with Tacón and a syndicate that shared its profits with Queen Mother Christina of Spain. In 1835, Spain signed a new treaty with Britain that provided for stronger measures against the slave trade. These measures merely caused a diversion of the trade from Spanish vessels to ships flying the American and other flags, while Spanish officials continued to co-operate with the traders. Trist made the American flag available to slavers.[50] Fast Baltimore clippers were specially built for the purpose. British cruisers were reluctant to stop and search vessels under the United States flag, and sometimes too slow to overhaul the clippers. The United States was now the only power refusing to concede the right of search. Public agitation in the United States led to the investigation of Trist. Alexander H. Everett was sent to Cuba by Secretary Forsyth. He found that the number of American ships in the Cuban slave trade had increased from 5 in 1836 to 22 in 1839. They were bought by the syndicate, sent to Africa with a token American citizen aboard, loaded with Negroes, and on the return voyage their ownership was transferred to the American whenever a British cruiser approached. Trist authenticated the papers necessary for these operations and signed blank forms for emergencies. He also used his consular seal and signature to authenticate papers of Portuguese vessels as a "favor" to the Portuguese consul while he was "on leave". The result was that papers provided by Trist were used by 61 of the 71 slavers that were known to put into Cuban ports in 1838. Trist's defense was a tissue of strange ambiguities.[51] He attempted a diversion by proposing

49 Trist to Forsyth, Havana, November 29, 1836. Department of State, *Consular Despatches: Havana*, VII.

50 Mathieson, *op. cit.*, 16-18, 27.

51 Everett to Forsyth, Washington, July 21, 1840, Department of State, *Consular Despatches: Havana*, XIV.

to Forsyth a scheme for the United States to purchase Cuba. This was the rather unsavory occasion of the first official statement of the desire to buy the island. Forsyth rejected the plan with a reproof to its author.[52] After Everett's report, Trist was relieved and Secretary of State Webster appointed James S. Calhoun as Consul in Havana. The Spanish authorities showed their displeasure at these proceedings by refusing to give Calhoun his exequatur. Nor were slave traders pleased when the United States agreed in the Webster-Ashburton Treaty of 1842 to provide warships to suppress the use of the American flag in the slave traffic.

While the Van Buren administration had tolerated Trist and co-operated with Britain and France against internal revolt in Cuba, it also had occasion to state in the strongest terms the opposition of the United States to any increase of British influence in the island. Victories of the Carlists in Spain had led to rumors that Queen Isabella II would go to Cuba and set up a separate government under British protection. Britain was also said to be negotiating for Cuba in exchange for a loan. United States Minister Stevenson protested to Lord Palmerston that " *it was impossible that the United States could acquiesce in the transfer of Cuba from the dominion of Spain to any of the great maritime powers of Europe*," and warned him that the United States would intervene for self-protection.[53] John H. Eaton, United States Minister to Spain, told the Spanish Minister of State for Foreign Affairs that the United States would regard British ownership of Cuba as a sign of " intended hostility ".[54] Secretary Forsyth in 1840 instructed the new Minister to Spain, Aaron Vail, to make an even stronger declaration to the Spanish government that if any plan

52 Forsyth to Trist, Washington, March 19, 1839. Department of State, *Special Missions*, I.

53 Stevenson to Forsyth, London, June 16, 1837. Department of State, *Diplomatic Despatches: Great Britain*, XLIV. Italics in the original.

54 Eaton to Minister of State for Foreign Affairs, Madrid, March 10, 1838. Department of State, *Diplomatic Despatches: Spain*, XXXII.

developed to change the title of the island, "the U. States will prevent it, at all hazard, as they will any foreign military occupation for any pretext whatsoever." Spain might depend on United States military and naval aid to help her preserve Cuba.[55] Britain made loans to Spain but, whether or not as a result of American influence, without compromising Spain's ownership of Cuba. These loans were quickly in default and led to new schemes to throw Cuba into the scales for payment.

The United States also found itself the victim of Spain's loose financial practices. In 1834, Spain had agreed to pay the United States $600,000 in settlement of old claims for depredations against American shipping in Cuban waters. Two of the annual installments of $30,000 were paid. After failing in further payments, the Spanish government placed the obligation in the Cuban Treasury. It paid one semi-annual installment. Webster in 1842 sent Tully R. Wise as his confidential agent to treat directly with the Captain-General. That official pleaded lack of authority to deal with the United States, and the negotiations collapsed as a result of unwarranted efforts to write off the payments against controverted Spanish claims on the United States.[56] Such difficulties frequently occurred when the United States attempted to deal with the governors of Cuba. Spain gave them responsibility in foreign relations but no authority to deal with a foreign government. The system encouraged evasion and caused more serious irritation on later occasions.

The Tyler administration faced a new situation as evidence accumulated that Great Britain, or at least some of the officers of its government, had begun active promotion of the abolition of slavery in Cuba. The evidence was interpreted by Americans as proof of British intention to foment a slave revolt. The

55 Forsyth to Vail, Washington, July 15, 1840. Department of State, *Diplomatic Instructions: Spain*, XIV.

56 Webster to Wise, Washington, February 16 and August 16, 1842. Department of State, *Special Missions*, I.

fate of slavery in Cuba was of intense concern to Americans because it was thought to be intimately associated with the fate of that institution in the United States. Appearing when slavery was emerging as the most divisive issue in American politics, the question of slavery in Cuba became at least as important as strategic and commercial problems in creating a climax of American interest in the island from 1848 to 1855. Its origins will therefore be examined in some detail.

By 1841 the slaves of Cuba outnumbered the whites by 436,-000 to 418,000. Free Negroes numbered 153,000.[57] The percentage of Negroes in the total population increased from 32 percent in 1774 to 58 percent in 1842. An official report of the Royal Hacienda in 1845 recommended gradual emancipation.[58] But such a measure was too detrimental to vested interests in Spain as well as Cuba to be undertaken except as a political weapon of last resort to discourage Creole revolutionists and also to make the island undesirable to annexationists of the American South. The report recommended immigration of free laborers, but little was done. Beginning in 1847, a few Chinese were imported under eight-year contracts as an experiment with "free" labor.[59] The planters preferred Negro slaves and resisted all measures to substitute other labor. According to the Spanish census, the slaves decreased to 322,-000 by 1850,[60] but serious doubt has been cast on the good faith of Spain in issuing this figure. The large increases in slaves registered by previous censuses had given the world proof that the slave trade was very active in defiance of Spain's treaties with Britain, and it continued notoriously active dur-

57 H. H. S. Aimes, *A History of Slavery in Cuba* (New York, 1907), 143.

58 Fiscal de la Superintendencia General Delegado de Real Hacienda, *Informe Fiscal sobre Fomento de la Poblacion Blanca en la Isla de Cuba y Emancipacion Progressive de la Esclava* (Madrid, 1845).

59 Henry Ashworth, *A Tour in the United States, Cuba and Canada* (London, 1861), 61.

60 Aimes, *op. cit.*, 158.

ing the forties and fifties, subject only to very brief periods of decline when British measures were effective.[61]

Slavery increased in Cuba for much the same reasons as in the American South during the same period, with sugar playing the part of cotton. But in Cuba there was no internal source of slaves comparable to the border states of the South and natural increase was low because few women were imported from Africa, hence, as sugar planting increased with the expansion of markets and mechanization of refining methods, Africa replenished the labor supply. The size and number of plantations grew as sugar exports increased from 90,000 tons in 1827 to 300,000 tons in 1850 and the number of *ingenios* from 1,000 to 1,500. By 1851, sugar accounted for 84 percent of Cuba's exports, and the island had taken the place of the French and British West Indies as the world's chief source of sugar.[62] Coffee and tobacco planting lost their importance and were relegated to small holdings operated by free labor. Church lands were confiscated by the government and sold to sugar planters, although tithes continued to be collected. Sugar production became a capitalistic enterprise requiring credit and heavy investments in land, steam-power machinery and slaves. The investment estimated to be necessary to produce 400 tons of sugar increased from $100,000 in 1825 to $320,000 in 1854. But prices kept up with this advance sufficiently to make the great Creole planting families exceedingly wealthy.[63] Many " sugar noblemen " bought titles from the Spanish crown at a standard price of $25,000.[64]

On the sugar plantations, the paternal relation of masters to slaves was lost and brutal exploitation by overseers for absentee owners took its place. During the cutting season, when the success of the crop depended upon speedy day and night

61 Vilá, *Historia de Cuba*, I, 351. Mathieson, *op. cit.*, 63, 143.

62 Jenks, *Our Cuban Colony*, 19-24.

63 Aimes, *op. cit.*, 157.

64 Maturin M. Ballou, *History of Cuba* (Boston, 1854), 140-1.

operation, slaves were sometimes worked to death. The newly-imported *bozales* were only partially broken to submissiveness in the traders' pens. In districts like Cardenas and Matanzas, where the slaves far outnumbered the whites, the latter lived in constant and justified fear of slave revolts.

The slaves were more loyal to the Spanish authorities than to their Creole masters. The former were charged with enforcing the ameliorative slave code of the ancient Laws of the Indies and were sometimes effective in supporting the slaves against their owners, especially as regards the slaves' right to buy their freedom. Insofar as they had political weight, the slaves were on the side of Spanish domination of the island. This did not prevent the Spanish authorities from suppressing abolitionism among whites and free Negroes or putting down with terror any insurrection of slaves. But the threat of an emancipation under Spanish auspices, not for idealistic purposes or by methods conducive to social peace, but through violence as a vengeful deterrent against attempts by whites to overthrow Spanish rule, was held out as the only alternative to that rule. Cuba would be Spanish or "African", but never free under Creole domination. This came to be understood as a sinister motive for promotion of the slave trade by Spain in defiance of treaties: to increase the slave population until it should overawe the Creoles and make them accept Spanish rule as their only available security. The slave-owners in their complaints against Spain turned against the slave-trade, but they did not stop buying *bozales*.

Free Negroes and *mestizos* provided some support and leadership in the movement to abolish slavery and make the island independent. The whites in this movement were drawn largely from the professional and small farmer classes rather than from the planters. Business men were divided between the liberals and the conservatives. The wealthiest merchants were dependent on the sugar trade and sided with the Creole planters. The numerous Spanish officials counted on transients from

Spain who went to Cuba to make their fortunes as the chief nucleus of government support. Some free Negroes were used at critical moments in the Spanish militia as a threat of " Africanization ". White Cubans were not allowed to bear arms. Timidity was often charged against the Cubans for enduring Spanish rule. The charge was just in regard to the planters and those who preferred the evils and profits of slavery rather than face the difficulties of emancipation. But many did not, and the number of liberals who lost their lives in the cause of freedom from Spain, and even freedom for the slaves, suggests that not moral weakness but the divisions in Cuban society produced by the island's economy and labor system, the greater efficiency of Spanish tyranny in Cuba compared with the former colonies of the mainland, and at many critical moments the opposition of the United States, Great Britain and France to Cuban independence are the sufficient explanations of Cuba's long torment.

The tensions of the island's social order mounted rapidly with the expansion of sugar planting and slavery. Local spontaneous uprisings of slaves occurred in various districts in 1832, 1835, 1836, 1837 and 1840. The Negro government of nearby Haiti was considered a standing incitement to the Negroes of Cuba, and the emancipation of slaves in the British West Indies in 1833 and French West Indies in 1848 contributed to unrest in the Spanish islands. In 1837 the liberal *Club de los Habañeros* organized the *Conspiración de la Cadena Triangular y Soles de la Libertad* to abolish slavery and free the island. Tacón's informers betrayed it and it was suppressed.

In November, 1840, the famous English abolitionist, David Turnbull, arrived in Havana as British Consul. Turnbull knew the island well from his years of service on the anti-slave trade mixed commission. He counted Cuban liberals among his friends, had travelled in the West Indies since 1837 as agent of the English Anti-Slavery Society, and achieved fame as the author of *Travels in the West,* in which he championed the cause of emancipation. The book was dedicated to Lord Clarendon.[65] Lord Palmerston, Minister of Foreign Affairs, wrote to Lord Acton that Turnbull's book and lofty ideals recommended him for the office in Cuba.[66]

Turnbull's arrival with another abolitionist, Francis Ross Cocking, as his Vice-Consul caused a sensation in Cuba. The *Junta de Fomento,* a semi-official organization of business men, protested that Turnbull should be expelled from the island as a menace to slavery. Tacón refused to recognize him, but he was shortly relieved by Captain-General Valdés, a moderate and a believer in Chinese and white immigration if not abolition, who was said to be the only captain-general of the period who failed to enrich himself through the slave trade. Valdés delivered his exequator to Turnbull. The object of the Consul as he busily organized leading white Cubans as well as Negroes was probably a revolt against Spain under leaders who supported abolition. His outstanding adherent was General Narciso López, a Venezuelan who had achieved renown in the Carlist Wars and was given several Cuban offices by his friend Valdés, including the Presidency of the Permanent Executive Military Commission. López had stood for liberalism within the limits imposed by Spanish service, and for a time he sympathized with Turnbull's program. Turnbull was acting in co-operation with British officials in Jamaica.[67] The conjunction of British power and disaffected Cubans, including the highest military official in the island, made Turnbull's activity formidable.

In October, 1841, fifty slaves who were building the palatial home of the Aldama family in Havana revolted and fought a pitched battle with Spanish troops. Valdés believed Turnbull

65 David Turnbull, *Travels in the West: Cuba; with Notices of Porto Rico, and the Slave Trade* (London, 1840).

66 Morales, *Iniciadores,* I, 228-9.

67 Cocking to Palmerston, Caracas, October 1, 1846. *Boletín de los Archivos Nacionales* (Havana, 1909), III (No. V), 3-9.

was responsible.[68] James S. Calhoun wrote Webster in April, 1842, that fears were entertained of the intention of the British in bringing two steamers loaded with munitions into Havana harbor in company with their Antilles Squadron.[69] When Turnbull began to journey through the island with a number of free British colonial Negroes, Valdés decided it was time to act. The Consul was arrested as he arrived at Cardenas and his Negro friends were shot down. He was expelled from the island, but Cocking remained.[70]

The Cuban planter Domingo del Monte wrote a warning against Cocking and British policy to Alexander H. Everett and urged that the United States frustrate them. Everett informed Webster and the latter sent instructions by special messenger to the new United States Consul, General Robert B. Campbell, to investigate and report in absolute secrecy on the scheme of Britain to ruin the island and erect a " *black Military Republic.*" The Secretary of State added that the Spanish authorities might " securely rely upon the whole naval and military resources of this country to aid . . . in preserving or recovering " Cuba, because:

> If this scheme should succeed, the influence of Britain in this quarter, it is remarked, will be unlimited. With 600,000 blacks in Cuba, and 800,000 in her West India Islands, she will, it is said, strike a death blow at the existence of slavery in the United States.[71]

John Quincy Adams, like most Secretaries of State, had earlier

68 Morales, *Iniciadores,* I, 251-2.

69 Calhoun to Webster, Havana, April 14, 1842. Department of State, *Consular Despatches: Havana,* XVIII.

70 Calhoun to Webster, November 4 and 6, 1842. *Ibid.*

71 Webster to Campbell, Washington, January 14, 1843. Department of State, *Special Missions,* I.

expressed similar fears,[72] but he had developed his views and now described Webster's instructions to Campbell as "putrid with slavery and the slave trade."[73]

Campbell's report does not appear in the archives, but Webster assured the Minister to Spain that the situation in Cuba was not dangerous.[74] Nevertheless during 1843 sporadic slave revolts occurred at Cardenas and elsewhere. A free Negro protegé of Turnbull, José Miguel Mitchell, was arrested as the instigator of a plot to bring an expedition of free Negroes from Jamaica to aid in a Cuban revolt.[75] The overthrow and flight from Spain of the dictator General Espartero led to rumors that he would be installed by Britain as ruler of Cuba. The Spanish Minister to the United States, Argaiz, asked President Tyler and his Secretaries of State and the Navy to make a naval demonstration in Cuban waters of American support of Spanish authority. Orders were accordingly drawn up, and executed by Commodore Chauncey who took a squadron to Cuba to assure that neither Espartero nor Britain should disturb the island. Consul Campbell in Havana offered co-operation to the Captain-General in "defending the city".[76] Secretary of State Upshur advised Argaiz that the Spanish authorities should execute anyone attempting rebellion in Cuba, or if a foreign government protected him, as Britain did Turnbull,

[72] *Supra*, 21; *cf.* Van Buren to Van Ness, Washington, October 2, 1829 and October 13, 1830. Department of State, *Instructions: United States Ministers*, XIII.

[73] *Memoirs of J. Q. Adams*, ed. C. F. Adams, XI, 351.

[74] Webster to Irving, Washington, March 14, 1843. Department of State, *Diplomatic Instructions: Spain*, XIV.

[75] Morales, *Iniciadores*, I, 252.

[76] Campbell to Upshur, Havana, November 12, 1843. Department of State. *Consular Despatches: Havana*, XIX. Jerónimo Becker, *Historia de las relaciones esteriores de España durante el siglo XIX: Apuntes para una Historia diplomatica* (Madrid, 1924), II, 59 ff.

the people of Cuba should lynch him and then it would be interesting to observe who objected.[77]

But the advice was unnecessary, for Spain replaced Valdés with Leopoldo O'Donnell, who effectively stamped out all opposition. At the same time Argaiz was removed from Washington for inviting United States intervention and replaced by Angel Calderón de la Barca. O'Donnell inaugurated his regime with a campaign against suspects in Cardenas and Martanzas. Torture was authorized to obtain confessions. In the middle of 1844, a widely-plotted conspiracy was discovered and attributed to British influence. It was suppressed with the utmost brutality. López was removed from the Permanent Executive Military Commission and in Matanzas alone it "tried" more than 3,000 persons, most of them free Negroes. Suspects were bound to ladders and lashed to obtain confessions, whence the name, *Conspiración de la Escalera*. The Commission condemned 78 to death, 1,292 to prison and over 400 to exile, and many died under the lash.[78] The best leaders of the free Negroes were wiped out, including the talented poet, Gabriel de la Concepción Valdés, called *El Placido,* who was thought to be Turnbull's agent, as well as scores of white liberals who had opposed slavery or the slave trade. A number of American mechanics employed by railroads and *ingenios* at Cardenas were arrested, and the consular rights of the United States in that "American city" and in other provincial centers were abolished. O'Donnell rounded out his policy by removing Cubans from all public offices and by encouraging the slave trade. He retired in 1848 with a fortune of a half million dollars.[79]

La Escalera was a turning point in the development of the Cuban situation. The independence and abolition movements were shorn of leadership, terrorized and discredited. They vir-

77 Argaiz to Minister of State, Washington, October 9, 1843. Becker, *op. cit.*, 65-6.

78 Morales, *Iniciadores*, I, 335.

79 Mathieson, *op. cit.*, 66-7, 141.

tually died out until after the American Civil War. Any thought of using the aid of Britain or any abolitionist government against Spain was rejected. Narciso López, stripped of his offices by O'Donnell, undertook various business ventures, none of which prospered. He turned to organizing a personal following of *guajiros,* cavaliers whose costume he affected, used his business activities as an excuse to travel extensively through the island, and made himself exceedingly popular among the rural Cubans. [80] He came forward in 1848 as the outstanding leader against Spain, freed of responsibility as an official, and devoted to the annexation of Cuba to the United States. Doubts of the sincerity of his annexationism exist, but none whatever of his desire to use American aid to prevent a slave insurrection as an incident of the liberation of the island. He had married into the wealthy Cuban de Frìas family of planters, and it was perhaps not surprising that he should turn to annexation as the solution of Cuba's dilemma. But José Antonio Saco, the exiled intellectual leader of Cuban liberalism, had pointed the way as early in 1837, when he wrote his famous statement:

> If Cuba, degraded by circumstances, should have to throw herself into foreign arms, in none could she fall with more honor or glory than in those of the great North American Confederation. In them she would find peace and consolation, strength and protection, justice and liberty.[81]

La Escalera was proof to Saco's followers of the wisdom of his advice. After a period of frightened silence under O'Donnell and of waiting while the United States showed its expansionist capacities by annexing Texas and half of Mexico, Cuban revolutionary activity broke out again, strengthened by

---

80 A Filibustero, *Life of General Narcisco Lopez* (New York, 1851), 12.

81 J. A. Saco, " Paralelo entre la isla de Cuba y algunas colonias inglesas," *Coleccion de papeles* (Paris, 1859), III, 174. Author's translation.

virtual unity on the program of the Creole planters to annex the island to the United States.

In the latter country, *La Escalera* had equally important effects. Sectionalism had not been significant in previous expressions of American interest in Cuba. In the South, fear that its peculiar institution was being surrounded by enemies—abolitionists in the North and a constricting ring of emancipated labor in Haiti, the Spanish-American republics and the British and French West Indies—and the needs of the plantation economy produced policies not merely of defense, but of aggressive expansion of slavery territory supported by the "positive good" doctrine to justify its protection and expansion. *La Escalera* made the apparition of a Negro republic under British protection and dangerously close to the cotton states seem real and imminent. The South consequently became the chief advocate of annexation and the security and expansion of slavery the chief motives of American interest in Cuba.

John C. Calhoun, the political and intellectual leader of the South, was alarmed by events in Cuba. The Cuban policy of Great Britain he interpreted as part of its general plan to surround the American South with abolition influence as a preliminary to attack on slavery in the United States. He believed that Britain's motive was the desire to eliminate production by slaves of staples which competed with those of free labor in her own colonies.[82] Great Britain was at work in Cuba as well as Texas, he wrote Secretary Upshur, "and both are equally important to our safety." [83] Early in 1844, the South Carolinian became Secretary of State and officially cognizant of events in Cuba. In answer to a famous note from Lord Aberdeen, he wrote that the President of the United States regarded with

[82] Calhoun to Duff Green, September 8, 1843. Quoted in St. George L. Sioussat, "John Caldwell Calhoun," *American Secretaries of State*, ed. Bemis, V, 137-8.

[83] Calhoun to Upshur, Fort Hill, August 27, 1843. Department of State; *Miscellaneous Letters.*

deep concern " the avowal, for the first time made to this Government, ' that Great Britain desires, and is constantly exerting herself to procure the general abolition of slavery throughout the world.' "[84]

The sensational news of *La Escalera* confirmed the fears of Calhoun and the South. But it came in the middle of the bitterly-contested election campaign which Polk won on the platform of annexation of Texas and Oregon, and Democratic leaders were concerned to postpone the Cuban question until Texas and Oregon should be safely in the Union. A popular campaign, supported chiefly in the South, for immediate annexation of Cuba became clamorous in 1845, and led to the proposal in the Senate of a resolution by Senator Yulee of Florida:

> *Resolved,* That, in the opinion of the Senate, it is advisable for the President to open negotiations with the Government of Spain for the cession to the United States of the Island of Cuba, the inhabitants of said Island consenting thereto.[85]

When the resolution was due for debate, Yulee withdrew it " in deference to the desire expressed to him by several of his friends," but only " for the present ". [86] Until the end of the Mexican War, Cuban annexation was advocated in Congress only once again, early in 1846, when Representative R. Smith of Illinois, in response to the demand of a public meeting in his state's capital, asked for a joint resolution in support of Yulee's plan.[87] He did not press the matter.

The preoccupation of the Polk administration with Texas, Oregon, and the war with Mexico made it seek a settlement of Cuban issues with Spain, particularly because it did not

84 Calhoun to Pakenham, Washington, April 18, 1844. Department of State, *Notes to British Legation,* VII.

85 *Congressional Globe* (29th Cong., 1st Sess.), 92.

86 *Ibid.*, 96.

87 *Ibid.*, 383.

want the island to be used by Mexico as a *point d'appui* against the United States. Congress in 1842 had struck another blow in the tariff war by raising still higher the discriminatory charges on Spanish ships entering American ports, besides a general increase in import duties. A high rate on sugar was enacted to satisfy Louisiana planters. Immediately after Polk took office, Minister Washington Irving initiated discussions with the Spanish government looking towards an agreement. He made an eloquent plea for the pacification of Cuba by liberal policies such as representation in the Cortes. The famous author wrote a moving description of the suffering caused Cubans by the high price of bread. Tyranny like Spain's had led the American people to revolt against Britain. The tariff on American flour should be lowered. He urged these measures because:

> The welfare of Cuba is, in a great degree, identical with the welfare of the United States: every blow to the internal quiet and safety of that Island vibrates through the southern parts of our Union and awakens solicitude at our seat of Government.[88]

Calderón de la Barca took up the discussion in a memorandum sent with a letter to Secretary of the Treasury Robert J. Walker. He pleaded Spain's need for the revenues derived from Cuban commerce and asked for a commercial convention which would reduce the United States tariff on Cuban sugar.[89] Congress in 1846 conciliated Spain by exempting Spanish vessels that came from Cuba and Puerto Rico from all discriminatory charges, and it refunded those paid since 1832 by Spanish vessels that had come from other than Cuban or Puerto

88 Irving to Narvaez, Madrid, March 10, 1845. Department of State, *Diplomatic Despatches: Spain*, XXXIV.

89 Calderón de la Barca to Walker, Washington, November 19, 1845. Library of Congress, Manuscripts Division, *United States Trade and Commerce*.

Rican ports. Secretary of State Buchanan told the Spanish Minister that this was an act of justice, and that he hoped the two governments might soon agree to remove all restrictions on trade between the United States and the Islands. [90]

Close watch was kept to prevent violations of neutrality in Cuba during the Mexican War. [91] The Mexican Consul in Cuba had letters patent for privateers but did not use them. Buchanan, on the other hand, found it necessary to justify the stopping of Spanish ships in Mexican waters by United States cruisers. [92]

Despite the submersion of the Cuban question during the war, it was widely expected that the Pearl of the Antilles, called by Spain her " Ever-Faithful Isle ", would be the next object of the boldly expansionist Polk administration. In Cuba, the desire for annexation was growing. And before the Mexican War was concluded, Americans interested in Cuba joined forces with Cuban annexationists and formulated the plan of action that Polk would make his own.

90 Buchanan to Calderón de la Barca, Washington, August 8, 1846. *The Works of James Buchanan,* edited by J. B. Moore (Philadelphia, 1909), VII, 54.

91 Buchanan to Campbell, Washington, December 10, 1846. Department of State, *Instructions to Consuls,* X. Buchanan to R. M. Saunders, Washington, June 13, 1847. *Works of James Buchanan,* ed. Moore, VII, 334-42, *et passim.*

92 Buchanan to Calderón de la Barca, Washington, October 9, 1846. *Ibid.,* 99-100.

CHAPTER II
POLK'S DECISION TO BUY CUBA

THE chief organizer of co-operation among American and Cuban annexationists and the Polk administration was John L. O'Sullivan. This volatile journalist and political promoter, a Master of Arts of Columbia College, was the creator of the phrase "Manifest Destiny", which comprehended all specific motives for expansion during the climaxes of American expansionism before and after the Civil War. According to Julius W. Pratt, the phrase meant to its originator that the American people would inevitably absorb their neighbors as a result of geography and the superiority of democratic institutions and the Anglo-Saxon race.[1] O'Sullivan first used the phrase in 1845 with reference to Texas in the *Democratic Review* of which he was editor. Later in the same year, he applied it to Oregon in the *New York Morning News* which he also edited. Then it was taken up in Congress and passed into a general expansionist meaning.[2]

The New Yorker called himself a Barnburner and a Free Soiler, and he has been accepted as such by Pratt and other students of his career. But further examination suggests that after 1844 O'Sullivan used the labels for purposes of disguise. The Barnburners originated in the thirties as the "Radical" faction of the New York Democracy opposed to extension of the state's canal system by bond issues. Their independence led them during the early forties to embrace reformist ideas on broader issues.[3] As a Barnburner member of the New York Assembly, O'Sullivan in 1841 proposed the abolition of cap-

1 Julius W. Pratt, "The Ideology of American Expansion," *Essays in Honor of William E. Dodd*, edited by Avery Craven (Chicago, 1935), 344.

2 J. W. Pratt, "Origin of Manifest Destiny," *American Historical Review*, XXXII (July, 1927), 795-8.

3 Herbert D. A. Donovan, *The Barnburners* (New York, 1925), 7-33.

ital punishment,[4] and the next year he advocated federal action in favor of William Ladd's plan for an international congress and court to preserve world peace.[5]

The Barnburners split off from the New York Democracy in 1844 and withdrew from the convention that nominated Polk for the Presidency because they opposed southern expansion. They favored the Wilmot Proviso to prohibit slavery in territory acquired from Mexico. In 1848, they again refused to support the regular party ticket and joined with the abolitionist Liberty Party, anti-slavery Whigs and Free Soil Democrats in support of Martin Van Buren for President. This loose association was called the Free Democracy or the Free Soil Party. It maintained the democratic-reformist traditions of Jefferson and Jackson after the regular Democracy dropped them in 1844 in favor of expansion and pro-slavery.[6] But in 1844 O'Sullivan deserted the Barnburners and supported Polk against Van Buren for the Democratic Presidential nomination. After Polk's victory, O'Sullivan was one of his distributors of patronage.[7] His greatest service to Polk and the expansionists was his propaganda in the *Democratic Review* and the *Morning News*. The magical phrase, Manifest Destiny, caught the imagination of Americans and made opponents of the war with Mexico seem pitted against Divine Providence.

The 1848 Free Soil Platform carefully distinguished between the expansion of free territory which it supported and the expansion of slavery territory it opposed.[8] But O'Sullivan's expansionism was neither anti-slavery nor as unconcerned

4 J. W. Pratt, "John L. O'Sullivan and Manifest Destiny," *New York History*, XIV (July, 1933), 226.

5 Merle E. Curti, *The American Peace Crusade: 1815-1860* (Durham, 1929), 60.

6 Jesse Macy, *Political Parties in the United States, 1841-1861* (New York, 1900), 100-1.

7 O'Sullivan to Polk, New York, April 12 and June 13, 1845. Polk Papers.

8 K. N. Porter, *National Party Platforms* (New York, 1924), 24.

with sectional issues as the interpreters of his phrase have believed.[9] He refused to support Van Buren for President on the Free Soil Platform, and came out for Senator Cass of Michigan, the regular Democratic candidate and an advocate of the expansionist program of the South, which by this time included annexation of Cuba. The *Democratic Review* called Van Buren's cry of free soil and no more slave territory hypo-critical and the basis of schemes of disunion.[10]

Annexation of Cuba was O'Sullivan's chief interest from 1847 and 1848, when he secured Polk's consent to his pur-chase plan, through the years of Whig rule when he was a leading organizer of the López and Quitman filibuster expedi-tions, in the 1852 campaign when he supported Pierce rather than John P. Hale, the Free Soil candidate, and as Minister to Portugal under Presidents Pierce and Buchanan. In 1860, John Bigelow entertained O'Sullivan at dinner in the Garrick Club and was shocked by his guest's " avowing himself a pro-slavery man and declaring that the Africans ought to erect the first monument they were able to erect by voluntary sub-scription to the first slave-trader." [11]

Why did O'Sullivan continue after 1844 to call himself a Barnburner and a Free Soiler? Like many pro-slavery northern Democrats, he resented and fought against capture by aboli-tionists of the Jacksonian mantle of democratic reform and the enormous prestige and political advantage it bestowed on its legitimate inheritors. The phrase Manifest Destiny was a first attempt to obscure in a cloud of fatalistic and fanatical emotionalism the sectional issues raised by expansion of slavery territory. Yet it was not enough, and in 1852, as will appear, a flat identification of slavery expansion with democratic idealism

9 Albert K. Weinberg, *Manifest Destiny* (Baltimore, 1935), 206 *et passim*.

10 *Democratic Review*, XXIII (July, 1848), 4-6. O'Sullivan did not end his editorial association with the *Review* when he sold it in 1846. Pratt, *op. cit.*, 225.

11 John Bigelow, *Retrospections of an Active Life* (New York, 1909), I, 280.

was asserted by O'Sullivan and the " Young Americans ". The Jacksonian passion to " extend the area of freedom " and the enthusiasm for the revolutions of 1848 in Europe were harnessed to the program for slavery extension. A brilliant journalist, O'Sullivan understood the semantic value of slogans with favorable connotations, and he exploited his talent in the cause of slavery. His major efforts, unlike his personal disguise as a Barnburner and Free Soiler, were extremely effective. Once the slogans were thrown out, they developed an independent life and were used by supporters of the expansion of free-soil territory as well as pro-slavery imperialists.

Cuban slave-owners were not excluded by O'Sullivan from the benefits Manifest Destiny should bring to their Anglo-Saxon neighbors. O'Sullivan's sister had married Cristóbal Madan y Madan, a wealthy Cuban planter, merchant, ship-owner and leader of the Creole annexationists.[12] O'Sullivan became an intimate associate of his brother-in-law in annexationist schemes. Madan moved freely between Havana and New York, and O'Sullivan often visited him in Cuba. This connection perhaps helps to account for the pro-slavery interpretation of Manifest Destiny that increasingly dominated the New Yorker's political activities after 1844. It certainly was the link that enabled him to bring together the Cuban leaders and the Polk administration.

Madan was President of the Cuban Council which delegates of revolutionary groups in the island organized in New York in 1847. This Council was the organizational expression of the unity of Cuban liberals and annexationists after the disaster to the liberal cause of *La Escalera*. Madan represented the *Club de la Habana* which he had helped organize among planters who had long espoused annexation to the United States as the means of achieving both separation from Spain and security for slavery.[13] The Club met in the Aldama palace in

12 Vilá, *Historia de Cuba*, I, 377.

13 H. P. Vilá, *Narciso López y Su Época* (Havana, 1930), I, 200.

Havana. The wealth and prestige of its members gave it a degree of immunity from interference by the Spanish authorities that no other group enjoyed. Herminio Portell Vilá, the leading Cuban historian of the period, designates most of its members as " annexationists for economic reasons," as distinguished from the liberals whom he calls "annexationists for patriotic motives". The character of the latter as Cuban nationalists is defended by Vilá, who points out that many of them lived to fight for independence in 1868 and 1895. Their annexationism during the earlier period, he writes:

> was a synonym of separatism, it meant the end of Spanish domination, and they contemplated with the greatest honesty and eagerness only that immediate result, because with the end of the colonial despotism and while the admission of the new state caused internal difficulties in the North American Union, they would be able to devote themselves with facility to the creation of the republic of which they dreamed.[14]

Certainly the schisms which presently revived found the " patriotic " and the " economic " annexationists the chief nuclei of contention.

The former were mainly active in provincial centers of the island. Their leader was Narciso López and their delegates to the Cuban Council in New York included José Aniceto Iznaga and Gaspar Betancourt Cisneros. The bold and impatient López was reluctant to place himself under the cautious leadership of the Havana Club or the Cuban Council. Since 1844 he had engaged in business enterprises that permitted him to travel through the island organizing support for a revolt. At his Cuban Rose Mines, machetes and pikes were forged and hidden. Other leaders feared that López intended to arouse the slaves and they worked to unite his efforts with their plans for peaceful annexation to the United States.

This was the task that O'Sullivan set for himself. In 1846

14 Vilá, *op. cit.*, 190-3. Author's translation.

his *Morning News* failed and he sold the *Democratic Review*. If he expected office under the Polk administration, he was disappointed. He did become a Regent of New York University, but that hardly satisfied the man who was, according to the son of his intimate friend, Nathaniel Hawthorne:

> always full of grand and world-embracing schemes, which seemed to him, and which he made appear to others, vastly practicable and alluring, but which invariably miscarried by reason of some oversight which had escaped notice for the very reason that it was so fundamental a one.[15]

The grand scheme O'Sullivan conceived may not have been one of those in which Nathaniel Hawthorne often saw him " on the verge of making a fortune, and always disappointed ", but it did attract " the fate he half-anticipates . . . to be shot or hung ".[16]

The first move in his scheme took O'Sullivan to Havana with his brother-in-law, Cristóbal Madan. Moses Yale Beach, the editor of the New York *Sun,* was there on a related mission. Beach was returning from Mexico where, as Polk's secret agent, he had engaged in intrigues that well prepared him for further adventures in Cuban affairs. He had arrived in Mexico City in January, 1847, with a British passport, plans for a canal across the Isthmus of Tehuantepec and a national bank, and letters from American and Cuban Roman Catholic prelates who introduced him into Mexican clerical circles. The Mexican government had resolved to sell Church property to raise funds for the war. Beach first attempted to negotiate a peace treaty. Failing in that, he created a diversion to cover General Scott's landing at Vera Cruz by encouraging the clerical party in Mexico City to revolt. He promised that the

15 Julian Hawthorne, *Nathaniel Hawthorne and His Wife* (Cambridge, 1884), I, 160.

16 Nathaniel Hawthorne to Franklin Pierce, Concord, December 3, 1861. Franklin Pierce Papers.

United States would support the freedom and property of the clergy, and supplied $40,000 to help finance the revolt. When Scott was safely ashore, Beach escaped.[17] As editor of the *Sun,* the pioneer of the penny press, Beach had retrieved his earlier failures as a manufacturer of a gunpowder engine for propelling balloons and other inventions of his own. The *Sun* thrived on journalistic exploits and, according to its rival, the *Herald,* hoaxes. After his trip to Mexico, Beach organized war news service for his paper that was 78 hours faster than the mails. The policy of the *Sun* was ardently Democratic with emphasis on unlimited expansion.[18]

Early in 1847, Beach, O'Sullivan and Madan met in Havana and attended meetings of the Havana Club in the Aldama palace. The Creole leaders appealed to the Americans to induce President Polk to buy Cuba from Spain, and thereby liberate the island without danger of internal disorder and secure their property rights, especially in slaves, as firmly as they were guaranteed in the American South. Besides their interests as planters and slave-owners, members of the Club, such as Aldama and José Antonio Echeverría, were active in the development of Cuban railroads, and others, like Madan, were leaders in trade between Cuba and the United States. They expected great commercial and industrial advantages when Cuba became a member of the Union. Such prospects were especially glittering to John S. Thrasher, the only American member of the Club. He had long been a resident of Havana and was editor of *El Faro Industrial,* a newspaper that celebrated the business life and potentialities of the island. Freedom from the restrictions and tyranny of Spanish rule and the fostering protection of slavery, commerce and industry

17 Buchanan to Beach, Washington, November 21, 1846. Department of State, *Special Missions,* I. Beach to Buchanan, New York, June 4, 1847. Department of State, *Special Agents,* XV. Justin H. Smith, *The War with Mexico* (New York, 1919), II, 11-13, 65, 331-2.

18 New York *Sun,* July 26 and November 30, 1847. Frank M. O'Brien, *The Story of the Sun* (New York, 1918), 139 ff.

that Cuba would receive in the American Union opened dazzling vistas to the members of the Havana Club, and they communicated their enthusiasm to Beach and O'Sullivan.[19]

Those two Americans decided that, with victory in Mexico in sight, the time was ripe for action by the United States on Cuba. It would be bought from Spain on the crest of popular enthusiasm generated by Scott's glorious deeds and as a corollary of Mexican annexations. Madan and the Creoles made lavish promises to pour out their wealth as compensation to the United States for the ransom it would pay to Spain. This would justify the United States in offering so large an amount of money that it would "pay" Spain to sell the island by making up for the loss of revenues and yielding profit besides. The extraordinary amount of $100,000,000 was the minimum sum on which they agreed.

Beach planned to launch a propaganda campaign in the *Sun* to focus attention on Cuba, present the purchase plan to the public, and create opinion in favor of action by Polk. Furthermore, the Cubans were ready to finance an annexationist newspaper in Spanish and English to be published in New York and serve as a propaganda organ in Cuba as well as the United States. Beach promised to print the paper on the presses of the *Sun*. The United States Consul, General Robert B. Campbell, became interested in these plans. He later admitted to Buchanan that he had entertained two Cubans at dinner with two Americans. Since, as he said, out of this meeting grew the plan to launch the New York annexationist newspaper *La Verdad*, the two Americans were doubtless O'Sullivan and Beach, the two leading promoters of the venture. Campbell denied that he encouraged opposition to the Spanish government, he said he merely told Cubans of the advantages of republican institutions and contrasted them with the evils of monarchy and despotism. However, he was satisfied that he knew more about

19 Vilá, *Historia de Cuba*, I, 364. Vilá, *López*, I, 241.

the members of the various Cuban revolutionary groups than they knew about each other.[20]

O'Sullivan opposed Beach's plan to make a newspaper sensation out of the plan to buy Cuba. He understood the passion for secrecy of President Polk, who was called by some a " mole ", and he feared that publicity would arouse opposition in Spain. He wanted to approach the President through Secretary of State Buchanan, convince them both of the wisdom of the plan and urge a swift and secret negotiation to be conducted preferably by himself. Returning to the United States, Beach and O'Sullivan each pursued his own course, and their efforts proved to be complementary.

In January, 1847, O'Sullivan had first proposed the purchase of Cuba to Buchanan. Now on July 6, he wrote a lengthy memorandum for the Secretary of State on the basis of the decisions of the Havana Club. This document became an important source of ideas on Cuba for the Pierce and Buchanan as well as Polk administrations. It began by asserting that the present moment afforded an opportunity for the acquisition of Cuba which might never return. Combined with accessions from Mexico, including an isthmian right-of-way, Cuban annexation, O'Sullivan wrote, " would stamp out the term of the Administration which should effect it, as one of the great epochs, not only of our country, but of the commercial history of the world ". O'Sullivan was aware that the Wilmot Proviso made annexation of slavery territory politically dangerous, and he stressed the strategic and commercial motives for annexation, which, he wrote, " would be no less popular at the commercial North and East & the grain-growing West, than at the South ". He dismissed the question of slavery extension with an unqualified statement that annexation of Cuba " would involve no extension of slavery." What he meant by this is unfathomable except in the light of Julian Hawthorne's remark

20 Campbell to Buchanan, August 9, 1848. Department of State, *Consular Despatches: Havana*, XL.

on the propensity of its author to ignore precisely that aspect of a project which ensured its failure.

The memorandum went on to point out that Cuban annexation would not disturb the sectional balance of the Union because it would accelerate acquisition of Canada. Cubans were afraid of servile insurrection and therefore did not want to be independent. It would be better to take Spain's "golden colony" now than to fight England or France for it later. Spain was doubtless ready to retreat before the "irresistible destiny" of the United States as manifested in Texas and Oregon. If the United States hesitated, France and Britain would combine to guarantee the island to Spain. This would not prevent annexation but only complicate matters. The Cuban planters themselves were ready to pay an enormous sum for the benefits of the American Union:

> I speak on the authority of some of the most wealthy and influential of them, when I say that for the Island to pay a hundred or a hundred & fifty millions of dollars, even with their present means, would be a great relief from their present burthens, under the Spanish colonial yoke.

Spanish pride must yield before such an irresistible temptation. But the negotiations must be "secret and rapid". Britain and France must be kept in the dark. O'Sullivan made the transaction seem quite simple: a treaty should be made and then "ratified by the stoppage of a few thousands of our troops at the Island on their return from Mexico, and by the rendezvous of Perry's squadron in the port of Havana to salute the change of flags on the Morro Castle". Britain and France would see themselves "baffled and anticipated, and the impregnable sway of the New World, together with the commercial predominance of the globe, secured forever to our Union".

In January, O'Sullivan had not wanted personally to conduct the negotiation with Spain. But now he thought that if the President wanted an unpaid agent to go as a private citizen and sound out the Spanish government, he would undertake the task. He would look for gratitude only to the people of Cuba, especially his personal friends.[21]

While Buchanan and Polk pondered this plausible temptation to try for a dramatic stroke that would crown the expansionist adminstration with glory, Moses Beach launched his propaganda campaign with the full resources of his skill in sensational journalism. First he sent his daughter, a clever writer keenly interested in politics, to Havana to send him material. She wrote under the name " Cora Montgomery " and was the wife of Willian L. Cazneau, a dabbler in West Indian political intrigues before and after the Civil War. In their New York home, Gaspar Betancourt Cisneros was a boarder.[22] On July 19 and 22, 1847, the first two of a pilot series of letters from Cuba appeared in the *Sun*. They were signed " Cora ", and appeared to be no more than travel sketches. In the first, the author declared she had arrived in the island prejudiced but had come to love its people and its natural beauties. The second attempted to dispel American notions that the Cubans were a backward people. Their progress in industrialization was offered as proof that their enterprising character could not be held in vassalage forever.[23]

On July 23, a *Sun* editorial presented the purchase plan devised by O'Sullivan, Beach, Madan, the Cuban Council of New York and the Havana Club. The headline was " Cuba under the Flag of the United States ". The editor professed to have met unnamed wealthy and influential men in Havana who assured him that Cubans were anxious to come into the Union. He had promised to lay the question before the American people as soon as Mexico was disposed of. Mexico was now ours.

21 Memorandum, O'Sullivan to Buchanan, Washington, July 6, 1847. Buchanan Papers.

22 Vilá, *López*, I, 237.

23 New York *Sun*, July 19 and 22, 1847.

Cuba by geographical position, necessity and right belongs to the United States, it may and must be ours. The moment has arrived to place it in our hands and under our flag. Cuba is in the market for sale, and we are authorized by parties eminently able to fulfil what they propose, to say that if the United States will offer the Spanish government one hundred millions of dollars Cuba is ours, and that with one week's notice, the whole amount will be raised and paid over by the inhabitants of the island.

Cuba would complete the territory of the United States and make it master of North America. It was the " Garden of the World, the key to the Gulf ". It was almost within cannon shot of Florida. It was rich. The island's revenues provided support for 25,000 soldiers, the Spanish civil service, fortifications and other works, and $7,000,000 besides. It produced the finest sugar, coffee, tobacco and tropical fruits in the world.

Cuba must be ours! . . . To us it is indispensible. We want its harbors for our ships to touch at to and from Mexico — for the accommodation of American and English transatlantic steamers — for its products and trade, and as the Grand key to the Gulf of Mexico. Give us Cuba, and our possessions are complete.[24]

This editorial reopened the Cuban question in the United States after it had been submerged by the outbreak of war with Mexico. Agitation for the annexation of Cuba would not again die out until internal division and a greater war distracted the country. In the meantime, the struggle over Cuba helped to divide the North and the South on the issue of expansion of slavery territory, which became the decisive issue between the sections. But Beach had studiously avoided raising the slavery issue in his initial editorial. He appealed only to the traditional strategic and commercial motives for interest in Cuba.

24 New York *Sun*, July 23, 1847.

The press responded with ridicule and apathy. In *Niles'
Weekly Register* it was dryly observed that "the appetite for
new territory would seem but to increase with its indulgence".[25] The *New Orleans Bee* called the *Sun* plan "the
inanimate nursling of Mr. Yulee . . . as ricketty and jointless
and languid an abortion as was ever spawned from the sickly
brains of progressive democracy".[26] As ardently expansionist
and Democratic a paper as the New York *Herald* ignored the
proposal of its rival.

By the end of August, the *Sun* admitted the slavery motive
for annexation of Cuba. Cora Montgomery described the
Creoles' fear of slave revolts and declared it to be their reason
for turning to "the powerful and abiding shelter of the
Union".[27] Presently Beach wrote an editorial to develop the
argument that the Spanish government did not give the Cuban
slave-owners sufficient aid against insurrections.[28]

The British threat to Cuba was brought home to Americans
fortuitously for the annexationists when Lord George Bentinck
on July 7, 1847, told Parliament that Britain should take Cuba
and Puerto Rico to satisfy British holders of defaulted Spanish
bonds. Lord Palmerston ominously answered for the government that Britain indeed had a right to go to war against Spain
to obtain redress and the question was merely one of expediency. Beach wrote that this proved not only the urgency
of annexation by the United States, but the rare magnanimity
of his plan, and he reprinted an editorial of the Springfield,
Massachusetts, *Gazette* which declared that if Britain took
Cuba she would have a "girdle of fire" around the United
States.[29]

25 *Niles' Weekly Register*, LXXII (July 31, 1847), 338.

26 *New Orleans Bee*, August 4, 1847. *Ibid.* (August 14, 1847), 378.

27 New York *Sun*, August 31, 1847. *Cf.* the same writer, *ibid.*, August 25,
1847.

28 *Ibid.*, September 10, 1847.

29 *Ibid.*, August 9, 1847.

During the fall, as his arguments became repetitious, Beach tried to meet the chief objection to his plan, namely, that the Cubans did not want to be annexed. He published an increasing number of letters by Cubans who demanded of the American people that, as the poet " Cubano " wrote:

> O, like Columbia's birth,
> Be ours! the stars and eagle hovering o'er each hearth.[30]

Possibly assisted by their patron, the Cubans caught the spirit of Manifest Destiny and begged the opportunity to submit to it. Their appeals reached a climax in the demand signed by José Vicente Brito:

> I have the commission and authority from [my countrymen] to demand protection and assistance from the United States in regard to the matter of annexing the Island of Cuba to this confederation . . . . We have been treasuring in our hearts, a burning wish for the emancipation of our country, from old dejected and corrupt Spain, since the year 1823.

Wrongs committed by Spain were to be avenged, Brito wrote, from those against the Indians described by las Casas to the cruelties of Tacón, " that savage tiger ", and of O'Donnell in *La Escalera*.

> If [the United States] government does not protect and aid us in our just claims, we shall then arise ourselves and never cease, until Cuba shall be emancipated . . . . We must continually keep our gaze fixed on this glorious land, to have our country annexed to which, and to see her, flourishing beneath this meteor flag is the living and dying wish of every Cuban Patriot.[31]

On January 1, 1848, *La Verdad* took over the main burden of convincing the American people that Cubans favored annexation. This semi-monthly newspaper in Spanish and Eng-

30 New York *Sun*, August 17, 1847.
31 New York *Sun*, December 21, 1847.

lish was distributed free in the United States and Cuba. Its expenses were paid by Cubans, who provided $10,000 initial capital.[32] It maintained high standards of writing, editing and printing, the last being performed on the new cylindrical press of the *Sun* across Nassau Street from the office of *La Verdad*. The editors were Gaspar Betancourt Cisneros and later José Teurbe Tolón, members of the Cuban Council, but for a time Cora Montgomery's name appeared on the masthead as sole editor. *La Verdad* published very little matter unconnected with Cuban annexation, but within that limitation it served fare of considerable variety and liveliness. News items and complaints against the horrors of Spanish rule from Cuba, news of American expansionist politics, articles on the affairs of the Cuban Council and annexationist ideology, and editorials ringing the changes on the wisdom of annexation were its staples. Public notices, commercial advertisements, shipping news and fiction were published to appeal to a wide public. Racial contempt for other Latin-Americans than Cubans was calculated to placate the Anglo-Saxon gods of imperialism and it provided a touch of absurdity.

The propaganda of *La Verdad* was highly flattering to Americans. Leading Cubans who claimed to speak for all the islanders represented themselves as inspired by passionate admiration for the United States, its institutions and people. They begged to be favored as the next object of America's Manifest Destiny, which an editorial defined as the

> decree of Providence, who has placed Cuba in America, and in America a people who are charged with the mission of liberty, morality, civilization and progress to all American nations.[33]

Annexation of Canada was advocated as the means of balancing sectional interests in expansion. The slavery motive

32 New York *Sun*, November 24, 1847.

33 *La Verdad*, November 3, 1848.

of the Creoles was frankly set forth. Northern criticisms that the large slave population of Cuba was a hindrance to annexation were answered with the statement that the slaves were

> the *most urgent cause,* if not the *principal,* which compels the Cubans to shake off the Spanish yoke, and place themselves under the protection of the United States, where the negroes *are not* an obstacle to the liberty or the political rights of the Americans; where the negroes *are not* an instrument in the hands of the government to terrify and subjugate its citizens; where the negroes *are not* an inexhaustible mine of taxes and contributions.

The United States could save Cuba from " volcanic fires " like those that had erupted in Haiti by making possible " pacific revolution, without bloodshed, reactions, hatreds, or retaliations sufficiently merited and therefore likely to be sufficiently cruel ". The revolutions of 1848 in Europe were greeted ardently as confirmation that for the whole world and especially Cuba, " The hour of liberty approaches! " However, in this year of splendid " Revolution upon Revolution! " a report of a Negro uprising in Haiti impressed the editors of *La Verdad* as too much of a good thing. And the abolition of slavery in the French West Indies was offered as a warning that the United States must take over Cuba in self-preservation.[34] Such admission of the slavery motive was unusual in American discussion of expansion.

The method usually advocated by *La Verdad* by which the United States should annex Cuba was, of course, purchase from Spain. Early in 1848, it urged renewal of Senator Yulee's resolution of 1845 in favor of opening negotiations with Spain. Cubans were advised to be ready to cast themselves into " the strong, friendly and protecting arms of the Union." [35]

34 *Ibid.,* April 27, 1848.
35 *Ibid.,* April 27, 1848.

La Verdad was chiefly important as the organ of the Cuban exiles, but it provided convincing proof that many Cubans desired annexation, and its articles were widely commented on and copied in the American press. Beach had sent bundles of the *Sun* containing annexationist propaganda to Cuba, but the Captain-General soon forbade its circulation or any public reference to it.[36]   *La Verdad* was also banned in Cuba, but an effective clandestine distributing organization used the government-subsidized United States Mail Steamship Company's vessels and Drake Brothers and Company, Havana agent of the line, to secure a wide circulation in the island. This collusion led to numerous incidents that troubled Spanish-American relations during the seven years of *La Verdad's* life.

The Spanish government was sufficiently concerned over the effectiveness of the Cubans' impudent newspaper to finance an organ of counter-propaganda in New York, *La Cronica,* which was established in offices next door to the *Sun* in October, 1848.   Its editor made an effort to present general news, but he reserved his special anger for the advocates of annexation of Cuba to the United States. He was accused of spying on the Cubans across the street as a side-line. In opposition to Anglo-Saxon expansionism and its Cuban friends, *La Cronica* developed the point of view of *Hispanidad,* the movement to bind all Spanish-speaking peoples together in a spiritual union capable of indefinite amplification which became important in Latin America and Spain later in the century.[37]   The editors of *La Verdad* tended to bog down in heavy rebuttals of *La Cronica's* litanies in praise of Spanish absolutism and in other controversies of parochial interest. Yet the annexationist newspaper continued to publish during the whole period of the climax of American interest in Cuba, and was far more influential in creating opinion favorable to annexation as well as longer-lived than *La Patria,* the organ of exiles in New Orleans

36 New York *Sun*, September 23, 1847.

37 *La Cronica*, February 17, 1849, *et passim.*

who favored Cuban independence, or *La Aurora* of Washington, which favored annexation. It was by much the most effective to date of any propaganda vehicle of a foreign group in the United States, and must be credited with some responsibility for the importance which the desire for Cuba began to assume in American politics after the Mexican War.

O'Sullivan at first deplored the public agitation of the Cuban question by Beach and his friends. He wrote to Buchanan on July 31, 1847, that he thought the "foolish" campaign of the *Sun* would do mischief unless, to be sure, it stimulated President Polk to "a little action". Buchanan had told O'Sullivan that Polk feared to alarm Spain by sending him to sound its attitude towards selling Cuba. O'Sullivan now wrote that in any case he could not afford to go, because Secretary of the Navy John Y. Mason would not allow a dock to be built at Pensacola in which he was interested. But no more harm could be done than Beach had already accomplished, so the President should make an attempt to buy the island. Surely, O'Sullivan wrote, the administration must heed the danger of British action as foreshadowed in Parliament.[38] Buchanan answered that the President did not want to act until the Mexican War was settled. O'Sullivan next pleaded that England had created "a proper occasion for some interference of our Minister at Madrid", who should announce that the United States would never allow Britain to take Cuba, and that his government was "willing to take the Island & the debt in case the Spanish government should be hard pressed by England on the subject".[39]

But the administration was not yet in a position to act on Cuba and O'Sullivan's importunities were unavailing. When Congress met in December, it became apparent that the first object of expansionists was to annex all of Mexico, and Cuba was neglected. Nicholas P. Trist's treaty arrived in February,

38 O'Sullivan to Buchanan, New York, July 31, 1847. Buchanan Papers.

39 O'Sullivan to Buchanan, New York, August 4, 1847. *Ibid.*

1848. Buchanan and Secretary of the Treasury Robert J. Walker wanted to reject it because it did not cede enough territory to the United States, but Polk, fearful of the House majority that had passed the Wilmot Proviso and accused him of waging the war for conquest, after painful hesitation, sent the treaty to the Senate as the best that was then obtainable. The President remained on the lookout for further opportunities for expansion, and only the vacillating attitude of Buchanan, which Polk attributed to his ambition to be President, disturbed the unity of the administration on the policy of further annexations.[40] In the Senate, extreme expansionists among the Democrats were so disappointed by the treaty that they joined Whig opponents of expansion to vote against it, but nevertheless, on March 10, a majority of two-thirds gave its consent.

O'Sullivan promptly renewed his urging to Buchanan. Surely, he wrote, the hour to strike for Cuba had now come. The Mexican affair was disposed of safely enough. Time was short to make a more valuable acquisition. Elections were coming and if a Whig, Clay or Taylor, became President, " God only knows what may be the fate of Cuba before a Democratic administration will again have a chance of renewing an effort for its acquisition ". Buchanan should urge Polk " that further delay now would be criminal—imbecile—almost treasonable to the destiny and policy of the United States ". The " bugaboo " of English and French intervention was entirely exploded now: " The French Republic (God bless it!) would be on our side, and England will have enough to do to mind her own business at home ". If they did try to interfere, ships and a few thousand American troops from Mexico would settle the matter. The action of Britain in claiming a protectorate over the Mosquito Indians of Nicaragua showed why the United States must have Cuba. Furthermore, the throne

40 *The Diary of James K. Polk: 1845-1849*, edited and annotated by Milo M. Quaife (Chicago, 1910), III, 348, 350 *et passim*.

was tottering in Spain, and Minister Washington Irving, O'Sullivan claimed, had written to him that Spain would accept an offer of $100,000,000. He had not Beach's faith that the Creoles would personally repay the sum, but the recent demonstration of the Rothschilds' confidence in American bonds proved that a new issue would be easily absorbed in Europe. The administration need not fear a split in the Democratic Party, because:

> We Barnburners will be as much pleased at [the purchase of Cuba] as the Southerners themselves. To the abolitionists we can point out that it is the only mode of stopping the slave trade; which is the fact. If the object can be consummated before the election, it would have an electric effect. If encouragingly in progress, it will do great good; especially to those who may be personally entitled to the credit of it. It will give great moral force to the party whose measure it will be, as contributing to prove that to be the true American party, the party entrusted by God & Nature with the mission of the American policy and destiny.

O'Sullivan suggested John Frémont as the agent to negotiate with Spain, and pointed out slyly that if he pretended to be on an engineering mission to work on Madrid's water system:

> it would not be the first time that in the service of his country he has combined with duties of scientific exploration, other simultaneous ones, of a political character, looking to the double object of acquiring a valuable country, and of defeating English intrigue in its aim of being beforehand with us.[41]

Two things still stood between O'Sullivan and success. Buchanan was discovered by Polk to be the source of secret documents and the Nugent Letters which much defamed the President, the split between them widened, and Buchanan was reluctant to urge on Polk Cuban annexation because he wished to reserve it for himself when he should succeed to the Presi-

41 O'Sullivan to Buchanan, New York, March 19, 1848. Buchanan Papers.

dency.[42]   And Polk himself was interested in exploring an opportunity to keep the door open for more Mexican territory which he found in the peculiar situation of Yucatan.

That state had asserted its neutrality during the war with the United States only to fall into civil conflict.   Justo Sierra presented himself to Buchanan in the fall of 1847 as the agent of a white government fighting a race war against the Yucatecan Indians and desperately in need of aid.   Soon the Governor of Yucatan offered the sovereignty of his state to Britain, France, Spain and the United States, whichever would send help.   On April 29, 1848, Polk submitted the offer to Congress without recommendation but with broad hints.   He said he had not enough troops to occupy the peninsula, warned that the Monroe Doctrine forbade its acquisition by a European power even with the consent of Yucatan, and made the strategic problem clear.   Yucatan, he wrote:

> is situate in the Gulf of Mexico, on the North American continent; and from its vicinity to Cuba, to the capes of Florida, to New Orleans, and indeed to our whole southwestern coast, it would be dangerous to our peace and security if it should become a colony of any European nation.[43]

Senator Hannegan for the Committee on Foreign Relations reported a Bill to authorize the President to take " temporary military occupation of Yucatan ", in order to assist its people in repelling " the incursions of the Indian savages ", and he stoutly denied that anyone dreamed of permanent occupation.[44] Polk noted in his diary that Walker favored ultimate annexation of Yucatan, and added: " I concurred with Mr. Walker, rather than see it fall into the hands of England." [45]

42 *Diary of Polk*, ed. Quaife, III, 400-6.

43 *Congressional Globe* (30:1), 709.

44 *Ibid.*, 727; *Appendix*, 596.

45 *Diary of Polk*, ed. Quaife, III, 444-5.

The Yucatan Bill reopened debate on expansion and, because of their intimate strategic relations, focused attention on Cuba as well. In fact, Congress showed itself more interested in Cuba than in Yucatan, and the work of Beach began to bear fruit. Hannegan reminded the Senators of recent British encroachments in Nicaragua, and warned that if England now took Yucatan it would soon be followed by her taking possession of Cuba. That island was the key to the Gulf of Mexico, he said, and " Yucatan and Cuba combined are the lock and key. Place them in the hands of England and she controls the mouth of the Mississippi, as absolutely as she controls the mouth of the Thames! " [46]

Senator Jefferson Davis of Mississippi agreed with Hannegan's analysis of British purposes, and added:

> Yucatan and Cuba are the salient points commanding the Gulf of Mexico, which I hold to be a basin of water belonging to the United States. Whenever the question arises whether the United States shall seize these gates of entrance from the south and east, or allow them to pass into the possession of any maritime Power, I am ready, for one, to declare that my step will be forward, and that the cape of Yucatan and the island of Cuba must be ours.[47]

The Whig Senator John M. Clayton of Delaware drew from Davis the statement that he would not hesitate for a moment to go to war if Britain occupied Cuba to put down a Negro insurrection according to the precedent proposed for the United States in Yucatan. Davis offered an amendment that would permit the President to raise new troops to replace those sent from Mexico to Yucatan, and for this purpose he wanted twenty regiments.[48] Davis was bold: a proposal in January

---

46 *Congressional Globe* (30:1), *Appendix*, 597.

47 *Ibid.*, 599.

48 *Ibid.*, 599-600, 607.

that ten regiments be raised to continue the war in Mexico had met bitter opposition.[49]

The debate shifted backward to the causes of the war against Mexico and forward to plans for unlimited expansion, but time and again it dwelt on Cuba. Senator Westcott of Florida stressed the interest of the South in the fate of Cuban slavery. Britain, he said:

> seeks to emancipate the slaves in Cuba, and to strike the southern portion of this Confederacy through its domestic institutions . . . Are the southern States of this Confederacy prepared to see the slaves in Cuba emancipated by the efforts of Great Britain, and then to see her in possession of Yucatan, and populate it with a colony of manumitted negroes from Jamaica? My State will not assent to such a state of things . . . Why, sir, Florida would be surrounded by a cordon of foreign colonial governments, the population of which would be emancipated slaves, under the control of the worst enemy of the United States.

He would go to war if Britain fomented incendiarism. If the United States obtained nothing more than a naval base in Yucatan, he would take it because that would render Cuba worthless to Britain.[50] Senator John C. Calhoun of South Carolina had become gloomy with forebodings of the fruits of expansion after the annexation of Texas, and he took the lead in opposition to the Yucatan Bill. He declared that Polk had dangerously extended the Monroe Doctrine. He would not oppose Britain in Yucatan. Nevertheless, he said, there were cases in which he would resort to the hazards of war. with all its calamities: "Am I asked for one? I will answer. I designate the case of Cuba." If Spain lost it, no other power but the United States might take it. British control and emancipation must certainly be prevented in Cuba.[51]

49 *Congressional Globe* (30:1), 214 ff.

50 *Congressional Globe* (30:1), *Appendix*, 608.

51 *Congressional Globe* (30:1), 712; *Appendix*, 631-2.

On May 10, Senator Cass of Michigan proposed the purchase of Cuba after asserting that the Gulf of Mexico " must be practically an American lake," and the importance of the island as a coaling station for the new steam vessels.[52] Twelve days later, Cass was nominated for the Presidency by the Democratic Convention in Baltimore. The well-known talent of the Michigan Senator for pleasing the South had borne fruit, but not without causing northern Democratic opponents of slavery extension to split the party rather than support him.

On the same day that Cass urged the purchase of Cuba, John L. O'Sullivan saw President Polk for the same purpose. He had finally realized that Buchanan was a poor advocate of his plan. Now he pressed the views on the President which he had vainly written to Buchanan. Senator Stephen A. Douglas of Illinois accompanied O'Sullivan and seconded him. The President wrote in his diary:

> I heard their views, but deemed it prudent to express no opinion on the subject. Mr. O'Sullivan read to me and left with me a paper embodying his views in favor of the measure. Though I expressed no opinion to them I am decidedly in favour of purchasing Cuba & making it one of the States of [the] Union.[53]

O'Sullivan had evidently connected the Cuban question with that of Yucatan, for later that day he sent Polk a passage from Senator Hannegan's speech on Yucatan to be inserted where he had left a blank in his written statement to Polk. Additional remarks of his own warned Polk that important Spanish interests enjoyed monopoly markets in Cuba because of discriminatory tariff and navigation laws and that they should not be alarmed by knowledge of the intentions of the United States " until too late ". An inconspicuous envoy should negotiate the purchase. Payment of the purchase

52 *Ibid.*, 614-7.

53 *Diary of Polk*, ed. Quaife, III, 446.

money O'Sullivan made to seem simple by a scheme which he outlined to require most of it to be paid by Cuba. He concluded with an explanation that if his interest in the speedy purchase of Cuba was

> somewhat quickened by a natural anxiety respecting the personal safety of some very dear members of my family resident on that island, I beg you to be assured that this motive is wholly subordinate to the higher ones, founded on the public reasons I have laid before you, by which I have been actuated ever since my visit to Cuba.[54]

On May 17, 1848, after a vote on an amendment to the Yucatan Bill indicated that the expansionists would carry the measure at least in the Senate,[55] news arrived that peace had been made by the contending factions in the peninsula, and Hannegan put through a motion that the Bill be passed over.[56] This ended the chance of making the Yucatan incident yield an increment of territory for the United States. On May 22, the Democratic Convention nominated for the Presidency Senator Lewis Cass, who had publicly called for the purchase of Cuba. The prospect of his election was dimmed by the defection of Northern Democrats who had supported the Wilmot Proviso, Barnburners and Free Soilers with Van Buren as their candidate. On the other hand, their defection removed many opponents of slavery expansion from the ranks of the Democrats, and a further effort would not improve the chance of a Whig victory. Polk resolved to buy Cuba. He refused to yield to the opposition of Northern Democrats to the extension of slavery territory. The successive frustrations of his desire for more of Mexico would be compensated. In the circumstances, the President's decision had pro-southern and pro-slavery significance which would not be revealed in official statements or in the always-guarded words of his diary.

54 O'Sullivan to Polk, Baltimore, May 10, 1848. Polk Papers.
55 *Congressional Globe* (30:1), 773.
56 *Ibid., Appendix*, 639.

Polk proposed the purchase of Cuba to his Cabinet on May 30, 1848, in virtually the terms suggested by the *Sun* and O'Sullivan, which were the terms of the Cuban planters who belonged to the Havana Club and the Cuban Council. He stressed the danger that Cuba might fall into the hands of Britain, although no specific threat from that quarter had been offered for almost a year.[57] The leader of Polk's Cabinet was Robert J. Walker, Secretary of the Treasury. He was a planter and land speculator of Mississippi who had initiated the program of southern imperialism commonly pursued by politicians of the South, especially Mississippi and Louisiana, during the period 1844 to 1860. He had been the chief engineer of the adoption by the Democratic Convention in 1844 of the expansionist platform and of Polk's nomination. Like Jefferson Davis of Mississippi in the Pierce administration and John Slidell of Louisiana in the Buchanan administration, Walker played the part of Warwick in order to commit the party leadership to pro-slavery policies, chief of which was expansion.[58]

Walker now took the lead in the Cabinet discussion of Cuba. He said, as Polk wrote in his diary, that he was " earnestly in favor of making the attempt to purchase [Cuba], and was willing to pay one hundred millions of dollars for it ". This commitment by the Secretary of the Treasury was considered by Polk to justify negotiation of a treaty of purchase without any assurance that Congress would appropriate the money or even knowledge on its part that the Executive was committing it to so large an expenditure. Secretary of the Navy John Y.

57 *Diary of Polk*, ed. Quaife, III, 469.

58 William E. Dodd, *Robert James Walker, Imperialist* (Chicago, 1914), 1-13. Walker's personal evolution reversed the normal progress of southern politicians of the period. He followed Douglas into the camp of popular sovereignty, opposed the South as Governor of Kansas under Buchanan, supported Lincoln in 1861 and became his financial agent in London during the Civil War. *Ibid.*, 14-7.

Mason of Virginia agreed with Walker. Postmaster General Cave Johnson of Tennessee " had objections to incorporating the Spanish population of Cuba into our Union, and did not seem to favour the idea of purchasing it ". Buchanan, Polk wrote,

> expressed a general wish to acquire Cuba, but thought that there were objections to making the attempt at this time. He feared [if] it became known that such a step was contemplated, that it might act prejudicially to the Democratic party in the next Presidential election.

But Polk expressed his " strong conviction " that the attempt should be made without delay.[59]

Two days later Buchanan sent Polk a letter from General Campbell. The Havana Consul declared that a revolt would soon occur in the island. A general, unnamed by Campbell but evidently Narciso López, was being restrained with difficulty :

> He is brave, and of some experience and it is understood wishes to retire into the Interior and make a pronunciamento immediately. If Revolution is attempted, and succeeds, immediate application would be made to the United States for annexation as the most intelligent of the Creoles have an abiding conviction of their utter incapacity for self government.

In the latter opinion Campbell concurred. The new Captain-General Roncali seemed conciliatory and was working to reduce taxes.[60] The next day, June 2, O'Sullivan called on Polk and told him that an agent of the Cuban planters had arrived in Baltimore with news that a revolution was imminent, aid from the United States was wanted, and annexation to the

59 *Diary of Polk*, ed. Quaife, III, 468-9.

60 Campbell to Buchanan, Havana, May 18, 1848. Department of State, *Consular Despatches: Havana*, XXI. The date, May 8, which Polk gives this letter in his diary (III, 475), is an error. Its actual date and contents suggest that it was inspired by events in Washington.

United States would be sought when the Spanish power was overthrown. Furthermore, a General of the United States Army then in Mexico had agreed to resign his commission and proceed to Cuba with a body of discharged American soldiers to aid in establishing Cuban independence. All of this O'Sullivan " detailed confidentially " to Polk.[61]

It is far from clear why O'Sullivan confided in Polk or what he expected the President to do. The island could not be bought quickly enough to forestall the events he anticipated. If he imagined that Polk would connive in aid to the revolutionaries and filibusters, he was disabused. Polk told him that if Cuba was ever obtained by the United States, " it must be by amicable purchase, and that as President of the United States I could give no confidence to such a step, and could not wink at such a movement." [62] If O'Sullivan actually wanted the plans of his Cuban friends and relatives to succeed, his confidence in Polk was misplaced.

What had happened was that the leaders of the Havana Club had sent an agent, Rafael de Castro, to Jalapa, Mexico, to make an offer to General William J. Worth. A Cuban doctor, Sedano y Cruzat, had been negotiating with several American generals since 1846. Worth drew his attention perhaps because he had been the leader of a group of officers who quarreled with General Scott and were arrested by him. De Castro was sent to make a formal agreement that General Worth would place himself and 5,000 volunteer American veterans under the orders of the Havana Club, which would pay him $3,000,000.[63] According to Ambrosio José Gonzalez, a later agent of the Club on the same mission and a friend of de Castro, General Worth, " the Bayard of the American army," accepted the offer, contingent upon his resignation of his com-

61 *Diary of Polk*, ed. Quaife, III, 476.

62 *Ibid.*, 476-7.

63 Vilá, *Historia de Cuba*, I, 366.

mission.[64]   The purpose of the Havana Club was to check the restless General Narciso López and safeguard the internal order of the island against a rising in which López might encourage Negroes to take part.   The General had fixed on June 24, when the festival of Saints Peter and Paul would permit public gatherings, as the day when the cry of rebellion would be raised by his supporters in provincial towns throughout the island. Late in May, López visited Havana, ostensibly to show specimens of coal from his mines to promoters, but actually to get in touch with the Havana Club.   In the Aldama palace, he was told of de Castro's mission and the plan to bring a strong force of American veterans under General Worth to land on the island.   The Creoles asked López to postpone the date of his uprising until the American filibusters should arrive.   The next day, López's friend Manuel Munoz Castro, Consul of Venezuela, presented him to General Campbell, who confirmed the plans of the Havana Club.

López was disgruntled by the realization that he was being placed in a secondary position to Worth and his leadership subordinated to the Havana Club.   But he agreed that annexation to the United States should be the objective, once the Spanish authorities were overthrown, and he decided to cooperate.   The date of his uprising was postponed to the middle of July, and he returned to the provinces to await instructions from the Havana Club.[65]

O'Sullivan apparently did not know of the agreement between the Havana Club and López when, on June 2, he told Polk of the projected uprising and Worth expedition.   He probably shared the planters' distrust of the provincial movement and its chief, and perhaps he detailed the situation to Polk in fear that López's activities would disrupt the administration's efforts to purchase the island. Polk transmitted the

64 Ambrosio José Gonzalez, *Manifesto on Cuban Affairs Addressed to the People of the United States* (New Orleans, 1853), 6.

65 Vilá, *López*, I, 241-2, 270.

information to his Cabinet. Walker proposed that capital be made of the situation by taking official action against the Cubans' plans and showing Spain how peaceable and amicable were the intentions of the administration. Orders were accordingly drawn up by the Secretary of War to General Butler in Mexico to prevent any Cuban expedition, and Buchanan wrote to Campbell insisting that his conduct be strictly neutral. Copies of these documents were transmitted to Minister Romulus M. Saunders in Madrid to show the Spanish government. Buchanan heartily approved of this plan and it, coupled with an assurance by Cass that the purchase of Cuba would not be detrimental to his candidacy, broke down the Secretary of State's opposition.[66]

The administration did not limit its efforts to frustrate the Cubans' plans to those mentioned by Polk in his diary. Those actions only assured Spain rather gratuitously that, after undefined lapses by American officials, the administration endeavored to correct their behavior. Either immediately or after the Cuban Council told Polk on June 23 of López's original date for the uprising, Buchanan gave the Spanish Minister in Washington, Calderón de la Barca, more concrete proof of the loyalty of the administration to Spain. He betrayed the López conspiracy to the Spanish Minister. The conspiracy was suppressed by Roncali on July 5. On August 15, Calderón wrote to Pidal, the Spanish Minister of State, that Buchanan had told him the revolutionary plans of the Cubans, and on September 16 Pidal answered that Buchanan's act had made the Queen very happy. Calderón, he said, should tender Buchanan a copy of the letter in proof of Spain's gratitude.[67] Campbell also may have exposed López to the authorities. Immediately after he had an interview with Cap-

---

66 *Diary of Polk*, ed. Quaife, III, 478-488.

67 Pidal to Calderón, Madrid, September 16, 1848. Annexed to Calderón to Buchanan, Washington, November 21, 1848. Department of State, *Notes from Legations: Spain*, XII.

tain-General Roncali, the latter's aide, Commandante Tres-
palacios, left Havana with orders to proceed against López and
his fellow conspirators.[68]   The letter from Buchanan to
Campbell of June 9 which enjoined neutrality upon him does
not appear in the volume of instructions to consuls for the
period in the archives of the State Department.[69]   Campbell
" neglected to acknowledge " the letter for two months, when
he denied that he had encouraged a spirit of revolution among
Cubans, although he had listened to their plans " without re-
buke " and brought together the Cuban and American promoters of La Verdad.   Rumors, he said, that the President of
the United States had betrayed López to the Spanish Minister
were "not generally believed".   Campbell's letters on this
subject were not placed in the archives until 1860, when
Buchanan was President and about to leave office.[70]   In 1855,
Senator John Slidell of Louisiana wrote to Buchanan, then
Minister to Britain, that Lawrence J. Sigur, a New Orleans
editor and intimate friend of López, would oppose Buchanan's
candidacy for the Presidency because Campbell had told the
editor Buchanan had betrayed López in 1848.   Campbell was
then United States Consul in London and, when Buchanan
faced him with the charge, denied that he had told Sigur and
claimed that in any case he remembered no Cuban revolution
in that year![71]   Nevertheless, the correspondence of Calderón
and Pidal cited above proves that Spain did obtain information
about the Cuban conspiracy from Buchanan.

O'Sullivan was not the administration's only source of information on developments in Cuba. On June 23, President
Polk recorded in his diary that Senator Jefferson Davis

68 Vilá, Historia de Cuba, I, 381-2.

69 Department of State, Instructions to Consuls, X (1841-1849).

70 Campbell to Buchanan, Havana, August 9 and 12, 1848. Department
of State, Consular Despatches: Havana, XL (1860).

71 Campbell to Buchanan, London, August 13, 1855. Quoted in Vilá,
Historia de Cuba, I, 384-5.

brought three Cubans to see him with a letter from Cuba which declared that the revolution would occur the next day. They wanted Polk to station troops at Key West and other points on the Gulf coast to protect the interests of American citizens in Cuba. Polk said that he would consider it.[72] The three Cubans were members of the Cuban Council: José Aniceto Iznaga, Gaspar Betancourt Cisneros and Alonzo Betancourt. Their letter was from the nephew of the first-named, José Maria Sanchez Iznaga, a lieutenant of López in Cienfuegos. The letter was dated May 25, 1848, and was written prior to López's agreement with the Havana Club to postpone his revolt.[73] The latter circumstance left time for the contents of the letter to be transmitted by Polk to Roncali by July 5 when the revolt was suppressed. The Havana Club was evidently not implicated in the information Roncali received. None of its members was apprehended. López received a few hours' warning from a friend among the Spanish officials and made good his escape after a dramatic flight across the island by horse, by train to Cardenas and coastal steamer to Matanzas, where he got aboard the American bark *Neptune* just as it set sail for Rhode Island. A number of López's leading supporters were captured and imprisoned, but this Conspiracy of the Cuban Rose Mines, which takes its name from the mines owned by its chief where he manufactured arms for it, was suppressed without the rigor that usually attended such affairs in Cuba. López himself was condemned *in absentia* to be shot. At the hearings, annexation to the United States was shown to be ultimate object of the rebels.[74]

The Polk administration also eliminated the danger that General Worth would lead a filibuster expedition to Cuba. After strict orders had been issued that no vessel with troops

[72] *Diary of Polk*, ed. Quaife, III, 499-500.

[73] José Maria Sanchez Iznaga to José Aniceto Iznaga, Cienfuegos, May 25, 1848. Vilá, *López*, I, 221-222.

[74] *Ibid.*, 284-292.

from Mexico should touch at Cuba, Worth was recalled and arrived in the United States on August 5.   He had not given up the plan.   In Newport, Rhode Island, he met Ambrosio J. Gonzalez, the new agent of the Havana Club, and confirmed the agreement.   He sent his aide, Colonel Bohlen, to Cuba with Gonzalez.   Bohlen returned, " satisfied with the ability of the persons connected with the movement to carry out their promises," and bringing the plans of cities and fortifications which General Worth had requested.   But the General was suddenly ordered to Texas, where a few months later he died.[75]

The policy of supporting Spanish possession of Cuba even against internal revolt, which John Quincy Adams had pursued because he expected the law of political gravitation to make the island fall one day like a ripe apple to the United States, was thus vigorously pursued by the Polk administration with the hope that the proof of loyalty to Spain and $100,000,000 would induce her to give the tree a shake and speed the operation of Adams' law.

On the same day that Walker proposed that policy to Polk, the news arrived that Mexico had ratified the peace treaty. This put a final end to possibilities of further expansion in Mexico.   The Cabinet that day decided to send instructions and full powers to Saunders to buy Cuba.   Buchanan had agreed to write the instructions but without taking any responsibility himself.   Polk believed that while his Secretary of State wanted to postpone the purchase until he himself should be President, he was unwilling to be uncompromising.[76]   The instructions Buchanan wrote and the efforts of the Minister to Spain to carry them out will be described in the next chapter.

75 Gonzalez, *Manifesto*, 7. Vilá, *López*, 239-240.

76 *Diary of Polk*, ed. Quaife, III, 497, 485-8.

CHAPTER III
THE NEGOTIATIONS OF ROMULUS M. SAUNDERS

THE instructions of Secretary of State Buchanan to Minister Romulus M. Saunders gave the official reasons for President Polk's decision to buy Cuba and exact orders as to how the Minister should negotiate the purchase. The basic policy of the United States that Cuba might be Spanish but the United States would resist with force a transfer to any other European power was reaffirmed by Buchanan particularly against British possession of the island. The justification for this policy was that Cuba would give Britain power to blockade the Gulf of Mexico, the Mississippi River and the western states of the Union and cut communications between the Gulf and Atlantic coasts. Britain's motives, Buchanan wrote, were commercial. It opposed economic development of Cuba and capture of its markets by the United States. The purpose of Britain to put the commerce of the United States at its mercy was shown by encroachments in Nicaragua that were intended to establish British control of the Isthmus communications between the Atlantic and Pacific Oceans. The nearness of Belize to Cuba emphasized the danger to the United States. Lord Palmerston had declared that Britain had the right to go to war and take Cuba to recover the debt Spain owed British subjects. A crisis was at hand since Spain had expelled the British Minister, Sir Henry Bulwer.

So far, Buchanan had followed the analysis of John C. Calhoun, but he did not go on to assert the interest of the South in Cuban slavery. On the contrary, he followed the suggestions of O'Sullivan and declared that the Cuban question was not a local one. If Cuba was annexed, not only would the security and commerce of the United States benefit, but " human foresight cannot anticipate the beneficial consequences which would result to every portion of our Union." The benefits he listed, however, were the same two: a naval station at Havana and fortifications there and at Tortugas would give the United States command of the Gulf and ample security for the foreign and coasting trade of the southern and western states; and, under the United States, Cuba would become the richest and most fertile island of the same extent in the world, its population would increase ten times and in like measure its trade.

Still, the United States refused to acquire the island " except by the free consent of Spain." The Creoles were anti-Spanish, and Cubans were inspired by the revolutions in Europe. Proof that the United States did not encourage them was in the appended copies of letters to the American Consul in Havana and the Commanding General in Mexico. Besides, an unsuccessful revolution would delay if not defeat annexation.

The amount of money to be offered might be based on Spain's net revenue from the island. Spain would cease to have certain expenses, and Minister Calderón had said that his government never received more than $2,000,000 net from Cuba. So $50,000,000 would be a generous offer. But the import duties which the United States would collect in Cuba after its development were estimated at $6,000,000. No revenues were expected from public lands. Therefore, if he could not procure it for less, Saunders might offer $100,000,000. Thus Buchanan showed the administration was willing to give Spain the benefit of the increased earning capacity of Cuba which would result from reorganization and improvements by the new owner.

The political consequences in the United States of annexation were assessed favorably by the Secretary of State. In the face of the Wilmot Proviso, the abolition and free soil agitations, and the counter-movements which were leading to threats of secession in the South, he wrote:

The apprehensions which existed for many years after the origin of this Government, that the extension of our federal system would endanger the Union, seem to have passed away.

He saw only one qualification of this happy situation: the mass of the population must be of the dominant race, or at least "educated in liberty." Under the United States, Cuba would be speedily "*Americanized*,—as Louisiana has been." The process had been started by the Americans already in Cuba. Annexation could only strengthen the Union by increasing the mutual dependence of the southern and western states and the shipping and naval interests of the Atlantic states. Mutual dependence on trade between Cuba and the other states "will insure the perpetuity of our Union." The Secretary of State did not repeat O'Sullivan's remarkable statement that annexation of Cuba would not be an extension of slavery territory, but he was no less determined to ignore the question.

Saunders was told to proceed with caution. Nothing should be put in writing and the Cortes must not know of the negotiations. He should initiate the subject by describing the revolution brewing in Cuba and showing the orders to Army authorities in Mexico and the "first part" of the instructions received by Campbell. The British danger should next be cited, followed by reaffirmation of the "no-transfer" policy of the United States. Then he should offer to buy the island. The example of Louisiana should be held up for Spain by reminding its government that Napoleon sold that territory to the United States "when he was at the zenith of his power and glory." This would dispose of hesitation prompted by Spanish pride. Saunders was sent full powers and told to use the Louisiana Purchase Treaty as a model. Secrecy in Europe should be guarded by sending his despatches by special messenger.[1] Secrecy on the American side was guarded by Polk's refusal to tell even O'Sullivan, " who first suggested to me the idea

[1] Buchanan to Saunders, Washington, June 17, 1848. Department of State, *Diplomatic Instructions: Spain*, XIV.

of purchasing Cuba," that his efforts had succeeded,[2] and by keeping out of the State Department's files all records of the correspondence until the eve of the administration's departure from office. This last precaution upset the numbering system of letters of instructions and left at least one letter missing even after the serial was reorganized.

Three weeks after the initial instructions were sent to Saunders, President Polk received evidence from a strange quarter that may have encouraged him to believe Spain was ready to sell Cuba. On July 6, Secretary Walker told him that Vice President Dallas had been approached by a person who said he was authorized by the Queen of Spain to sell Cuba. Polk told Walker to bring Dallas to the White House, and within two hours the Vice President arrived. He said the person was a native of Spain, a lawyer of good reputation long resident in Philadelphia, and the agent of Isabel II and her morganatic husband charged with the investment of large sums of money. Polk confided in Dallas the plans on foot to buy Cuba (which Dallas called "a good bargain" at the price offered) and told him to explain the situation to the Spaniard and to require the latter to show credentials.[3] The demand for credentials evidently closed the episode, and leaves to speculation the question whether this Spaniard was the source of the failure of the administration to keep Saunders' negotiations secret. He is not mentioned again in the President's diary, nor is Cuba, as Polk seemed to find nothing worthy of note in the diplomacy of his envoy Romulus M. Saunders.

This American Minister to Spain, like several before and after him, had an unenviable task. His own equipment was sketchy in the extreme. An inveterate officeseeker who had failed of election as senator from North Carolina in 1842,

2 *Diary of Polk*, ed. Quaife, III, 493. The credit Polk gives O'Sullivan can hardly mean that the President had been unaware of Yulee's Resolution of 1845.

3 *Ibid.*, IV, 4-5.

he had served Polk by moving the two-thirds rule that helped defeat Van Buren in the Democratic National Convention of 1844. John Quincy Adams said of him: " There is not a more cankered or venemous reptile in the country." [4] He stayed in Paris during most of 1847 and then quarreled with his Secretary of Legation, Thomas C. Reynolds, whom he had left in charge of the Madrid mission, and had him dismissed. Saunders lacked knowledge of Spanish or French and in his conversations with Spanish officials was forced to depend on their knowledge of English. Most serious of his disqualifications was his proneness to assert his own judgment of proper policy and carry it out against the instructions of the Secretary of State. This led him in the Cuban negotiations to give away the card which Polk and Buchanan thought the strongest in their hand, and incidentally to reverse the basic policy of the United States towards Cuba which had stood for many years.

The rupture in diplomatic relations between Spain and Britain in the spring of 1848 gave rise to a situation which made Saunders decide that previous American policy was a mistake. After the Carlist Wars, the feeble hold of the dissolute Queen Isabel II and Queen Mother Maria Cristina on the distracted country was strengthened by a group of army chiefs who rotated in office and vied with each other in oppression and waste. General Narváez took power for the third time in October, 1847. He easily suppressed republican uprisings that followed the French Revolution of February, 1848, and was hailed as the savior of the throne by those who overlooked gross administrative mismanagement and scandals. In March, Lord Palmerston told Sir Henry Bulwer, British Minister to Spain, to urge the Spanish government and the Queen Mother to adopt a constitutional government and put liberals in office in order to avoid the fate of Louis Philippe. Bulwer gave a copy of

4 Quoted by J. G. de R. Hamilton, " Romulus Mitchell Saunders," *Dictionary of American Biography*, edited by Dumas Malone (New York, 1936), XVI, 382-3.

these demands to Narváez. He asked the Queen Mother to call a meeting of the Cortes and to free its imprisoned members. These interventions were offensive enough, but Bulwer had made himself personally intolerable to the reactionary and corrupt court and government of Spain by direct encouragement to the domestic enemies of both. He sheltered in his house in Madrid rebels who had fought the government at the barricades, and Palmerston's note he gave to an opposition newspaper before he gave it to the government. The Duque de Sotomayor, Minister of Foreign Affairs, told Bulwer that another such note would be returned without an answer. Bulwer promptly wrote another insisting on Britain's right to give advice and be heeded because of its great services to Spain. Sotomayor asked Palmerston to recall Bulwer. The British Foreign Minister refused, Bulwer was given his passports, and Palmerston gave his to the Spanish Minister to Great Britain.[5]

In the midst of the crisis and before he had received instructions to buy Cuba, Minister Saunders received a call from Sir Henry's private secretary, who said that Spanish officials claimed to have had " positive assurances " of support from the United States and France in the event of difficulties with Britain. The Minister's secretary said he thought this " strange." Saunders denied that he had given such assurances. The incident awakened Saunders to the realization that Spain relied on promises by previous American administrations of support by the United States " so far at least as Cuba is concerned." He feared that Spain would feel it unnecessary to pay attention when the United States asked that burdens on commerce be removed. He wrote to Buchanan what had happened and stated he thought it better to " change our tone." Indeed, he would do so on his own initiative if occasion arose. He

5 Becker, *Historia de las Relaciones Exteriores de España durante el Siglo XIX*, II, 131-43.

would not excite distrust, but he would leave Spain in doubt as to American support.[6]

Saunders had already made this extraordinary decision when Buchanan's instructions to buy Cuba arrived and gave the Minister an unexpected opportunity to apply the new policy he had formulated for the United States. Notwithstanding explicit orders and the excellent opportunity offered by the rupture between Spain and Britain, Saunders refused to exploit the situation in the classical way that quarrels among the powers were made to yield American diplomatic successes by a Franklin and a Jefferson.

The North Carolinian did not apply his new policy immediately. He received Buchanan's instructions of June 17 five weeks later at La Granja, where he had followed the court. He wrote a brief note to Buchanan to ask that the President be thanked for the confidence he had shown his Minister to Spain. Narváez, he continued, had just told him that Sotomayor was to be replaced as Foreign Minister by Pedro J. Pidal, a change by which the United States had "nothing to loose [sic]." Tomorrow he would communicate with Narváez, but he dared not hold out "any great prospects of success." [7] Five days later he wrote to Buchanan greatly discouraged. Difficulties surrounded the subject of Cuba. In the first place, he hardly knew whom to approach. The Duque de Sotomayor, a "timid and cautious man," was pro-English and anti-United States, Saunders had heard, although he had never noticed it himself. On the contrary, Sotomayor always spoke to him with pride of his American grandfather, Governor McKeon, and with respect of the United States. Saunders had asked him for an interview, but unfortunately he was suffering an attack of gout. The incoming Foreign Minister promised to be a "bold, rough, independent man." General Narváez was a "bold, fear-

6 Saunders to Buchanan, Madrid, June 27, 1848. Department of State, *Diplomatic Despatches: Spain*, XXXV.

7 Saunders to Buchanan, La Granja, July 24, 1848. *Ibid.*

less man, the Soul of the Cabinet," and at the moment anti-English, yet he was " difficult of approach, and might not like the responsibility of having the subject, in the first instance broached to him."

Another difficulty and, Saunders feared, an insurmountable one, was the influence of the Queen Mother over her daughter and the ministry. He suspected she would " most decidedly " object to the cession:

> She has considerable investments in Cuba, from which she derives great profits. These investments are loudly complained of by the people of Havana as interfering with their private matters, and such as the Queen Mother should not meddle with. Such as gas light companies and other associations in a small way.

While she could only be silenced by a prospect of gain or indemnity for her losses, " at this stage of the business it is not necessary she should know anything about it, unles the minister should see fit to consult her."

It seemed also that the Spanish officials placed a much higher estimate on their revenues from Cuba than had Buchanan. They believed they derived a net profit of six millions of dollars from the gross revenues of twelve millions, and other benefits totaled fifteen or twenty millions.

The greatest problem, Saunders wrote, was the mistaken previous policy of the United States. Spain felt secure in Cuba ever since Secretary Forsyth had told Minister Vail in 1840 to assure Spain that the United States would use its military and naval resources to protect her possession. It was commonly said on the street during the present crisis in Anglo-Spanish relations that the United States would aid Spain in the protection of Cuba. Saunders, however, wanted to tell the Spanish government:

> In a war between Spain and England, the United States might feel greatly embarrassed from her friendly relations with

England. That she is not only our ally with whom we are at peace, but with whom at present, we have the most intimate commercial relations. That whatever we may think of her colonial policy . . . the United States would feel great reluctance in an open rupture with her at this time. Besides she might claim from us the same neutrality in a war with Spain as she had observed in our late contest with Mexico.

Saunders saw dimly the possibilities of the situation his instructions directed him to exploit: he observed to Buchanan that Spain might turn to the United States as a result of the trouble with Britain. He was content to wait and see whether this happened.

While he waited, he had an interview with Narváez. The latter said he was entirely satisfied with the orders to Campbell and Butler, wanted copies, and asked Saunders to transmit " *muchas gracias*, many thanks to the President for his course in the business." The possibility that the Spanish government would have a special interest in learning of Campbell's intimate knowledge of revolutionary activities in Cuba, Saunders dissipated by reaching with Narváez an " understanding that the information given by Mr. Campbell was not to be used in any way to excite prejudices against him as our Consul." This letter containing " information given by Mr. Campbell," which is missing from the archives, evidently contained more than Buchanan's charge to Campbell to observe neutrality in Cuba. Saunders described the information as " relative to the threatened insurrection in the Havana." Since Buchanan had cautioned Saunders to show Spanish officials only the " first part " of the letter to Campbell, it is likely that Saunders showed too much. However, information on the Cuban revolutionaries was probably becoming redundant to Spanish officials.

Saunders was not sure whether he had made his real object clear to Narváez. He repeated the considerations which made the United States interested in Cuba as Buchanan had charged him, he did not in this first interview withdraw the standing promise of the United States to support Spanish possession against third powers, but he carefully avoided the word " cession" and only hinted that the President had given him authority "to treat on the subject of Cuba, if it should be the pleasure of Her Catholic Majesty to enter into such a negociation." Narváez replied that he received the information with much pleasure, and thought the new Minister of State should be told. The interview ended with Saunders, as he wrote:

> well satisfied nothing will induce the Spanish Government to part with Cuba, but the apprehension of a successful revolution in the Island, or the fear of its seizure by England.

For the latter contingency and its possible result he would wait. He wished the President to be assured that he felt highly flattered to be entrusted with a negotiation which might produce "one of the most important events in our diplomatic history." [8]

Pidal was not willing to play hide and seek with Saunders. At their first interview on August 15 he bluntly asked the American whether he "proposed to treat for the cession of Cuba to the United States, or for its security to Spain, and in the event of a difficulty with England, whether Spain could rely for any aid from the United States." Saunders answered that

> it was from the fear of a difficulty with England and the threat on her part to seize on Cuba, which had in part, induced the President to give me the special authority he had done at present. That as his Excellency would see, an open rupture between Spain and England, the allies of the U. States, might greatly embarrass her as to the part she as a neutral might find it necessary to take. That whilst self-preservation and the interest of her commerce, might prevent her from remaining passive, in the event of any pressing danger, she would greatly prefer a direct purchase of Cuba to involving herself in a war with England on that account.

8 Saunders to Buchanan, La Granja, July 29–August 4, 1848. Department of State, *Diplomatic Despatches: Spain*, XXXV.

Thus the Minister broke down the foundation of American policy towards Cuba on which Polk and Buchanan wanted the case built for the purchase of the island.

The Spanish Foreign Minister responded that " it was but candid in him to say, he could not hold out any prospect at present of a cession." Saunders, in his letter reporting this interview, seemed unaware that he had violated his instructions.   He hoped that the President would approve his acceptance of an invitation to be present at the " accouchment " of the Duchess of Monpensier, the Queen's sister, because, although the ceremony might seem comical to Americans, his prompt acceptance " was quite gratifying both to the Queen and her mother." [9]

Saunders was not solely responsible for the futility of his efforts. Buchanan himself sometime during the summer denied to Calderón that Saunders had been instructed to buy Cuba. Pidal wrote Calderón on September 16 that he was glad to hear this.[10] Buchanan's motive for repudiating Saunders is difficult to determine unless Polk's deepest suspicions of him are credited. Furthermore, the efforts of the Polk administration to show friendship for Spain hardly lasted through the summer. At best, those efforts were bound to appear ineffective to the government of Spain. Given the nature of the American government, they could not be thorough. Suppressed in the island, the center of Cuban revolutionary activity was transferred with López to the United States. *La Verdad*, the bitterly anti-Spanish organ of the Cuban Council, continued to be published in New York and circulated in Cuba. It openly threatened the island with a filibuster expedition of American veterans.[11]

9 Saunders to Buchanan, Madrid, August 18, 1848. *Ibid.*

10 Pidal to Calderón, Madrid, September 16, 1848. Department of State, *Notes from Legations: Spain,* XII.

11 *La Verdad,* July 30, 1848.

The actions of the American Consul in Havana were far from conciliatory. Campbell demanded the full rights of an American citizen for José Maria Sanchez Iznaga when he was arrested as a leader in the Conspiracy of the Cuban Rose Mines. Like many Cuban revolutionaries, Iznaga had taken the precaution during a trip to the United States of establishing legal citizenship under the lax regulations of the period. Campbell told Captain-General Roncali that the United States had fought the War of 1812 in defense of the right of expatriation.[12] Campbell made a direct threat of war to Roncali in the course of obtaining the freedom of John Lytle, a free American Negro who was abducted and held in slavery in Cuba, and in whose fate John L. O'Sullivan had interested Buchanan. Roncali was conciliatory enough, freed Lytle, and Buchanan was constrained to point out to Campbell that the war-making power belonged exclusively to Congress.[13]

A serious dispute grew out of the third of Campbell's aggressive representations to Roncali. William H. Bush, steward of the American bark *Childe Harold*, served as messenger between Cuban exiles in the United States and fellow-conspirators in the island. The Spanish authorities caught him delivering letters and copies of *La Verdad*, arrested him aboard his ship, and held him incommunicado. Upon demand, Campbell was allowed to see the prisoner and to learn that the charge against him was *infidencia y subversion*.[14] Campbell translated the

12 Campbell to Roncali, Havana, July 14, 1848. Department of State, *Consular Despatches: Havana*, XL (1860). Campbell to Buchanan, Havana, August 12, 1848. *Ibid.*

13 O'Sullivan to Buchanan, Washington, April 28, 1848. *Ibid.*, XXI. Buchanan took up Lytle's case only on May 11, the day after O'Sullivan's first interview with Polk, and the Secretary of State told Campbell to keep O'Sullivan's name out of the case. Buchanan to O'Sullivan, Washington, May 11 and July 5, 1848. Department of State, *Consular Instructions*, X. Buchanan to Campbell, Washington, July 27, 1848. *Ibid.*

14 Campbell to Buchanan, Havana, October 23, 1848; Galdiano to Campbell, October 28, 1848; Count of Alcoy (Roncali) to Campbell, Havana, October 30, 1848. Department of State, *Consular Despatches: Havana*, XXII.

charge as treason, and told Roncali that as an American citizen Bush was incapable of committing that crime against Spain.[15] Obtaining no satisfaction, Campbell told the Captain General he would turn the matter over to his government, which, he wrote, used the same " force and energy " to extend the " protection of her stripes and stars " over the humblest citizen as though he were the highest. This letter became particularly offensive to the Spaniards when " stripes " was translated " *azotes*," that is, " lashes " or " scourges." [16] At the same time, Campbell made a formal protest against Roncali's " gross, palpable, and wanton violation " of the seventh article of the Treaty of 1795 by holding Bush incommunicado, denied the possibility of treason, and charged violation of a law of Spain which limited incommunication of prisoners to twenty-four hours. Bush's only offense according to the American Consul was evasion of the Spanish posts, for which Spanish law limited the punishment to a fine of one ducat. The protest was delivered November 5, after Roncali had failed to keep a promise to put Bush in communication.[17] That same day, the Consul wrote Buchanan that he did not fear for Bush's safety but was determined to stop the Spanish practice of holding American citizens incommunicado, and that a naval force would be of assistance.[18]

A larger issue was introduced by Roncali in response to Campbell's protest. He told the Consul he was " a mere commercial agent " without the right to invoke treaties or make protests in other than mercantile affairs.[19] Campbell rejected this view because, he told the Captain-General, Cuba was in

15 Campbell to Roncali, Havana, October 31, 1848. *Ibid.*

16 Campbell to Clayton, Havana, March 21, 1849. *Ibid.*

17 Campbell to Roncali, Havana, November 2, 1848. *Ibid.*

18 Campbell to Buchanan, Havana, November 5, 1848. *Ibid.*

19 Roncali to Campbell, Havana, November 6, 1848. *Ibid.*

fact a vice-royalty, and he threatened that the President would decide " the most appropriate measure to be pursued." [20]

On the narrow issue, the Captain-General gave way to these threats. He ended the incommunication of Bush immediately and at the end of a fortnight put the steward at liberty without any further penalty. Campbell believed his intervention to have been " efficient and beneficial," and told Buchanan that after " one excited interview " he and Roncali were again on the best of terms.[21] But on the larger issue of the status of American consuls in Cuba, the Spanish government was not reconciled to Campbell's view. On January 2, 1849, Pidal instructed Calderón to ask Buchanan to relieve Campbell because Spain could not allow him to exercise diplomatic functions. In the same letter, the Spanish Foreign Minister made clear his conclusion as to the meaning of Campbell's actions. He wrote that the Consul made the United States government appear to take part in Cuban revolutionary activity.[22]

The question of Campbell's removal was inherited by Secretary of State John M. Clayton after the Polk administration left office. But the aggressive championing of the rights of Cuban revolutionaries and the threats of war by Campbell during the months when Saunders was trying to buy Cuba made absurd the efforts of the administration to strengthen Saunders' hand by proving its friendship for Spain. Coupled with Saunder's own withdrawal of American promises to support Spain's possession of Cuba against the British threat, Campbell's actions made the co-operation with Spain which the Polk administration initiated as the basis of negotiations for Cuba degenerate to hostility against Spain before the negotiations actually began. Nevertheless, Buchanan approved these

20 Campbell to Alcoy, Havana, November 7, 1848. *Ibid.*

21 Campbell to Buchanan, November 11 and December 30, 1848. *Ibid.*

22 Pidal to Calderón, Madrid, January 2, 1849. E. S. Santovenia, *El Presidente Polk y Cuba* (Havana, 1936), 136-7.

actions of both Saunders and Campbell.[23] It was as if Polk's plan to buy Cuba could not be taken seriously enough by the officials charged with its execution to make them overcome their preference for Spain's enemies.

By the time of the Bush affair, Saunders too had taken up the cause of one whom Spain conceived to be an enemy. The Minister's servant, Fernando, was arrested in September while helping Mrs. Saunders into her carriage. He was charged with desertion from the Spanish army because he had not obeyed a conscription order, and Saunders entered with enthusiasm into a long wrangle with Pidal over the question whether his own immunity from arrest extended to his servants. Pidal finally admitted the point of law, but insisted that Saunders discharge Fernando.[24]

When in November Saunders recalled his task and again mentioned Cuba to Pidal, it was to apologize and disclaim responsibility for the publicity the negotiations were receiving in the press of the United States and Europe, including Spain. On October 20, the New York *Herald* had created a sensation by publishing a letter from its Madrid correspondent containing accurate information of Saunders' efforts to buy Cuba. Their failure to date was attributed to the Minister's " utter ignorance " of Spanish or French, which threw him into the hands of other diplomats who used the information they gained to defeat the cession. If Saunders had as much knowledge of good manners and diplomacy as he did about tar, turpentine and chewing tobacco, he could buy Cuba in less than two months.[25] The Spanish press raised a strong protest against

23 Buchanan to Saunders, Washington, October 2, 1848. Department of State, *Diplomatic Instructions: Spain*, XIV. Buchanan to Campbell, Washington, December 11 and 14, 1848. Department of State, *Instructions to Consuls*, X.

24 Saunders to Pidal, Madrid, September 30, October 5 and 16, 1848. Department of State, *Diplomatic Despatches: Spain*, XXXV.

25 New York *Herald*, October 20, 1848.

the project. Pidal told Saunders that the affair was annoying and produced a bad effect in the colonies. Saunders reported this to Buchanan, and assured the Secretary of State that he was not the source of the leak, because he did not use interpreters, the Spanish Foreign Ministers he had dealt with spoke English.[26] As an afterthought, a few days later he added to his letter a statement that he had received no encouragement to renew the subject of Cuban purchase. The public and Pidal were against it; Narváez said nothing. This was in cypher.[27]

The victory of General Zachary Taylor at the polls in November opened the prospect to Spain of relief from the diplomacy of the expansionist Democrats and, coupled with Buchanan's repudiation of Saunders, made the definitive and rather insulting answer Pidal gave Saunders in December not indiscreet. Saunders asked for it, at least insofar as it was definitive, because expansionists at home were grumbling that his efforts were too feeble. He confided this to Pidal. First he got onto the general field of Cuba by asking whether Cubans did not want their tariffs lowered. Pidal replied that Spanish wheat-growers wanted high rates. The Queen, Saunders admonished him, should have learned a lesson by this time from the retaliations of the United States during the last fifteen years. Then he explained that American publications had created the impression that if he increased his efforts and offered sufficiently liberal terms, Spain would sell Cuba. Did the Foreign Minister wish to hear anything more on the subject? Pidal said he thought Saunders was not empowered to make an offer but only to negotiate, and would do so only if Her Majesty wished it. With this understanding, he had denied to the Queen the rumors in the newspapers, and he wanted matters to stand thus so he could also deny them to the Cortes. Saunders agreed. However, his present object was

26 Saunders to Buchanan, Madrid, November 17, 1848. Department of State, *Diplomatic Despatches: Spain*, XXXV.

27 *Loc. cit.*, postscript of November 21, 1848.

" a simple enquiry to enable me to learn and to state, whether any terms however liberal would induce Her Majesty to make the Cession." Pidal said he could answer most positively:

> That it was more than any Minister dare, to entertain any such proposition; that he believed such to be the feeling of the country, that sooner than see the Island transferred to *any power,* they would prefer seeing it sunk in the Ocean.

This celebrated answer ended the negotiations without them having officially started: Pidal had not even heard the offer of $100,000,000. Prior to the American elections, Spain had conceded or postponed every demand of the United States; now it rejected with unexampled bluntness a request merely to discuss cession of Cuba.

Saunders told Pidal he would not again renew the subject unless he was especially invited to do so. To Buchanan he agreed that Spanish opinion was against the cession, especially since the public believed that the money received would not go to the relief of the nation but would be diverted by officials. He had actually feared a flat rejection of an offer and so was glad not to make it. The island could not have been obtained, he believed, by the " most skillful diplomat," and he wanted to be relieved of his post.[28]

The attitude of President Polk towards the collapse of his Cuban plans is not clear. After the letter of Buchanan to Saunders of October 2, in which the President was said to approve Saunders' course, no further communication to the Minister appears in the archives except one concerned exclusively with efforts to reorganize serial numbers preliminary to placing some of the correspondence in the files of the State Department. The apparent dates of missing letters make it appear likely they preceded the failure of Saunders' negotiations.[29]

28 Saunders to Buchanan, Madrid, December 14, 1848. *Ibid.*

29 Buchanan to Saunders, Washington, February 28, 1849. Department of State, *Diplomatic Instructions: Spain,* XIV. *Cf.* Saunders to Buchanan, Madrid, October 3, 1848. Department of State, *Diplomatic Despatches: Spain,* XXXV.

If Polk's omission of Cuban affairs from his diary after July 6 concealed disappointment, Buchanan was apparently not disturbed by the turn they took. Shortly after John M. Clayton succeeded him in office, he exchanged letters with the new Secretary of State on the subject of Cuba. Clayton wrote his predecessor that he was busy " covering up and defending all your outrageous acts," especially the projected purchase of Cuba, which he designated "a blunder worse than a crime." When the devil called him to give evidence against his predecessor, " what a tale I shall be compelled to tell on you!... Do you still wish like Sancho to have an island...?"[30] Buchanan answered that Clayton's letter gave him great pleasure. The late " Loco Foco administration " played into Clayton's hand by committing itself in favor of acquiring "'the gem of the ocean'" for which he was now longing. Buchanan continued:

> It must be admitted that a more skilful agent might have been selected to conduct the negotiation in Spain, as our present minister speaks no language except English, & even this he sometimes murders;...
>
> We must have Cuba. We can't do without Cuba, & above all we must not suffer its transfer to Great Britain. We shall acquire it by a coup d'etat at some propitious moment, which from the present state of Europe may not be far distant.... Cuba is already ours. I feel it in my finger ends.[31]

Buchanan had occasion later to try again for Cuba. Clayton, far from " covering up and defending " Buchanan's action, repudiated it in a highly uncomplimentary way, as will subsequently appear.

The attitude of Congress towards the attempt to purchase Cuba was indicated before Polk left office. On December 18, 1848, Senator Jacob W. Miller, a Whig of New Jersey, introduced a resolution that the President inform the Senate whether he was negotiating to buy the island, and if so that he send

30 *Works of Buchanan*, ed. J. B. Moore, VIII, 359-60.
31 *Ibid.*, 360-1.

the documents to the Senate.[32] The next day, Senator Berrien of Georgia wanted the subject discussed only in executive session in order to preserve the President's legitimate secrecy. Miller asserted he could not believe the President was actually negotiating for Cuba, he only wanted to suppress the public excitement by proving the rumors to be untrue. But he was willing to allow the resolution to be passed over.[33]

After the Christmas recess Miller and others demanded a record vote on the resolution. The New Jersey Senator admitted he was now suspicious that Polk was negotiating. Foote of Mississippi challenged him to say whether he would oppose the purchase of Cuba, and Miller answered that he would oppose Cuban annexation " at all times and under all circumstances." In that case, Foote retorted, Miller would be in an awkward position in March because President-elect Taylor had declared himself in favor of annexation. Senator Dickinson, Democrat of New York, moved to lay the resolution on the table, and this motion passed, 23 to 19. This vote was a fair index of sentiment in favor of Polk's attempt to buy Cuba. Of the 23 Senators who refused to challenge him, 21 were Democrats, 16 represented slave states, and 4 came from Illinois and Michigan, 2 from New England and 1 from New York. Among the 19 Senators who wished to " smoke out " the President, 14 were Whigs, 12 represented free states, 6 came from border slave states and 1 from Florida. Westcott of Florida and Benton of Missouri were the only Democrats from slave states who voted against the motion. The announced opinions of Westcott makes his stand inexplicable. No Whig from a free state voted for the motion and none from a slave state voted against it.

This vote was the closest either House came to a commitment on Cuban purchase during the Polk administration, and it indicates that sentiment in favor of the policy cut across

32 *Congressional Globe* (30:2), 46.
33 *Ibid.,* 58.

party lines and was strongly concentrated in the cotton slave states. But the North was not as united against it as the South was united in favor of it.[34] The situation was summed up by the *Herald* in an editorial declaring that fanatics in the North opposed, but the South and the West favored annexation of Cuba.[35] But it is unlikely that an annexation treaty could have carried two-thirds of the Senate.

The peculiar diplomacy of Buchanan, Saunders and Campbell ensured defeat of Polk's attempt to buy Cuba. It provided no fair test of Spain's willingness to sell the island. The Americans threw away every opportunity to influence favorably the Spanish government, Saunders by his disobedience to his instructions, failure to exploit the break between Spain and Britain and general incompetence, Buchanan by his seeming treachery in denying to Calderón the instructions he had sent to Saunders, and Campbell by his challenges to Spanish authority in Cuba. It was an inglorious defeat of the South's desire for more slavery territory, of Polk's hope to end his administration with a crowning triumph, and of the scheme concocted by O'Sullivan, Beach and the Cuban slave-owners.

But the groups in and out of the United States government that worked for Cuban annexation during the Polk administration did not abandon hope of success after the failure of Saunders and the Democratic defeat at the polls. For eight years after the Taylor-Fillmore administration, Cuban annexationists, led finally by President Buchanan, were influential in Democratic regimes highly sensitive to southern demands. And during the Whig interlude, they were far from inactive as O'Sullivan turned from promoting action by the government to organizing filibuster expeditions to invade Cuba.

34 *Ibid.*, 162-3.

35 New York *Herald*, October 20, 1848.

CHAPTER IV
THE TAYLOR ADMINISTRATION AND CUBA: 1849

GENERAL ZACHARY TAYLOR, a slave owner of Mississippi and hero of the Mexican War, won election to the Presidency because the northern Free Soilers and Van Buren broke the unity of the Democratic Party. " Old Zach " was the candidate of the Whigs, but they in their Convention voted down all proposed platforms for the campaign, and their candidate refused to admit that he campaigned on the ticket of any party. In actuality, the " Young Indians " in Congress, Whigs chiefly from the South, engineered Taylor's nomination. On the advice of John J. Crittenden, after Henry Clay had made himself " unavailable " for nomination by offending the South, Taylor abandoned his plan to oppose annexations south of the Missouri Compromise line. Taylor's strength in the Convention came chiefly from a solid block of delegates from the Deep South. Still no evidence appears to exist for Senator Foote's statement that Taylor favored annexation of Cuba. And by March, 1850, President Taylor was dominated by the leading Whig opponent of southern ambitions, William H. Seward.[1]

This did not mean that Taylor or Seward and his supporters were opposed to expansion. But it was commercial expansion they favored while territorial annexations, for which they looked to the free soil of Canada rather than to Latin America, were secondary and, in the existing state of weakness of their party, impracticable. The outstanding achievement of the administration in the foreign sphere was to check British expansion in Central America and thereby secure American communications across the Isthmus where Americans were building the Panama Railroad and the transit by steamer and

1 George R. Poage, *Henry Clay and the Whig Party* (Chapel Hill, 1936), 157-215.

carriage through Nicaragua. Coaling stations at points like Samana Bay in the Dominican Republic for the steamship lines that received government subsidies were the objects of the only efforts by the administration to win new territorial positions, and none was obtained. For the rest, the administration showed a strong nationalizing tendency by the assertion of American rights and ideals in ways that pleased believers in Manifest Destiny but did not raise the sectional issues involved in the annexation of any specific territory.

All of these policies were effectively carried forward by John M. Clayton of Delaware, the new Secretary of State. Accordingly, he distinguished between two aspects of the previous administration's Cuban policy. The attempt to buy the island and Saunders' disruption of the traditional policy of American support of Spain in Cuba against third powers Clayton determined to repudiate. But Campbell's efforts to protect the rights of American citizens and to win recognition of his diplomatic powers in relation to the government of Cuba would be sustained. In these and other ways Clayton would strengthen the more national commercial and stategic interests of the United States while he ignored the interest of the South in the fate of Cuban slavery.

The Cuban problem was brought to Clayton's attention shortly after he assumed office by a letter from Calderón requesting that Campbell be relieved of his office. Calderón had postponed the request until the new administration took office because he feared that Buchanan would not accede to it, whereas the new Secretary would welcome an opportunity to give the post to a Whig.[2] Now he asserted to Clayton that the Consul's attempt to treat diplomatically with the Captain-General in the case of Bush was " as absurd in its nature, as unusual in its form." The terms Campbell had used were:

passionate, and improper — offensive to the dignity of Spain,

2 Calderón to Pidal, Washington, February 22, 1849, *Boletin del Archivo Nacional*, XVI (September, 1917), 407.

lead to the conclusion that the American Consul has been
guided in this affair, by persons by no means impartial, who
have placed his character in jeopardy, and may to a certain
extent have rendered his Government apparently liable, to
be regarded as a participator, in the subversive plans of the
conspirators.

The Spanish government had too high an opinion of the
United States government to admit such feelings of distrust
and therefore considered the recall of Campbell would be " ad-
vantageous to the common interests of both Cabinets . . . ."
Otherwise Campbell, " not comprehending the duties of his
mission, may, one day, bring on a contest between the two
Governments," which Spain wished to " ward off forever."
If he was not recalled, Spain would cancel his exequatur.[3]

Clayton referred Calderón's request to President Taylor,
who refused to repudiate Campbell's assumption of diplomatic
powers and defense of American citizens. The Secretary of
State wrote to the Spanish Minister that the President " con-
curs in opinion with his predecessor, the late Executive, in
declining to recall the Consul." However, the President wanted
Campbell informed of Spain's request, " leaving it to his sense
and discretion to quit voluntarily." [4]

Campbell was not seriously pressed to resign. Clayton told
him the Department fully approved his conduct. The Queen
had a right to revoke his exaquatur but the United States
government refused to recall him.

Under all the circumstances of the case, I have thought
proper, to submit for your consideration, whether, it would
not be more agreeable to you, to retire from a situation, the
occupation of which, by you, is not acceptable to the Authorities of the country, where you reside, rather, than invite a pro-

3 Calderón to Clayton, Washington, March 9, 1849. Department of State,
Notes from Legations: Spain, XII.

4 Clayton to Calderón, Washington, April 3, 1849. Department of State,
Notes to Legations: Spain, VI.

ceeding, on their part, unpleasant in its character to your Government and yourself, & leading ultimately to the same result.[5]

The Consul refused to resign. He assured Clayton that the revocation of his exequatur by Spain would not injure the administration, while for him to resign would be to admit that he had been wrong in the Bush affair.[6] Clayton did not insist. Calderón advised Pidal not to take action against Campbell because the Bush case was before the Senate and the Democratic majority of that body would undoubtedly support the Consul.[7] The latter remained in office for another year until his involvement in the affairs of filibusters and new assertions of diplomatic powers had still further aroused the distrust of Spain.

The Taylor administration made no objection to Campbell's connections with Cuban revolutionaries. It could not have been unaware of them because, apart from correspondence in the files, Campbell took courage from the support he received from the new administration and sent Don Cristóbal Madan, head of the Cuban Council, to Clayton. His letter of introduction called Madan a planter of "large fortune, extensive connexions," the best informed of the Cuban Creoles, and well able to give information to the Secretary of State.[8] What Madan's purpose was does not appear, but the fact that Clayton accepted such a contact from Campbell heightens the contrast between his refusal to heed Spain's desire to be rid of Campbell, who had given serious offense to that power, and the contemporaneous dismissal by the United

5 Clayton to Campbell, Washington, April 2, 1849. Department of State, *Instructions to Consuls*, X.

6 Campbell to Clayton, Havana, June 5, 1849. Department of State, *Consular Despatches: Havana*, XXII.

7 Calderón to Pidal, Washington, April 9, 1849. *Boletin del Archivo Nacional*, XVI (September, 1917), 412.

8 Campbell to Clayton, Havana, June 22, 1849. Clayton Papers.

States of the French Minister Poussin purely for reasons of diplomatic punctilio.[9]

A special agent of Clayton, Benjamin E. Green, was entrusted with a mission to the West Indies. This mission has been called " a preface to the purchase of Cuba " by the Taylor administration,[10] but the correspondence that passed between Clayton and Green shows only the administration's interest in the political situation in Cuba. The main object of the mission was to make a treaty for a coaling site on Samana Bay with the Dominican Republic.[11] Before Green could achieve that object, his instructions were canceled.[12]

From Cuba, Green wrote Clayton in July, 1849, that he had omitted no opportunity to ascertain the state of opinion. His first report declared that Cuban fellow-travelers returning from the United States were eager for annexation. Exiles remaining in the United States numbered 600. The opening of the new steamship line between Charleston and Havana, Green thought, would hasten annexation.[13] After a short stay in the island, Green again wrote to Clayton. He was satisfied that the Cubans were " unanimous in their desire to throw off their dependence on Spain, and that nine tenths of them desire annexation to the United States." But the difficulties were many. Fear of each other and of Spain, especially that it would incite the Negroes to insurrection rather than relinquish control to the Creoles, explained why

9 Mary W. Williams, " John Middleton Clayton," *The American Secretaries of State*, ed. S. F. Bemis, VI, 19-24.

10 Walter L. Wright, Jr., and Fletcher M. Green, " Benjamin Edwards Green," *Dictionary of American Biography*, VII, 538-9. The quotation is based on papers in the possession of Professor Green which are not available for investigation.

11 Clayton to Benjamin E. Green, Washington, June 13, 1849. Department of State, *Special Missions*, I.

12 Clayton to Green, Washington, February 16, 1850. *Ibid.*

13 Green to Clayton, Bay of Guasabacao, Cuba, July 7, 1849. Clayton Papers.

many are anxiously looking to the United States for the initiative of annexation. Any such step on the part of our Government or people would be hailed with delight by the whole Creole population of the Island.

Green said he learned that several of the wealthiest Cubans had recently contributed $200,000 towards a revolutionary movement.[14]

The Taylor administration was not interested in such temptations. Early in 1850, James Robb, a banker of New Orleans, offered to finance a secret mission to Spain to buy Cuba. Joel R. Poinsett of South Carolina, former Minister to Mexico, was eager to undertake the mission, but President Taylor refused to sanction it and the scheme was dropped.[15] The administration also opposed the filibuster expedition that General López organized during the spring and summer of 1849. Once the administration's support of Campbell had been made clear to Spain, Clayton worked to obtain the confidence of that country in the friendship and co-operation of the United States. The first task was to liquidate the policies of Polk and Saunders. On May 22, 1849, in a conference with Calderón, Clayton went so far as to impugn the veracity of his predecessor in order to obtain the good will of the Spanish Minister. He himself exaggerated in telling Calderón that Saunders had been sent to Spain on a " special" mission to secure Cuba. Calderón recalled that Buchanan had assured him the rumors that Saunders was trying to buy Cuba were false. Clayton exclaimed that it was shameful: " ' Buchanan was lying to you about it all that time. Here is all the evidence that proves the contrary.' " Saunders would be recalled, Clayton said, and a new minister would be ordered to nullify his predecessor's instructions and make known to Spain that the United States

14 Green to Clayton, Havana, July 21, 1849. Department of State, *Special Agents*, XV.

15 J. Fred Rippy, *Joel R. Poinsett, Versatile American* (Durham, 1935), 230.

wanted Cuba to remain under Spanish dominion. Besides this, the United States desired only to end the tariff war between the two countries.[16]

Clayton's instructions to the new minister, Daniel M. Barringer of North Carolina, were not quite as strong as his words to Calderón. He wrote that the administration did not desire to renew the proposition of Cuban purchase. Spain had considered it a " national indignity." Should Spain desire to part with the island, the offer of its cession must come from her, in which case Barringer should merely transmit it to his government for consideration. On the subject of the no-transfer policy:

> The President cannot comprehend or appreciate the motives or expediency of openly declaring to Spain that the whole power of the United States, would be employed to prevent the occupation in whole or in part of Cuba, from passing into other hands; because he has reason to believe that this declaration on our part has led to counter-declarations, being made to Spain, against us, of a similar character, by other interested powers.
>
> Whilst this Government is resolutely determined that the Island of Cuba shall never be ceded by Spain to any other power than the United States, it does not desire, in future, to utter any threats, or enter into any guaranties, with Spain, on that subject. Without either guaranties or threats, we shall be ready, when the time comes, to act. The news of the cession of Cuba to any foreign power would, in the United States, be the instant signal for war. No foreign power would attempt to take it, that did not expect a hostile collision with us as an inevitable consequence.

Barringer's main task, Clayton added, would be to get Spain to abolish her discriminating duties against American trade with Cuba and Puerto Rico.[17] Barringer was delayed and did

16 Calderón to Pidal, Washington, May 24, 1849. *Boletin del Archivo Nacional*, XVI (September, 1917), 415.

17 Clayton to Barringer, Washington, August 2, 1849. Department of State, *Diplomatic Instructions: Spain*, XIV.

not arrive in Madrid until October 20, 1849. In the meantime, Calderón's letter to Pidal of May 24 containing Clayton's promises to reverse the policies of Polk and Saunders had arrived, and Clayton furthermore had had opportunities to put into practice his dual program of strong defense of American rights and strong support of Spanish possession of Cuba.

The decision of Cuban exiles to launch a filibuster expedition against the island was conditioned not only by the realization that Clayton and the Whigs would not renew Polk's attempt to buy Cuba, but also by the shift to American soil of the center of Cuban revolutionary activity when López fled after the betrayal of the Cuban Rose Mines Conspiracy. The fiery General and many provincial leaders who succeeded in reaching the United States believed that their own efforts were their best reliance for freedom from Spain. An expedition from the United States meant to López chiefly the means of returning to take command of his true army, the provincial liberals and *Guajiros,* whom he expected to rise when his landing gave them a rallying point and a leader with arms. He subordinated all other problems to the great one of his own return to Cuba in force. Whatever anti-slavery sentiments he had entertained were submerged in deference to the American South and in hope of its support. His program for Cuba was an ambiguous mixture of annexationism and independence. He held out the former to American supporters while his manifestos to the Cuban people spoke only of a Cuban republic. When pressed to clarify his position, he said the Cuban people would determine their own future after independence was achieved. His plan was calculated to appeal to the broadest possible range of support, and he won the adherence of American adventurers, enthusiasts of Manifest Destiny and partisans of the South and slavery, European liberal revolutionary exiles, and Cuban slave owners and liberals.

Yet the coalition was weakened by the continuing distrust for each other of the " patriotic " and the " economic " Cubans,

so that it never reached the full strength López labored to
assemble around his leadership.   The cautious members of the
Havana Club and their agents in the Cuban Council of New
York refused to make the impetuous General their leader.
López, refusing to submit to them, founded his own *Junta
Cubana* in New York late in 1848.   Ambrosio José Gonzalez,
agent of the Havana Club to General Worth, attempted after
the American was ordered to Texas to substitute López for the
American General as leader of an expedition under the auspices
of the conservative Creoles.   Failing in this, Gonzales joined
López's Junta along with José Maria Sanchez Iznaga, who
had escaped the island after imprisonment and the intervention
of Campbell.   Juan Manuel Macias completed the leadership
of the Junta.   The break with the Council did not prevent a
certain amount of co-operation. Gaspar Betancourt Cisneros
and Cristóbal Madan acted as liaison between the two groups,
and provided funds for López's expeditions.   John L. O'Sullivan had a foot in each camp and served as the filibusters' business agent.   Cisneros wrote later that López had been "the
pupil of no one" and preferred the advice of men who had
more confidence in him than the members of the Cuban
Council.[18]

La Verdad remained the organ of the Cuban Council.   After
Polk's failure to buy Cuba, the newspaper became narrowly
concerned with the affairs of the exiles, it dropped general news
and advertising, issued only a single tabloid sheet, and its
chief American appeal was to the South and fear of emancipation in Cuba.   It took no responsibility for López in 1849,
but it did not attack him.[19]

The newspaper vigorously fought the ideas of José Antonio
Saco when in 1848 he turned against annexation.   This out-

18 Cisneros to José Luis Alfonso, New York, May 13, 1852. Morales,
Iniciadores, II, 64.

19 *La Verdad*, July 16, 30, November 3, December 15, 1848; May 18,
June 1, 1849, ff. *A Series of Articles on the Cuban Question*, Editors of
La Verdad (New York, 1849).

standing intellectual leader of the Cubans contributed to their disunity by launching a series of striking polemics against annexationism at the moment when it had become the dominant tendency among the opponents of Spain. Saco was accused of making his about-face, with its effect of a "thunderbolt bursting on a picnic," [20] because of jealousy and hatred of López, who had won their competition for the hand of the latter's wife. But Saco changed his opinion before López had emerged as a leader of movements against Spain. He was a Cuban nationalist of lofty ideals, political acuity and great literary talent who did much to give form and direction to the struggles of the Cubans for self-realization, and his work bore fruit in the revolutions of 1868 and 1895. Meanwhile, he was partially responsible for the failure of the annexation movement in mid-century, as his pamphlets and letters were widely read and highly influential, although they were written from exile in Paris.

On March 19, 1848, Saco wrote to Cisneros that Cuban nationality could not survive annexation by the United States because the population would be absorbed by American immigrants. He wanted the island to be "*Cuban*, and not *Anglo-Saxon*." Spain should be endured heroically and liberals should work to weaken slavery, increase white immigration, and improve the economic life of the country while they waited for a better day.[21] These ideas were fully developed in the famous pamphlet Saco published on November 1 of the same year: "Thoughts on the Incorporation of Cuba in the United States." [22] Thereafter he conducted spirited debates in public and private especially with the exiles in the United States. Cristóbal Madan wrote the most comprehensive rebuttal of Saco and revealed the views of the outstanding Cuban annexa-

20 Morales, *Iniciadores*, II, 25.

21 Saco to Cisneros, Paris, March 19, 1848. *Ibid.*, 94-101.

22 J. A. Saco, "Ideas sobre la incorporación de Cuba en los Estados Unidos," *Contra la Anexion*, I, 33-67, *Coleccion de Libros Cubanos*, compiled by Fernando Ortiz (Havana, 1928), V.

tions. He wrote that Saco's pamphlet was the only moral obstacle in the way of union with the United States. He believed Saco had unfortunately been imbued with the ultra-liberalism of Europe. But Cuban slave-owners were good liberals who merely asked for time and gradual measures to do away with slavery. In the United States, slaves made slow but certain progress towards freedom. The South was wise, tenacious and daring in the counsels of the nation. Saco's " *negrophitism* " made him blind to the virtues of American slavery. As for his fear of loss of Cuban nationality, Louisiana refuted him, because forty-five years in the American Union had not destroyed its French character. The failure in self-government of the Spanish-American republics was a warning to Cuba. All races and the Catholic religion flourished in the United States. Annexation would end the corruption of the Cuban clergy. Indeed Cuba would find her salvation in the great republic, Madan wrote:

> From an humble and oppressed colony, trampled on by oriental despotism, she would rise to be, like her sister republics, a nation within a nation, and for the first time would Cuban nationality, essentially Spanish in character, have an existence.

Southern interest in Cuban slavery was a sure guaranty of annexation, he continued:

> The Pearl of the West Indies, with her thirteen or fifteen representatives in Congress, would be a powerful auxiliary to the South, and her value as an immense outlet for American manufactures, and a source of vast tropical production in exchange, and also as a military post, would surely make the attainment of Cuba a bond of peace and union for all the states.

As it was, Cuba like a wall divided and interrupted the growth of the United States. But if tyranny might oppress, democracy might use force to strike the chains from Cuba.[23] In spite of

23 Leon Fragua de Calvo [pseudonym of Cristóbal Madan], "Thoughts on the Annexation of Cuba to the United States," in R. B. Kimball, *Cuba and the Cubans* (New York, 1850), 214-51.

such pleas, Saco saw his followers grow until annexationism was a dead issue among Cubans twenty years later. For his epitaph he wrote: " Here lies José Antonio Saco who was not an annexationist because he was more Cuban than all the annexationists." [24]

Thus as López planned his expedition the exiled annexationists, lacking unity among themselves, struggled against Cuban as well as American and Spanish opposition. López looked to southern leaders for aid. Gonzalez had interviewed General Taylor before his inauguration, but received no encouragement. The Junta feared that the new administration would oppose any change in the political condition of the island.[25] The Cubans turned to the Democrats. Gonzalez obtained an introduction to Senator Daniel S. Dickinson of New York.[26] In Washington, Gonzalez, López and Iznaga met Senator Calhoun. The South Carolinian called on López twice and then arranged a meeting in a committee room of the capitol between the three Cubans and himself, Senators Foote, Davis, Douglas and Dickinson. López described the sufferings of the Cubans, their ardent desire for liberty, and their need for aid " in some way or other " from the United States. According to John F. H. Claiborne, the friend and biographer of General John A. Quitman who became the filibusters' leader in 1853, Calhoun at this meeting in early 1849 was deeply impressed by López, declared himself in favor of annexation, and said the American people could lawfully aid an insurrection.[27] However, after Calhoun had died, Representative Venable of North Carolina told the House that he had been present when the legislators interviewed the Cubans and Calhoun had opposed their plans and annexation of Cuba. Venable himself

24 Saco, *Contra la Anexion*, II, cxliii.

25 Gonzalez, *Manifesto*, 7.

26 J. M. Storms to Dickinson, New York, January 4, 1849. Polk Papers.

27 John F. H. Claiborne, *Life and Correspondence of John A. Quitman* (New York, 1860), II, 53-5. Vilá, *Historia de Cuba*, I, 414.

opposed annexation.[28] General López claimed to have Calhoun's support after the interview. O'Sullivan wrote to Calhoun in August, 1849, when the expedition was ready to set forth: " The South ought (according to an expression which Gen. López has quoted to me from you) to flock down there in ' open boats,' the moment they hear the tocsin." [29]

Jefferson Davis was offered the command of the expedition, but he proposed Major Robert E. Lee. The latter consulted Davis on the propriety of accepting. He decided it would be wrong to take command of the army of a " foreign power " while he held a commission in the United States Army.[30] Lee's decision is interesting in the light of his more famous one in 1861 to follow his state out of the Union. In the episode of 1849, both Davis and Lee evidently had no objection to the filibusters' plans on grounds of principle or political expediency. Service in the expedition was accepted by other American Army officers, including Colonels Briscoe and White. The latter had commanded a Louisiana company in the Mexican War and then took part in the civil war in Yucatan.[31] López became chief of the expedition and Gonzalez was made a general and second in command.

Funds for the enterprise came from Cuban and American sources. Estimates of their amount vary from $200,000 at the disposal of Colonel White alone,[32] to $70,000 as the total for the whole expedition.[33] López tried to raise 1200 men by mak-

28 *Congressional Globe* (32:2), 189-92.

29 O'Sullivan to Calhoun, Atlanta, August 24, 1849. *Calhoun Correspondence*, edited by J. Franklin Jameson, Annual Report of the American Historical Association, 1899 (Washington, 1900), II, 1202-3.

30 Vilá, *López*, I, 39. R. G. Caldwell, *The López Expeditions to Cuba: 1848-1851* (Princeton, 1915), 49.

31 P. Hamilton to Clayton, Mobile, August 4, 1849. Department of State, *Miscellaneous Letters*.

32 *Loc. cit.*

33 Morales, *Iniciadores*, II, 155.

ing lavish promises of rewards. Ordinary recruits were not told the precise object or destination of the venture. The personnel of this first expedition lacked the political character of later ones. An agent of Clayton who observed the recruits of 1849 described them as the "most desperate looking creatures as ever were seen would murder a man for ten dollars." [34] The steamships *Fanny* and *Sea Gull* were purchased and the *New Orleans* was chartered. Chief points of embarkation were New York and Cat and Round Islands on the coast of Mississippi at Pass Christian. On the last day of July, 200 men arrived at Round Island from New Orleans and camped.

Newspaper rumors had already led Clayton to initiate an investigation of the filibusters through his secret agent, Malcolm W. Mears. The latter was instructed on July 31 to continue providing information "of the enlistment and equipping of an armed expedition in the U. States for some foreign destination," and to go to Baltimore, Philadelphia and New York for the purpose. [35] On August 4, United States Attorney Hamilton of Mobile, Alabama, wrote Clayton that the lighthouse keeper on Round Island was alarmed by the encampment of several hundred men. They did not appear to be armed, but were being paid eight dollars a month and promised a thousand dollars bonus at the end of a campaign in unnamed foreign parts. [36]

As evidence accumulated that a serious offense against Spain was imminent, news also came that the Spanish Consul in New Orleans was to be prosecuted by the state of Louisiana for a violation of American sovereignty. On August 3, Logan Hunton, United States Attorney at New Orleans, telegraphed Clayton that Consul Carlos de España had been arrested by

34 M. W. Mears to Clayton, New York, September, 1849. Department of State, *Special Agents*, XVIII.

35 Clayton to Mears, Washington, July 31, 1849. *Ibid.*

36 P. Hamilton to Clayton, Mobile, August 4, 1849. Department of State, *Miscellaneous Letters.*

the state authorities for the abduction on American soil and forcible return to Cuba of one Juan Garcia, *alias* Francisco Rey.[37] If the arrest and subsequent proceedings against the Spanish Consul were not planned by the Louisiana authorities to distract attention from the filibusters and focus it on Spain as the initial violator of international law, the coincidence was remarkably fortuitous. The situation certainly gave the Taylor administration an opportunity to fall in with the Louisiana officials, direct its activity against the Spanish violation of American rights, and ignore the filibusters' plan to violate Spanish rights.

The administration refused to exploit this opportunity, despite the fact that the President had already contemplated war with Spain over the Garcia affair. Garcia had been turnkey of a Havana prison who, in the spring of 1849, released Cirilo Villaverde, the private secretary of General López, and another prisoner in his care and escaped with them to the United States. Agents of the Spanish Consul in New Orleans induced Garcia to sign a paper listing fifty Cubans as guilty of plotting the overthrow of Spain and annexation of the island to the United States. The Consul claimed that Garcia, disgruntled when his former prisoners deserted him in the United States, agreed in return for a promise of pardon to go voluntarily to Cuba and testify against the annexationists. If so, Garcia changed his mind by the time his ship reached quarantine in Havana harbor, because he appealed to Consul Campbell for aid, charging that he had been abducted and forced to return. Campbell asked the Captain-General for permission to see Garcia but received no answer.[38]

Newspapers in the United States made a sensation of the alleged abduction. The President asked Clayton to draft in-

37 Hunton to Clayton, New Orleans, August 3, 1849. *Ibid.*

38 Campbell to Clayton, Havana, July 31, 1849. Department of State, *Consular Despatches: Havana*, XXII. *Cf. Abduction of Juan Francisco Rey: A Narrative of Events from His Own Lips*, compiled and edited by Daniel Scully (New Orleans, December, 1849).

structions to Campbell in strong terms.   If the Consul found
reason to believe that " an outrage so gross " had occurred, he
should demand that the Captain-General surrender Garcia,
ship him back to the United States, and punish the guilty.
Campbell should write a note to the Captain-General declaring
in the name of the President that if a " violation of the sovereignty of the United States " had been committed by Spanish
officials and was not " satisfactorily and promptly atoned," the
President would refer the matter to Congress

> with a view to such action on their part, as the occasion may
> demand, and their patriotism and wisdom may dictate.   Under
> the circumstances if they prove to be as alleged, the Executive
> would not hesitate to recommend immediate war.[39]

At this juncture, only the lack of a few thousand dollars
which had failed to arrive from Cuba and was demanded by
their creditors prevented López and his followers from
sailing.[40] As it was, the administration had time to prevent the
Garcia affair and the filibuster expedition from creating a
crisis in Spanish-American relations. The prosecution of the
Spanish Consul was removed to the Federal Circuit Court,[41]
where the Grand Jury eventually freed him, not because it
doubted that he had abducted Garcia, but for lack of sufficient
evidence to obtain a conviction. The President thereupon re-
voked de España's exequatur on the ground that public opinion
of his guilt was so strong in New Orleans that his usefulness as
a consul was impaired.[42] But, notwithstanding the decision in
August of Federal Commissioner Cohen that evidence justified

39 Clayton to Campbell, Washington, July 28, 1849. Department of State,
Instructions to Consuls, X.

40 José Maria Sanchez Iznaga to Friends in Cuba, New Orleans, May 4,
1853. Morales, *Iniciadores*, II, 194.

41 Hunton to Clayton, New Orleans, August 14, 1849. Department of State,
Miscellaneous Letters.

42 Clayton to Calderón, Washington, January 4, 1850. Department of
State, *Notes to Legations: Spain*, VI.

holding de España for the Grand Jury, and some substantiating evidence of the latter's guilt sent by Campbell, Clayton did not instruct Campbell to deliver the quasi-ultimatum called for in his earlier instructions if the Spanish Consul appeared guilty. Rather he enjoined him to prevent the consequences fatal to peace " which must inevitably flow from any attempt to justify or uphold the conduct of the Spanish Consul, if he be really guilty." [43] Campbell had already obtained Garcia's freedom. On a face-saving application by the Cuban for pardon, the Captain-General turned him over to Campbell who sent him to the United States.[44] In Cuba, the prosecution of annexationists languished for lack of the turnkey as witness, while in the United States his best efforts as a witness failed to put the Spanish Consul on trial.

In a letter to Calderón, Clayton gave the credit for the Captain-General's liberation of Garcia to his own earlier instructions that a quasi-ultimatum be delivered to the Spanish official.[45] However, Campbell had not even demanded Garcia's freedom,[46] and it is more likely that the news of President Taylor's Proclamation against the López expedition inspired the conciliatory action of the Captain-General.

The first definite information on the objective of that expedition came to Clayton from Thomas Ewing, Secretary of the Interior. He wrote on August 7 that 800 men under Colonel White intended to embark from Round Island about August 20 or 25 for the south side of Cuba. Corresponding numbers were preparing to sail from Baltimore, New York and

43 Clayton to Campbell, Washington, August 20, 1849. Department of State, *Instructions to Consuls*, X.

44 Campbell to Clayton, Havana, August 18 and 20, 1849. Department of State, *Consular Despatches: Havana*, XXII.

45 Clayton to Calderón, Washington, September 3, 1849. Department of State, *Notes to Legations: Spain*, VI.

46 Campbell to Clayton, Havana, August 18, 1849. Department of State, *Consular Despatches: Havana*, XXII.

Boston.[47] The next day Clayton ordered the Federal Attorney at New Orleans to proceed against violators of the neutrality laws.[48] On August 9, Commodore F. A. Parker, commander of the Home Squadron based at Pensacola, was ordered by the Secretary of the Navy to patrol the coast of Mississippi and prevent the sailing of the expedition. If necessary, he should go to Cuba and prevent a landing.[49] Two days later the Proclamation of President Taylor declared the duty of the government to prevent aggression by its citizens, warned them against taking part in an enterprise " grossly in violation of our laws and our treaty obligations . . . in the highest degree criminal," and that as pirates their claim to protection would be forfeited. The President exhorted all good citizens to prevent the expedition by all lawful means, and he called upon every civil and military officer of the government to arrest for trial and punishment every offender against the law.[50]

Despite the last clause of the Proclamation, no one was arrested or tried and the filibusters retained possession of their arms and other property, including the *Sea Gull* and the *New Orleans* after they were temporarily attached by the federal authorities in New York. Commander V. M. Randolph, in the absence of Commodore Parker, blockaded Round Island with six naval vessels and cut off the filibusters' supplies until, in early September, they consented to be taken in naval vessels to the mainland, where they were set free.[51]

The lenient treatment of the expeditionaries General Gonzalez attributed to " protection from high places." [52] The

47 Ewing to Clayton, Washington, August 7, 1849. Clayton Papers.

48 Clayton to Hunton, Washington, August 8, 1849. Department of State, *Lopez Expedition: 1849-1851: Cuba.*

49 Preston to Parker, Washington, August 9, 1849. Navy Department, *Confidential Letters*, II.

50 *Messages and Papers of the Presidents*, compiled by James D. Richardson (Washington, 1911), VI, 2545-6.

51 Randolph to Preston, Off Ship Island, August 25, 28; September 1, 5, 14, 1849. Navy Department, *Commanders Letters*, August-December, 1849.

52 Gonzalez, *Manifesto*, 7.

organizers of the expedition had no intention of obeying the Proclamation and set September 2 as the day of departure. In the meantime, O'Sullivan wrote to Calhoun, pleading:

> Now, my dear sir, can not you write to fifty points and fifty proper persons to act and act with the requisite energy, prompitude, head and heart, in this matter? Your aid thus extended would be a tower of strength. All going may rely on generous compensation from opulent Cuba, once liberated. But independent of such motives there are considerations enough of a different character which I should think ought to rouse all the youth and manhood of the Southern States in particular to rush down and help the Cuban Revolution. . . .
>
> If I, a "New York Free Soiler" am so deeply interested in behalf of this movement, what ought not to be the enthusiasm of Southern gentlemen? [53]

Rose Greenhow, wife of a translator in the State Department, after giving a "parting breakfast" to López on August 29, wrote to Calhoun enthusiastically of the filibusters' chances of success, and declared that the administration had "done no more in the matter of the *Proclamation* than *regard for appearances demanded*.[54] Campbell reported to Clayton rumors that a revolution had broken out on the south side of Cuba where support of López was strong. An army officer who had cried "Viva Lopez!" had been shot. Campbell was convinced that a strong expedition could effect the overthrow of Spanish authority in ninety days. A British naval force was expected, and the American Consul requested that American vessels be sent to provide refuge for American citizens. The Navy Department despatched the sloop *Germantown,* but it did not arrive in Havana until after Campbell decided that the rumors of revolution had been exaggerated.[55]

53 O'Sullivan to Calhoun, Atlanta, August 24, 1849. *Calhoun Correspondence*, ed. Jameson, II, 1202-3.

54 Greenhow to Calhoun, Washington, August 29, 1849. *Ibid.*, 1203-4.

55 Campbell to Clayton, Havana, August 27, 28, September 7, 1849. Department of State, *Consular Despatches: Havana*, XXII.

The blockade of Round Island and attachment of the filibusters' ships finally broke up the expedition of 1849, although López and his aides retrieved their investment and were left free to apply the lessons of American law and politics they had learned, reorganize, and set out on another " buffalo hunt," as the *Herald* called it, when the season opened in 1850.

Clayton had co-operated intimately with Calderón to frustrate the 1849 expedition,[56] and the administration won the praise of the Spanish government for its efforts. When Barringer presented himself to Pidal as the new United States Minister, Pidal expressed to him:

> the profound admiration and pleasure with which his whole country had viewed the conduct of the President of the United States in regard to the late attempted invasion of the Island of Cuba.

Barringer told Clayton that everywhere on his trip through Europe he had heard the same remark and commendation: the President had elevated the character of the United States.[57]

56 Clayton to Calderón, Washington, August 9 and 17, 1849. Department of State, *Notes to Legations: Spain*, VI. Calderón to Clayton, Washington, August 13, September 4, 1849. Department of State, *Notes from Legations: Spain*, XII.

57 Barringer to Clayton, Madrid, October 25, 1849. Department of State, *Diplomatic Despatches: Spain*, XXXVI.

CHAPTER V

THE CARDENAS EXPEDITION: 1850

THE failure of the Round Island expedition led General López to adopt significant new methods when he organized his next attempt to invade Cuba. He broke relations with the cautious slave-owners of the Havana Club and Cuban Council, who feared violence in the island, the public clamor aroused by López, and the opposition of the Taylor administration. They sold the ships intended for the 1849 invasion, refused to turn over to López the arms which had been purchased, and maintained only a shadowy organization called the *Junta Suprema Secreta*, later the *Consejo de Organización y Gobierno Cubano*. Its chief activity was the publication of *La Verdad*, which came out strongly in favor of peaceful measures of annexation to prevent emancipation of the slaves by revolution, English influence, or legislative enactment under an independent republic.[1]

López was determined to organize a new expedition in the open as a legal enterprise. Violation of the Neutrality Act of 1818 would be avoided by sending the filibusters out of the United States as emigrants to California via Panama in unarmed vessels and without military organization. A rendezvous at an uninhabited island off Mexico would bring together arms and men and make possible military organization and drill prior to the descent on Cuba. The organization of the *Junta Publica Promovedora de los Intereses Politicos de Cuba* was announced to newspapers of New York and the South with an invitation to the friends of Cuban liberty to make honorable and legal contributions to the cause. Communications were directed to a Post Office box in Washington, as the leaders of the Junta, López, Gonzales, Sanchez Iznaga,

1 *La Verdad*, 1850, *passim*. Cf. Cora Montgomery, *The Queen of Islands and the King of Rivers* (New York, 1850), 17-27.

Villaverde and Macías, made Washington their headquarters during the winter. Wealthy Cubans were no longer providing funds, so bonds were issued on the credit of the future Cuban republic. They were sold to Americans with considerable success at discounts up to seventy-five percent. General John Henderson, former Senator from Mississippi, was a leading contributor to the Junta's treasury. With these funds, extensive propaganda in Cuba was undertaken and arms and ships were assembled for the new expedition.[2]

Calderón bitterly complained of these impudent activities to Secretary Clayton. The filibusters' pretense of legality, he said, propagated the false and pernicious notion that their actions were approved by the administration. Their propaganda in Cuba and the threat of an expedition caused Spain heavy expenses for counter-measures. The Spanish Minister proposed that the " voice of a respected and acknowledged authority " should warn the public not to be led astray.[3] This proposal was ignored, but Clayton assured Calderón that the President had sent instructions to the District Attorneys of New York, Washington and New Orleans to prevent violations of the Neutrality Act.[4]

The administration and Congress were preoccupied with the critical struggle over slavery in the territories ceded by Mexico. President Taylor opposed compromise measures offered by Clay. Southern leaders threatened secession if their full demands for protection and extension of slavery were not met. Senator Calhoun, fighting the compromise until he died in April, 1850, believed that the attention of the South should be concentrated on this issue and therefore considered the plan of López inopportune. Calhoun largely controlled the strategy of the South in Washington. The discouragement López met

2 Morales, *Iniciadores*, II, 46-54, 195-6. Claiborne, *Quitman*, II, 70.

3 Calderón to Clayton, Washington, January 19, 1850. Department of State, *Notes from Legations: Spain*, XII.

4 Clayton to Calderón, Washington, January 22, 1850. Department of State, *Notes to Legations: Spain*, VI.

there even from the southerners who sympathized with his cause led him to transfer his headquarters to New Orleans. There he found politicians of the extreme " southern rights " school who opposed the Compromise of 1850 after as well as before it was enacted and favored annexation of Cuba at the same time that they advocated secession of their states from the Union. The enterprises of López were henceforth intimately associated with the dreams of a slavery empire entertained by extremists of the Deep South.

Outstanding among them was General John A. Quitman, Governor of Mississippi. He was perhaps the most uncompromising pro-slavery expansionist and secessionist politician in his state, the home of fire-eaters. A planter of German antecedents who had migrated to Mississippi from New York, he had led filibusters into the Texas Republic, won fame as a general in the Mexican War in a hand-to-hand combat at the gates of Mexico City, and was rewarded by the voters of his state with the governorship. His passionate southern nationalism and love of slavery as the best of all possible labor systems made him look upon the purely tactical compromises of a Jefferson Davis or Henry S. Foote as treason to the South and slavery. States' rights was for him a religion that sanctioned any measures to strengthen his section and its peculiar institution. He was a Democrat except during the period of Jackson's heresy on nullification. Truculent and outspoken, he commanded the devotion of the extremists of the Gulf states.[5]

On their way to New Orleans, López and Gonzalez stopped at Jackson and offered the Governor military command of the Cuban revolution. Claiborne provides a description of his friend's state of mind:

Quitman was ambitious, and these grand ideas of revolution and progress, of changes to be accomplished by liberal prin-

5 J. F. H. Claiborne, *Quitman*, I-II. A. C. Cole, *The Whig Party in the South*, Prize Essays of the American Historical Association, 1912 (Washington, 1913), 50, 185-6.

ciples and energetic rule, were his own. To lead such a movement in aid of an oppressed people, and for the introduction of American civilization *and Southern institutions,* had been the dream of his life. The battle-field and its glory, the clangor and the charge rose up like a gorgeous pageant to dazzle his imagination.[6]

López played on the warrior's pride, led the conversation to Chapultepec and the Belen Gate. Confidential friends who had been invited to the interview urged that the Governor accept. But he decided that he could not personally desert his post to invade Cuba while the struggle to concert measures of secession was pending. He could only " put his heart in the enterprise and contribute some pecuniary aid." And, laying the map of Cuba on the table, he freely offered his advice on military strategy.[7]

The offer of López to place himself second in command to the American General may have been an attempt to secure the co-operation of the Havana Club and Secret Junta. One of their agents had earlier written to Quitman:

Gen. Lopez, who is now in the United States, and whose impetuous anxiety to go to Cuba may occasion the neglect of all the elements of success and order which we desire, would certainly join were he to know that such a person as you headed the expedition. [Our plan is] to tie into one single action Southern interest and Cuban annexation; to create an intelligent American centre of action for the purpose of examining the subject, adopting a course, commanding and executing: a secret Southern committee for the annexation of Cuba . . . as the first step. . . .[8]

However, Quitman never found López too impetuous for his support, he favored him over the more conservative Cubans,

6 Claiborne, *Quitman,* II, 56. Italics added.
7 *Ibid.,* 57-8, 383-5.
8 *Ibid.,* 381-3.

and encouraged him to lead the invasion himself. Quitman was later indicted in the Federal District Court of Eastern Louisiana for his part in the 1850 expedition, which he seems to have aided not only with money and advice but by recruiting personnel.[9]

Cotesworth Pinckney Smith, Judge of the Supreme Court of Errors and Appeals of Mississippi, supported López and placed his own signature on the bonds of the " Cuban Republic." [10] Quitman, Smith, Henry S. Foote, and Henderson, the most important political leaders to support López, were all from Mississippi, which was also the chief center of secessionist activity in 1850. In New Orleans, Lawrence J. Sigur, owner and editor of the *Delta,* supported López in his newspaper and with funds, and the Cuban took up his residence in the editor's home.

The atmosphere of New Orleans was congenial to the plottings of filibusters. The city romanticized the famous pirates of its past and filibusters had long since become their natural successors. Bank's Arcade on Magazine Street had been the accepted headquarters of filibusters since Davy Crockett, James Bowie, and William B. Travis had organized their expeditions to Texas. López set up his headquarters there and might have recruited a full complement among the vagabonds and adventurers who frequented the place. Instead, he attempted to give a political character to his little army in order to identify it with the cause of the South. Veteran officers of the Mexican War were appointed in several states to raise regiments that bore their states' names. Ultimately a regiment was organized for each of three states: Kentucky under Colonel Theodore O'Hara, Mississippi under Colonel Bunch, and Louisiana under Colonel Chatham R. Wheat. The latter in the Civil War became the leader of the famed Louisiana Tigers. Many

9 John I. Goode to Quitman, Moscow, Alabama, May 30, 1850. Quitman Papers. *Cf. Senate Executive Documents* (31:2), no. 41, pp. 56-8.

10 *House Executive Documents* (32:1), no. 2, p. 28.

of the officers were young men of education and ability, although the privates, especially those of the Louisiana Regiment recruited at Bank's Arcade, were largely deficient as soldiers. Lavish promises were made to them, arms were obtained, among other sources, from the state arsenals of Mississippi and Louisiana, and two sailing vessels, the *Georgiana* and the *Susan Loud,* and the steamer *Creole* were purchased. American Army officers stationed at New Orleans were friendly. Early in May, the expeditionaries, numbering more than five hundred men, were ready to set forth in the mingled moods of a lark and a crusade.[11]

The motives for embarking on this strange venture of an intelligent filibuster, Captain J. C. Davis of the Louisiana Regiment, are revealed in the account he published after his return:

> 1st.   Because the inhabitants of Cuba wished to be free.   But it was said that they were told that the moment they made the effort, the blacks would be armed and turned loose upon them. No government capable of conceiving such an idea, or making such a threat, either deserves the respect or allegiance of its subjects.   2d.   Because I believe it to be right and proper to propagate republican principles . . . and multiply republican governments.   3d.   Because, if it was praise-worthy in Lafayette . . . how much more glory would there be in striking the first blow for an oppressed people. . . .   4th.   Because it was whispered about certain places that there was *gold* as well as *glory* in Cuba. . . .   5th.   Because it would be a very pretty little operation for the summer; there being but twenty-five or thirty thousand troops on the Island, we would, perhaps, have a right smart brush or so. . . .[12]

Notably absent from Davis' list is the desire to annex Cuba to the United States. López presented to his followers only

11 F. C. M. Boggess, *A Veteran of Four Wars* (Arcadia, Florida, 1900), chs. II-III. Herbert Asbury, *The French Quarter* (New York, 1936), 172-9.

12 O. D. D. O., *The History of the Late Expedition to Cuba* (New Orleans, 1850), 3-4. Author identified as J. C. Davis by Caldwell, *Lopez Expeditions,* 131.

the first step of his plan, the liberation of the island. But the Texas model for evolution from an independent republic into a state of the Union was the one his supporters expected Cuba to follow. Meanwhile, the red shirts of the liberal revolutionaries of Europe, which were the filibuster army's only uniform, expressed the most popular and praiseworthy motive of the expedition: to win freedom from European despotism for the white people of Cuba.

The activities of the expeditionaries as they gathered in New Orleans did not escape the notice of Spanish agents. The new Consul, Juan Laborde, was nervous and several times sent the Federal Attorney, Logan Hunton, on false scents to search innocent vessels. One of the owners claimed losses from being detained and sued the Consul. Legal vexations, the latter suspected, were intended to intimidate him from making further efforts. The upshot was that the filibusters' three vessels slipped away separately and without hindrance, took on arms from fishing smacks that followed them to sea, and made for their rendezvous off Yucatan. Hunton did not deny that he knew what was happening, and he did not justify his inactivity entirely by his interpretation that the Neutrality Act had not been violated. The law, he wrote Clayton, did not forbid every kind of hostile action by citizens against a power with whom the United States was at peace. But apart from that, he had not

> deemed it politic in the Government, to be engaged in abortive efforts to arrest by judicial proceedings, these attempts at invasion, conducted as they have been. The effect of such efforts would only have served to inflame the public mind, and to have emboldened these adventurers.[13]

This confession, more than any flaws in the Neutrality Act, perhaps reveals why not a year passed during the eighteen-

13 Hunton to Clayton, New Orleans, May 23, 1850. Department of State, *Lopez Expeditions.*

fifties in which federal officials did not fail to prevent an invasion by armed Americans of Cuba, Mexico, or Nicaragua.

The port authorities of New Orleans, accepting the disguise of the men as emigrants to the gold fields of California, cleared the filibusters' three vessels for Chagres. The Spanish Consul penetrated the disguise, but the federal officers refused to detain the vessels for lack of proof of an overt act. Laborde appealed to Calderón, who asked Clayton to require the District Attorney and Collector to co-operate with the Consul, but it was too late.[14] The administration, however, had already taken precautionary measures. Even before it received " credible evidence " of the expedition's departure, three war vessels had been sent to the coasts of Cuba to prevent the landing of any Americans who might proceed " under the American flag " to invade Cuba, and two more were sent within a few hours after such evidence was received.[15] The earlier warships might have intercepted the filibusters off the mouth of the Mississippi had not the local officials accepted their legal disguise. At it was, neither the five American nor nineteen Spanish warships guarding the Cuban coasts were able to prevent López's landing at Cardenas.

The expedition assembled at the uninhabited island of Contoy in Mexican territorial waters. About fifty men, some of whom had from the beginning intended to desert at Chagres and go on to California, were left with the *Georgiana* and the *Susan Loud* to return to New Orleans. On the way to Cardenas, the *Creole,* heavily overloaded, narrowly missed an encounter with the Spanish steam frigate *Pizarro,* which went on to Contoy, captured the party of deserters and took them with the two sailing vessels in tow to Cuba.

López and his band surprised the garrison of Cardenas on

14 Calderón to Clayton, Washington, May 8, 1850. Department of State, *Notes from Legations: Spain,* XII.

15 Clayton to Calderón, Washington, May 18, 1850. Department of State, *Notes to Legations: Spain,* VI.

the morning of May 19, took it prisoner after a few shots, fired the Governor's mansion and took him prisoner, and were masters of the town. The plan called for an advance along the railroad while Cuban volunteers should swell the ranks for an attack upon Havana. In the afternoon, an advance party of Spanish lancers arrived and a sizeable force was reported behind it, cutting off the railroad. The inhabitants of Cardenas were not unfriendly, but none responded to a recruiting party that marched through the streets with drum and flag of the " Cuban Republic." Sugar plantations surrounded the town, and whites feared that López intended to incite the slaves to revolt. After a brief encounter with the lancers, the filibusters re-embarked. López was eager to land again west of Havana, but arms had to be thrown overboard when the *Creole* grounded in the harbor, the men were discouraged and mutinous, and López reluctantly consented to head for Key West. The *Pizarro* chased the *Creole* into that port, and her captain demanded that the filibusters be arrested. The people of Key West hailed the men as heroes, helped them make their getaway, and a federal officer contented himself with seizing the *Creole*.[16]

The filibuster movement was not discouraged by the failure of the Cardenas Expedition. The exploit of capturing the town was held to be a warrant of future success, and López publicly proclaimed his intention to organize another expedition. In the South, he was fêted as a conquering hero. In Gainesville, Mississippi, cannon salutes, banquets and toasts were climaxed by a parade in which appeared " a band of music, some one hundred ladies, the pupils of the academy, Gen. López and friends [the leaders of the Junta], the masonic brethren, and the Sons of Temperance." [17]

16 Richardson Hardy, *The History and Adventures of the Cuban Expedition* (Cincinnati, 1850), 3-54. O. D. D. O., *The History of the Late Expedition to Cuba*, 6-81.

17 Claiborne, *Quitman*, II, 61.

Members of Congress who sympathized with the aims of the filibusters tried to call the administration to task for sending naval vessels to frustrate it. In the House, Representative Inge of Alabama introduced a resolution challenging the President's efforts to prevent the redemption of Cuba from the dominion of Spain. Not quite two-thirds of the members present voted for a motion to suspend the rules and debate this resolution.[18] Senator Yulee of Florida introduced similar measures. Use of the Navy to prevent landing of the expedition, he said, was a serious usurpation of power by the Executive. It violated the personal civil rights of emigration and expatriation, deprived American citizens of life, liberty, or property without due process of law, and was an act of war without authority of Congress against one belligerent in a civil war. The President, he suspected, leaned toward despotism against republicanism. Senator Webster defended the administration, but a resolution calling for any correspondence tending to show the existence of a revolutionary movement in Cuba passed. The President denied he had any such information and sent correspondence which showed, his message said, that the government had faithfully executed the laws and treaties bearing on the López expedition.[19] Yulee wanted to debate Cuban policy, and Foote of Mississippi threatened to answer Webster, but Clay, concerned over the fate of his Compromise Bill, refused to allow further interruptions which might reveal the limitations of his measure before it passed.[20]

While many citizens and Congressmen continued to support the filibusters, Secretary Clayton faced the difficult diplomatic tasks that resulted from the Cardenas Expedition. During the preceding months, a foretaste of these problems came to him when he attempted to obtain the freedom of two American citizens resident in Cuba who had been arrested for smuggling

18 *Congressional Globe* (31:1), 1021.

19 *Ibid.*, 1030-4, 1055, 1110.

20 *Ibid.*, 1130.

and hiding 20 kegs of what they claimed was "blasting powder" and 40 canisters of "sporting powder." For four months the Spanish authorities made no decision while they held the accused, James H. West, a merchant, in town arrest at Sagua la Grande, and his employee, Edward R. Lambden, in prison. At the moment when the López expedition headed for Cuba, Barringer and Campbell were making vigorous demands for the Americans' freedom. The former was rebuked by Pidal for "the vehemence and the unusual warmth" of his representations. The authorities in Cuba, Pidal wrote, could not overlook so large an amount of gunpowder, which made the Americans seem to Spanish officials implicated in revolutionary activities, "as they do see organized in the United States a perpetual conspiracy against the Island of Cuba." [21] In the light of the new problem López was making, Barringer's reply was unfortunate. It ran to sixteen pages of recriminations and sarcasm on the theme of Pidal's "fancy" of a conspiracy, and assured him that the United States would never intervene in favor of those who proved to be offenders against Spain.[22] Pidal stiffly answered that everything in his earlier note, which he said Barringer had only imperfectly understood, still represented his views.[23] Campbell also pressed the cause of West and Lambden, despite the fact that they were under the consular jurisdiction of Trinidad rather than Havana.[24]

Campbell gave particular offense when a letter he wrote to Clayton on the day the filibusters took Cardenas was published in the American press. The Spanish authorities considered it provocative and insulting. The Consul was evidently unaware that López had landed. He described the public excitement

21 Pidal to Barringer, Madrid, May 6, 1850. Department of State, *Diplomatic Despatches: Spain*, XXXVI.

22 Barringer to Pidal, Madrid, May 10, 1850. *Ibid.*

23 Pidal to Barringer, Madrid, May 15, 1850. *Ibid.*

24 Campbell to Villanueva, Havana, May 16, 1850. Department of State, *Consular Despatches: Havana*, XXIII.

over rumors and measures of defense. The Spanish warships,
he wrote, were inefficient. If the filibusters came in steamers
he did not doubt they would be able to make good their landing. The government had assembled 3,000 militia in Havana,
but their officers had never fired a gun or discharged a military duty. He expected disorder if civil war broke out. The
lower classes were ignorant, idle and debased, and might try
to please the authorities by attacking American citizens, all
of whom were thought to connive with the filibusters. He
feared a slave revolt and hinted that the President might well
" intimate to this Government any opinion of the course of
policy to be pursued by the United States in the event of the
slaves of Cuba being armed." [25] The event which his friends
of the Havana Club most feared seemed to Campbell a reason
for intervention by the United States.

Even before the Contoy prisoners arrived in Havana, the
American Consul addressed a letter to the Captain-General
with pointed inquiries whether they were American citizens
and their vessels under the United States flag. He wanted full
information regarding the circumstances of their arrest and
the nature of the offense with which they were charged.[26]
Clayton's first desire was to send a diplomatic agent to Havana to supersede Campbell and treat with the Captain-General, but Calderón was positive that " so strange a novelty "
might be " dangerous as well as useless " because the Captain-General lacked power to receive such an agent.[27] Campbell
was without instructions for ten days which he used to good
advantage. With Captain Randolph of the *Albany*, he called
on the Captain-General. The latter refused to receive a letter
Campbell had prepared because, he said, diplomatic powers
were not invested either in himself or the Consul. The prisoners and their vessels had not yet arrived in Havana, but Ron-

25 Campbell to Clayton, Havana, May 19, 1850. *Ibid.*

26 Campbell to Roncali, Havana, May 20, 1850. *Ibid.*

27 Calderón to Clayton, Washington May 20, 1850. Department of State,
Notes from Legations: Spain, XII.

cali called them pirates and admitted that the vessels were American. Campbell demanded that they be sent to the United States for trial. Roncali refused. This refusal, Campbell believed, brought into operation the Act of Congress that authorized the United States Navy to capture any ship that "unnecessarily" detained an American merchantman in the Gulf of Mexico, an Act which was supported by the law of nations and Webster's correspondence with Lord Ashburton. Therefore he sent out the *Albany* and Captain Lowndes of the *Germantown* to pursue the *Pizarro* and seize her prizes.

An encounter that might have led to war was prevented by Captain Tattnall of the *Saranac,* who met the *Albany* and *Germantown* and ordered them to abandon the hunt. Captain Tattnall also reminded Campbell that his main duty was to preserve good relations with the Spanish authorities and he induced the Consul to transmit to Roncali a warning that another contingent of filibusters was expected, a service for which the Captain-General was grateful. The *Saranac* brought to Havana Collector Douglass of Key West and Judge Marvin. The Captain-General received them, but refused to allow anyone to see the Contoy prisoners.[28] Campbell saw trouble wherever he looked. The Count of Mirasol arrived in the island from Madrid, and the Consul warned Clayton that the visit presaged an effort by Spain to conquer the Dominican Republic, or perhaps Guatemala. Men were being enlisted. That Mirasol might represent Spain's concern to defend the island against filibusters did not occur to the American. He sent Clayton minute details of the armaments of Spanish warships in Cuban waters.[29]

Even Campbell was satisfied when he finally received instructions from the Secretary of State. The administration

[28] Campbell to Clayton, Havana, May 31, 1850, and enclosures. Department of State, *Consular Despatches: Havana,* XXIII.

[29] Campbell to Clayton, Havana, June 4, 1850. Department of State, *Lopez Expeditions.*

had decided to claim full credit for enforcing the laws and treaties against the filibusters and to take strong ground against the seizure of the Contoy deserters and their ships. The United States, Clayton wrote, would prosecute anyone concerned with the expedition within its jurisdiction. But justice might be defeated in these cases if American citizens met injustice in Cuba, which might even render it impracticable to prevent more serious violations of the Neutrality Laws. Even if the Americans captured at Contoy intended to invade Cuba, Clayton said he could not recognize the right of Spain to "hang, garote, or shoot them for that intention." They might be guilty of violating American but not Spanish laws. Then followed a passage that, while repudiating annexationism, appealed to national pride in the vocabulary of the orators of Manifest Destiny:

> The President has resolved that the Eagle must and shall protect [the Contoy prisoners] against any punishment but that which the tribunals of their own nation may award. Tell the Count of Alcoy to send them home to encounter a punishment, which, if they are honorable men, will be worse than any, he can inflict, in the indignant frowns and denunciations of good men in their own country, for an attempt to violate the faith and honor of a nation which holds its character for integrity of more value and higher worth, than all the Antilles together. [Warn him that] if he injustly sheds one drop of American blood, at this exciting period, it may cost the two countries a sanguinary war.

The *Albany, Germantown,* and *Saranac,* Clayton added, "ought to be able to protect our countrymen, who were not guilty of the invasion." [30] These instructions were immediately given to American newspapers. John J. Crittenden, a Whig leader of Kentucky, complimented the Secretary of State. The instructions, he said, were masterly: "popular, proud and

30 Clayton to Campbell, Washington, May 31, June 1, 1850. Department of State, *Instructions to Consuls,* XIV.

national." [31] They were obviously calculated to answer the charge that the administration " leaned toward despotism," and were not the last attempt of the Whigs to appropriate the enthusiasm for Manifest Destiny that Democrats looked upon as their private property.

Newspapers containing the instructions reached Havana before Campbell could induce the Captain-General to accept a copy of them, so the Consul, dissatisfied with a garbled version telegraphed to New Orleans, copied them from a Savannah newspaper and handed them to Roncali. The latter had protested that the demand for the prisoners should be made to Calderón or through Barringer at Madrid, and agreed to receive it only in order himself to send it to Calderón.[32]

Clayton had already told Calderón that the President did not concede the right of Spain to punish the Contoy prisoners. He denied that the filibusters were pirates because murder and robbery were committed by them in Cuba and not on the high seas. To accuse Americans of piracy who did not even invade Cuba would lead to errors, and Clayton hoped that the authorities in Cuba would not in their triumph jeopardize the relations he and Calderón worked so hard to maintain.[33] After much prodding from Washington, federal officers arrested López, O'Sullivan and other filibusters.[34]

When the news arrived of the Captain-General's refusal to consider Campbell's demand for the prisoners, the administration determined to increase its pressure on Spain, in spite of a confidential warning from Campbell that the Spanish authorities, convinced that in any case they would soon lose Cuba

31 Crittenden to Clayton, Frankfort, June 22, 1850. Clayton Papers.

32 Campbell to Clayton, Havana, June 19, 1850. Department of State, *Consular Despatches: Havana*, XXIII.

33 Clayton to Calderón, Washington, June 3, 4, 25, 1850. Department of State, *Notes to Legations: Spain*, VI.

34 Clayton to Taylor, Washington, June 9, 1850. Hunton to Clayton, New Orleans, June 22, 1850. Clayton Papers.

to new expeditions, seemed ready for war.[35] A diplomatic
agent, Commodore Charles Morris, was ordered to Havana
in a naval vessel to take over Campbell's duties regarding the
prisoners and demand their release by the Captain-General.[36]
Calderón was informed of this action. His contention, bol-
stered by a United States Supreme Court decision, that " piratical " actions were not only those which the law of nations
called piracy but also any actions committed by pirates, Clayton turned with a quotation from Story that pirates did in
all cases operate against shipping. The President's designation
of filibusters as pirates in his 1849 Proclamation justified
Spain in shooting the invaders at Cardenas, Clayton now admitted, but the Contoy prisoners did not even intend to commit a hostile act against Cuba, they were *bona fide* passengers
for Chagres.[37]

Calderón made much of Lopez's new attempts to organize
an expedition against Cuba and he provided captured documents to aid the prosecution of the ringleaders.[38] He asked
that Campbell be removed. Complaints had piled up against
him, and publication of his dispatch to Clayton of May 19 had
given " serious offense " to the government of Her Catholic
Majesty. By a remarkable triple coincidence, according to the
official correspondence, Calderón's request for Campbell's removal was dated July 8,[39] the same day that Campbell in Havana wrote to Clayton asking for a leave of absence,[40] and the

35 Campbell to Clayton, Havana, June 13, 1850. Clayton Papers.

36 Clayton to Morris, Washington, June 29, 1850. Department of State,
Special Missions, I. Clayton to Campbell, Washington, June 29, 1850.
Department of State, *Instructions to Consuls*, XIV.

37 Clayton to Calderón, Washington, July 9, 1850. Department of State,
Notes to Legations: Spain, VI.

38 Calderón to Clayton, Washington, May 24, 27, 31, June 7, 22, 24,
28, 1850, and enclosures. Department of State, *Notes from Legations:
Spain*, XII.

39 Calderón to Clayton, Washnigton, July 8, 1850. *Ibid.*

40 Campbell to Clayton, Havana, July 8, 1850. Department of State,
Consular Despatches: Havana, XXIII.

very day that Clayton wrote the Consul permission to take leave " during this extremely warm weather." Clayton referred to a grant of leave in his previous dispatch,[41] which, however, is not there.[42] Campbell never returned to Havana. Clayton's ill-disguised concession was made while President Taylor lay dying from the effects of a Fourth of July celebration. It did something to break the log-jam and open the way for Spain to release the Contoy prisoners. On July 1, Clayton had instructed Barringer to demand their release. The death of President Taylor on July 9 suspended further negotiations in Washington until after President Fillmore had appointed Daniel Webster his Secretary of State.

In the meantime, conversations of Barringer and Pidal in Madrid took a serious turn involving threats of war by the United States and counter-plans of Spain to organize a European coalition against the United States. When news of the Cardenas Expedition arrived in Madrid, the American Minister had no instructions but only newspaper reports to aid in facing the angry Spanish Foreign Minister. He tried to assure the latter that the United States government had done and would do everything required by its obligations to Spain. Pidal replied that Spain had faith in the sincerity and good intentions of the President, but it appeared that he was very badly served by his subordinates. He rehearsed the occurrences which led to this conclusion, and they were damning enough. Spain and Europe did not understand them, Pidal said, nor could they be squared with the assurances of the present administration and its predecessors that the United States would use force to maintain Spain in the sovereignty of her West Indies possessions. Barringer was brought up sharply by Pidal's next statement that Saunders had offered to conclude with Spain a treaty guaranteeing to her the island of Cuba.

41 Clayton to Campbell, Washington, July 8, 1850. Department of State, *Instructions to Consuls*, XIV.

42 Clayton to Campbell, Washington, June 29, 1850. *Ibid.*

Pidal must be mistaken, Barringer said. But the Foreign Minister insisted that he had just finished reading the notes of the conversation with Saunders on the occasion when the latter referred to measures of his government to prevent soldiers returning from the Mexican War from landing in Cuba, and that Saunders had then declared his readiness to sign a treaty of guaranty.

Whether Saunders' ineptitude in his conversation with Narváez to which Pidal referred, or the latter's deliberate intention was behind this misunderstanding cannot be determined. Pidal mentioned the supposed offer of a treaty of guaranty by the United States to justify the course he proposed to Barringer for Spain now that it appeared the United States lacked power to prevent invasions of Cuba: " Spain & the rest of Europe will be obliged to make other arrangements, & combinations." The United States, he continued, was not the only government interested in Cuba:

> Other great powers had important rights and possessions among the West India Islands & near the Gulf of Mexico, and the deepest interest in whatever fortune awaited them; they also could never be indifferent to anything touching the sovereignty of the Island of Cuba—chief of the Islands & key of that Gulf. Spain had therefore guarantees of security to her sovereignty over the Island from other governments than that of the U. S.

These governments, Pidal said, were England, with whom Spain had recently restored friendly diplomatic relations, and France. Barringer inquired as to the nature of the guaranties, and was given to understand that they provided military and naval aid to secure the island to Spain against any other power.

Barringer attempted to reassure the Spanish Minister and clarify the policy of the United States, but he multiplied confusion as he declared that the United States would " resist at all costs any attempt on the part of any other power to acquire by cession or force " the whole or any part of Cuba, and in the next breath said he was " not authorized " to assure Spain " that the whole power of the U. S. would be employed to prevent the occupation in whole or part of Cuba from passing into other hands." This invisible distinction made, the American Minister thought the moment appropriate to say he was not authorized to open negotiations for the cession of Cuba to the United States, on the contrary, Spain would have to originate such a measure for it to be entertained by his government. " Spain might indeed lose the Island, but sell it, never !" Pidal exclaimed.

He returned to his main theme. Spain did not ask aid or guaranties of the United States. What she did desire was that the United States repress hostile and piratical expeditions. That done, Spain might be left to defend Cuba. But the present state of things could not long continue. Cuba was kept in perpetual agitation, in time of peace Spain was obliged to maintain war expenses. Either the United States had or had not the power to suppress filibustering; if not, " Spain & Europe must make other dispositions & new relations towards the United States." Barringer, having explained the difficulties for his government created by a free press, the gold rush to California which provided easy cover for the filibusters, and the scarcity of legal proofs against them, repeated that it would do its whole duty, and the interview ended with mutual congratulations by the American and the Spaniard for their frankness.[43]

A few days after this interview, Pidal addressed a Circular to Spain's representatives in European capitals requesting them to make known to the governments to which they were accredited Spain's efforts to obtain from the United States satisfaction for the past and guaranties for the future. If the filibusters went unpunished, the Circular stated, Spain would

[43] Barringer to Clayton, Madrid, June 19, 1850. Department of State, *Diplomatic Despatches: Spain,* XXXVI.

appeal to the moral sentiment and good faith of the European nations to oppose the irruption of a policy and doctrines destructive to the foundations on which the peace of the civilized world rested. Europe's silence in the face of American offenses would prepare an era in which might made right and popular passions of the worst sort were substituted for the rights of states. If the United States, degraded by popular passions, was unable to fullfill its international obligations, the Spanish diplomats were instructed to request the European governments to make a solemn protest to the United States and to take all possible measures to make the protest efficacious.[44]

Several of the governments instructed their agents in Washington to co-operate with Calderón, others waited to learn the attitude of Great Britain. Pidal directed a special note to the governments of that country and France. He imputed bad faith to the efforts of the United States government to suppress the filibusters and pointed out the danger to British and French interests of American annexation of the island. If the present scandalous state of affairs was not anathematized by all governments, evils almost as great as those of war would result. Therefore, Spain invited a joint guaranty by Britain and France of her possession of Cuba. Lord Palmerston seemed favorable to the proposal, and during July Pidal pushed the negotiations for a tripartite convention.[45]

While Pidal thus strengthened the position of Spain, the American Minister at Madrid was left until early August to fret over his lack of instructions and suspicions that his official mail was being opened en route.[46] Clayton's letter of July 1 finally arrived. It instructed the Minister, in terms similar to those Campbell had received, to demand the release of the

44 Becker, *Relaciones Exteriores de España*, II, 181-3.

45 *Ibid.*, 184-9.

46 Barringer to Clayton, Madrid, June 20, 27, July 4, 25, August 1, 1850. Department of State, *Diplomatic Despatches: Spain*, XXXVI.

prisoners, and added that if in the meantime they were executed, " I need not say to you, what I think will be the consequences." [47]

The issue between the two countries was clearly joined on August 5 in a conversation between Barringer and Pidal. The latter said that some of the prisoners would be discharged, but Spain had a right to capture them and try them, and " *insisted on that right*." All nations had the right to seize their enemies on the high seas, and the island of Contoy was equally deserted. Barringer answered that seizure of Americans on neutral territory under the jurisdiction of Mexico was illegal and in derogation of the rights of the United States. The President, he said, had instructed him to demand the immediate release of American citizens thus taken. Pidal requested a formal written demand. Barringer agreed, and said he and his government were " fully aware of the grave consequences of such a demand if resisted." The United States had done its duty. Spaniards abusing the hospitality of the United States had organized the expedition, deluded some few of its citizens, and but for the preventive measures of the government, the expedition would have comprised 20,000 men. Spain should consider all this before endangering peace. Pidal said he was chiefly concerned about the danger of future expeditions and the necessity of acting on the principle he asserted in defense against them. This consideration seemed to reconcile him to the idea of a war with the United States. He said: " Much as Spain would dislike a *rupture* with the United States, this state of things was not right & it could not long continue." Present conditions " must have an unfriendly termination."

Barringer wrote to Clayton that he believed Spain expected war with the United States if the Contoy prisoners were not freed or at any rate in defense of Cuba, and that active prep-

47 Clayton to Barringer, Washington, July 1, 1850. Department of State, *Diplomatic Instructions: Spain*, XIV.

arations were being made for it. Large new loans had been made to increase the military and naval forces, 5,000 picked troops had already been sent to Cuba, and General José Concha would presently replace Roncali and strengthen the military character of the Cuban administration. The Spanish government, Barringer thought, would refuse his formal demand for the prisoners. To avoid serious results from haste, and in deference to the new administration of President Fillmore whose wishes he expected soon to learn, he would postpone presentation of the demand for a few days.[48] The American Minister occupied three weeks with complaints against mistreatment of American citizens by Spain, the most flagrant case being that of West and Lambden, but he obtained satisfaction on none.[49]

Secretary Webster on July 29 instructed Barringer to insist on the immediate release of West and Lamden, but he said nothing about the Contoy prisoners.[50] On the other hand, the new Secretary did not revoke his predecessor's explicit instructions on that subject, so Barringer decided he could delay no longer.

The formal demand for the release of the Contoy prisoners was made on August 27 and, no reply coming from Pidal, was repeated on September 4. Two weeks later the Foreign Minister answered. He announced that most of the prisoners but not the vessels or their crews had been released. In regard to the latter and the principle that Spain had a right to make the seizures at Contoy, the American demand was rejected. The American "pretension" was "mistaken." Spain, Pidal reiterated, could not accept a rule that was incompatible with the defense of Cuba against pirates. The United States itself had formerly pursued pirates on foreign soil, specifically, in

48 Barringer to Clayton, Madrid, August 7, 1850. Department of State, *Diplomatic Despatches: Spain*, XXXVI.

49 Barringer to Pidal, Madrid, August 19, 22, 1850. *Ibid.*

50 Webster to Barringer, Washington, July 29, 1850. Department of State, *Diplomatic Instructions: Spain*, XIV.

Cuba. He insisted that the expeditionaries were pirates, and that when captured:

> I could not regard the said vessels as Anglo-American, nor those who manned them as citizens of the United States, because having undertaken an expedition of piracy, declared such by the law of nations, and by the government of the confederacy itself, and having put themselves on their own account, in war with Spain, they had lost by that sole act their nationality and the right to be regarded and protected as citizens of the Union.[51]

In his reply, Barringer expressed his deep regret that Spain insisted on the right asserted by Pidal and declared the American demand was not withdrawn. Beyond that, he contented himself with a long and close argument that the filibusters were not pirates because they did not commit robbery on the high seas and that Contoy was not a desert outside the jurisdiction of Mexico. In chasing real pirates, he said, the United States had only once and then in " fresh pursuit " trespassed on desert isles around Cuba.[52]

An impasse was reached as Pidal, doubtless emboldened by the mildness of Barringer's reply, cut off further debate with the remark that the latter had not and could not add significantly to the question because it had already been sufficiently debated on both sides. Still no instructions arrived for Barringer from Webster. The " neglect " of that statesman has been attributed to his ill health,[53] but he had in fact taken the essential negotiations into his own hands.

Webster's initial tone was far from calm. He rejected a note from Calderón that recapitulated the grievances of Spain regarding presumed laxity of the American government

51 Pidal to Barringer, Madrid, September 16, 1850. Department of State, *Diplomatic Despatches: Spain,* XXXVI.

52 Barringer to Pidal, Madrid, September 19, 1850. *Ibid.*

53 French E. Chadwick, *The Relations of the United States and Spain* (New York, 1909), 235.

towards filibusters, and the Spanish Minister reported his heated words to Pidal. The note, Webster said, was a prosecuting attorney's accusation and it could not be accepted. Calderón refused to withdraw it. Webster finally agreed to answer another note that the Minister drew up in more acceptable terms.[54] In his answer, Webster offered proof to Spain of an aggressive campaign by federal officers to suppress a new expedition to Cuba.[55] Next he told Campbell that existing relations with Spain involving commercial interests of high importance and other matters induced the President to withdraw his commission.[56] Thus failed the strenuous efforts of the doughty General and friend of Cuban annexationists to secure recognition of diplomatic powers for the American agent at Havana. Webster capped his work of conciliation by writing a personal letter to Pidal praying that Her Majesty might pardon the last Contoy prisoners.

At the same time, the striking outcome of Spain's effort to win British support against the United States helped to clear the air. On October 3, Barringer wrote Webster that he had learned of Spain's efforts to organize an European coalition " in case of the existence of certain emergencies between the United States & Spain." [57] On the same day, he wrote another letter describing the extraordinary result of those efforts. Lord Howden, the new British Minister to Spain, had called on Barringer and volunteered to read a despatch from Lord Palmerston on the question at issue between the United States and Spain. The latter country had sounded the disposition of

54 Calderón to Pidal, Washington, August 26, 1850. Becker, *op. cit.*, 169-71. Calderón to Webster, Washington, August 2 and 20, 1850. Department of State, *Notes from Legations: Spain*, XII.

55 Webster to Calderón, Washington, September 3, 1850. Department of State, *Notes to Legations: Spain*, VI.

56 Webster to Campbell, Washington, September 5, 1850. Department of State, *Instructions to Consuls*, XIV.

57 Barringer to Webster, Madrid, October 3, 1850. Department of State, *Diplomatic Despatches: Spain*, XXXVI.

the European powers towards aid and protection of Cuba and
other West Indian possessions. But Lord Palmerston admitted
the " justice and reason, both in law & fact " of the United
States demand for the release of the Contoy prisoners. Lord
Howden was instructed to advise the Spanish government of
this view, and to warn it that if any prisoner was executed, the
United States would have " just cause of complaint " and that
the most serious consequences might result. Furthermore,
Barringer had permission to use this information in present-
ing demands to Spain. The American did not ask, but estimated that Britain had refused to give assurances of aid to
Spain in the protection of Cuba against the United States.[58]

Palmerston's instructions to Howden were the first indication that Spain could expect no support from Britain. The
British Foreign Minister had decided that Spain was chiefly
responsible for her difficulties in Cuba and, after lecturing the
Spanish Minister to Britain several times on the way in which
heavy taxes, arbitrary administration and the slave trade provoked attempts by Cubans to obtain relief through annexation
to the United States, he rejected in December the Spanish proposal of a tripartite guaranty.[59] Britain also had an obvious
interest in opposing the " principle " of international law on
which Spain acted at Contoy.

After his interview with Lord Howden, Barringer hastened
to see Pidal and found he had already retreated from his former position in substance if not in principle. Orders had been
sent to suspend execution of any sentence against the Contoy
prisoners until it was submitted to Madrid. Barringer said he
was acquainted with Lord Palmerston's views on the subject,
but Pidal preferred to relate his government's conciliatory attitude to the disposition of the " new government " of the
United States to suppress filibusters and to the " calm tone "

58 Barringer to Webster, Madrid, October 3, 1850. *Ibid.*
59 Istúriz to Pidal, London, July 15, October 9, December 26, 1850. Becker,
op. cit., II, 191, 192, 196.

of Webster as compared with Clayton, under whom, he said, the correspondence had become " a little animated and a little vivid." The American Minister objected to what he thought was a slur on General Taylor. Pidal said that his government was interested chiefly in the principle involved in the Contoy affair and could agree with the United States on the men in custody because they mattered little to Spain. Barringer concluded that if the United States maintained its demand, all the prisoners would be released.[60]

The strong support of the United States by Great Britain as conveyed by Lord Howden was in part responsible for Spain's concessions in the Contoy affair, while disinterest in maintaining Clayton's demand and dismissal of Campbell opened a way out that permitted Spain to retrieve a victory " in principle." All of the prisoners were released in Cuba except a captain and two mates of the *Georgiana* and the *Susan Loud,* who were sentenced to ten, eight and four years in the mines of Ceuta. Webster's letter to Pidal secured their pardon. The Queen granted it, Pidal told Barringer, in order to show Spain's desire for friendship with the United States, and it was done while the prisoners were at sea so that they served none of their sentences in the notorious mines.[61] The two vessels were sold by order of a " prize court " in Cuba. This action, against which the United States had grounds for serious complaint, was not objected to by Webster until February, 1851, when he directed Barringer to seek indemnity,[62] a request which the Minister apparently ignored. A year later, Webster admitted to the House of Representatives when it called for information that a copy of the judicial proceedings which resulted in condemnation of the vessels had not yet been

60 Barringer to Webster, Madrid, October 9, 1850. Department of State, *Diplomatic Despatches: Spain*, XXXVI.

61 Pidal to Barringer, Madrid, November 6, 1850. Barringer to Webster, Madrid, November 21, 1850. *Ibid.*

62 Webster to Barringer, Washington, February 5, 1851. Department of State, *Diplomatic Instructions: Spain*, XIV.

received. When that was obtained, he said, the case would be examined.[63] Nothing was done about the vessels, even after Secretary of State Marcy tried to revive the question in 1856.[64] Two years later the Senate passed a resolution that characterized the action of Spain as " in derogation of the sovereignty of the United States,[65] and there the matter rested.

The case of one unfortunate sailor remained. William Wilcox, a fireman on the *Creole,* had failed in his attempt to desert at Contoy, but jumped overboard and swam to an island near Cardenas to avoid implication in the invasion. He was discovered later, shackled in solitary confinement for some weeks and then sentenced to ten years in Ceuta. At Cadiz, United States Consul Burton saw the hapless prisoner and, encouraged by Webster, Barringer was able to obtain a pardon for him. However, Wilcox spent five months in the mines while the pardon was delayed, Barringer said, by Spain's dissatisfaction with the trials of the filibuster leaders in the United States.[66]

Those trials gave the American government no more satisfaction than Spain. Calderón was particularly anxious that López and his followers be tried and punished because they were planning a third expedition to Cuba. He sent to the Secretary of State during the summer and fall a stream of notes providing evidence against the filibusters from Cuban and American sources and urging the utmost severity and haste.[67] The administration did its part. True bills were obtained from the Grand Jury at New Orleans against López, Gonzales, the eight highest ranking American officers in the expedition, and six outstanding organizers and supporters: O'Sullivan, Sigur,

63 *House Executive Document* (32:1), 83, pp. 1-2.

64 *Ibid.* (34:1), 98.

65 Chadwick, *United States and Spain,* 236.

66 Barringer to Webster, Madrid, April 18, 1851. Department of State, *Diplomatic Despatches: Spain,* XXXVI.

67 Calderón to Clayton and Webster, Washington. May 24 to November 28, 1850. Department of State, *Notes from Legations: Spain,* XII.

Henderson, Smith, the Louisiana militia general Donahen Augusten and, most sensational of all, John A. Quitman, the Governor of Mississippi. Quitman pondered whether, as the embodiment and jealous protector of the sovereignty of his state, he ought not to save its dignity by forcibly resisting arrest. The failure of the Nashville Convention and his isolation politically as an opponent of the Compromise of September, 1850, possibly influenced the Governor to resign his office early in 1851 and submit to arrest. At the same time, he was active in the organization of a third expedition. As General Henderson wrote, those who were under indictment took " special pride " in conducting another conspiracy while they were being prosecuted for the previous one.[68]

Henderson was tried first. Three juries divided and failed to convict in spite of effective prosecution and charges by the judge that were favorable to it. This miscarriage of justice was striking evidence of the popular approval the filibusters enjoyed. The remaining cases were dropped.[69] Webster regretfully explained to Calderón that no change of venue was legally possible.[70]

The year 1850 ended with American-Spanish relations surprisingly amiable. But the removal of Campbell and two small sailing vessels were Spain's only compensations for the injuries she had suffered from the Cardenas Expedition. That event had exposed her isolation in Europe as well as the vulnerability of Cuba to attack and the lawless extremes to which Americans, especially southerners, would go in their desire to annex the island while even an administration that opposed annexation seemed hopeless to enforce its will against them.

Southern enthusiasm for Cuba rose higher after the failure at Cardenas. The passage of Clay's Compromise had been

68 Claiborne, *Quitman*, II, 70.

69 William H. Trescot, " The Late Cuba State Trials," *Democratic Review*, XXX (April, 1852), 307-19.

70 Webster to Calderón, Washington, March 19, 1851. Department of State, *Notes to Legations: Spain*, VI.

aided by Taylor's death and the ascension of the more conciliatory Fillmore, who replaced Seward with Webster as the chief Presidential adviser. But formal consent to the Compromise by all factions in the country except abolitionists and southern extremists did not mean that the South was content with the opportunity for slavery extension that popular sovereignty permitted in New Mexico. Frank Blair, President Jackson's chief advisor and veteran editor of the *Globe,* who had disowned the Democratic Party when its leaders abandoned reform and took up pro-slavery expansion, wrote to Martin Van Buren that the Compromise would not solve the troubles of Fillmore, Webster and Clay because southerners

> aim to gratify their slave state ambition & avarice by the conquest of Mexico, Cuba, & the surrounding slave coasts on the Gulph of Mexico. Lieut. Maury who was made president of the Memphis [Southern Commercial] Convention by his friend Calhoun has prefigured all this scheme of buccaneering in his Report. Nothing easier he thinks than for the Southern Saxons to make way with the degenerate Spaniards, to seize their possessions round the Gulph & make it the Mediterranean of a modern race of Greeks & Romans of the old caste, glorifying themselves & extending civilization by subjecting all the barbarians around it. . . . The South therefore will be up in arms again, the moment New Mexico presents herself for admission as a state.[71]

The filibusters did not wait for New Mexico to create another crisis. The Captain-General of Cuba issued a decree to garrote the Cuban leaders whenever they were caught, but this dampened their spirits no more than did the American prosecutions. A newspaper correspondent in New York witnessed their reaction:

> A merrier set of fellows I never saw in my life than were these proscribed Cubans. . . . They laughed, and smoked,

---

[71] Francis Preston Blair to Van Buren, Silver Spring, Maryland, July 15, 1850. Martin Van Buren Papers.

and sipped toddy till they were all as blue as indigo, and the way in which they ridiculed the Count of Alcoy and all his crowd, was a caution to tyrants. By the way, there are rumors afloat of another intended descent on that island....[72]

Spain faced the filibustering season of 1851 with nothing but her faith in Webster's assurances and the defenses organized by General Concha to stave off another attempt to overthrow her rule in Cuba. As the tragic event proved when those assurances availed nothing, Cuba's defenses sufficed.

72 *Weekly Alta California*, November 9, 1850.

CHAPTER VI

THE BAHIA HONDA EXPEDITION: 1851

THE filibusters planned their next expedition to sail from Savannah, Georgia, in the spring of 1851. The Fillmore administration was determined to prevent it. In his Message of December 2, 1850, the President declared: " We instigate no revolutions, nor suffer any hostile military expeditions to be fitted out in the United States to invade the territory or provinces of a friendly nation." [1] Calderón obtained accurate information on the activities of López and his followers from a spy, Duncan Smith, who posed as " Doctor Henry Burtnett " and was admitted to the counsels of the conspirators.[2] The Spanish Minister relayed information to Secretary Webster during the fall and winter. On September 3, 1850, the Minister was assured that Federal officers had been ordered to maintain vigilance and enforce the laws.[3] Still the administration required that an overt act be committed before it risked repetition of the failure of the Cardenas trials.

A flaw in the legality of the filibusters' plan appeared when John L. O'Sullivan, in charge of securing ships and arms in New York, sent them by sea to southern ports. The *Fanny* was despatched to New Orleans, where the Collector found her cargo of guns consigned to " respectable houses " and refused to act.[4] Calderón insisted that the vessel had a false bottom which should be investigated, but nothing was done in this

1 *Senate Executive Documents* (31:2), no. 1, p. 3.

2 Duncan Smith, "Narrative of Events Connected with the Late Intended Invasion of Cuba," edited by L. M. Perez, *Publications of the Southern History Association*, X (November, 1906), 345-362.

3 Webster to Calderón, Washington, September 3, 1850. Department of State, *Notes to Legations: Spain*, VI.

4 Freret to Webster, New Orleans, February 1, 1851. Department of State, *Lopez Expeditions to Cuba*.

case.[5] In March, the Federal Court in New Orleans abandoned the Cardenas trials and the filibusters prepared to depart. Sir Henry Bulwer wrote to Webster a full description of their plans.[6] Closer watch was kept in New York and when the District Attorney reported that vessels were about to depart, the President insisted that they be apprehended,[7] and he issued a Proclamation against the expedition. Unlike his predecessor, Fillmore did not call the filibusters pirates, but their motives were declared to be " plunder and robbery " and they were warned that they would forfeit their claim to protection or any interference in their behalf by the United States government no matter to what extremities they were reduced.[8]

When the steamer *Cleopatra* and a sloop stood out of New York harbor, they were attached and a number of the leaders in New York were arrested. The Grand Jury indicted John L. O'Sullivan and two of his subordinates on the evidence of Duncan Smith, but after a mistrial they and their vessels were freed.[9] O'Sullivan had failed to keep his threat, made to the Federal Attorney, that he would " implicate Mr. Clayton " if forced to testify.[10] Ambrosio Gonzalez, in charge of preparations in Georgia, was arrested and gave bond but was never tried.[11] These inconveniences caused López merely to sell the vessels in New York, return to New Orleans as the friendliest point of departure, and postpone the date of his expedition.

5 Webster to Hunton, Washington, January 28, 1851; Statement of John F. Gruber, New Orleans, February 7, 1851. *Ibid.*

6 Bulwer to Webster, Washington, March 10, 1851. *Ibid.*

7 William L. Derrick, Acting Secretary of State, to J. P. Hall, Washington, April 23, 1851. Derrick to Tallmadge, Washington, April 25, 1851. *Ibid.*

8 *Messages and Papers of the Presidents*, comp. Richardson, VI, 2647-8.

9 Trescot, " The Late Cuba State Trials," *Democratic Review*, XXX (April, 1852), 307-19.

10 Logan Hunton to Clayton, New Orleans, June 22, 1851. Clayton Papers.

11 Gonzalez, *Manifesto*, 10.

Amos Kendall, a veteran of President Jackson's Kitchen Cabinet who, like Blair, opposed the southern orientation of his party, informed Attorney General John J. Crittenden of the new plans of the filibusters. He believed Quitman was now in command.[12]

But Spain was grateful for the President's Proclamation. The Marquis de Miraflores, Spain's new Minister of Foreign Affairs, instructed Calderón to render "most emphatic and sincere thanks to His Excellency, the President, for his loyalty and noble uprightness of purpose."[13] The Spanish government had recently received information on the President's Cuban policy that threw strong light on his general views if not on the failure to take effective action against the filibusters. In March, 1851, a number of American Senators had called on the Captain-General in Havana. The latter wrote to his government that in order to go beyond social compliments he entertained Henry Clay and a few others privately at dinner. In the conversation that followed, Clay assured Concha that he was a "faithful interpreter" of President Fillmore's sentiments when he complimented the new Captain-General for the strengthened military organization of the island. The Kentuckian sketched the economic and strategic interests of the United States in Cuba, the difficulties, in spite of good intentions, of suppressing filibusters, and expressed his "profound horror" of their expeditions and of war between the United States and Spain. However, he expected that some day the United States would find it necessary to acquire Cuba, and it would do so through mutually satisfactory negotiations.[14] If to this were added that the Fillmore administration was inclined to appease the extremists in the South among whom López found his chief

12 Amos Kendall to Crittenden, Louisville, May 30, 1851. Crittenden Papers.

13 Calderón to Webster, Washington, July 11, 1851. Department of State, *Notes from Legations: Spain*, XIII.

14 Concha to Miraflores, Havana, March 31, 1851. *Boletin del Archivo Nacional*, XVI (September, 1917), 390-2.

support, and unwilling to use the stringent methods required to enforce the Neutrality Act, Senator Clay's summary of administration policy would be complete.

The administration was off guard when López sailed for Cuba early in August. He left suddenly on hearing that revolution had begun in the interior of the island. After the Cardenas Expedition he had worked to synchronize his landing with the outbreak of internal revolt by the provincial groups he had abandoned in 1848. The capture of Cardenas by López stimulated his followers in Cuba to intensify their activity. They organized the *Sociedad Libertadora* under the leadership of the lawyer and ardent patriot Joaquin de Agüero with headquarters in Puerto Principe and branches in many towns. A clandestine printing press issued propaganda that circulated throughout the island. Fair communications were maintained with the exiles in the United States. Freemasonry provided further ties when Agüero and his followers founded in 1850 the Revolutionary Lodge of Camaguey.[15] López became a Freemason in Savannah and urged O'Sullivan and Sanchez Iznaga to join. Links were possible also with disaffected elements of the Spanish army and officialdom who belonged to the revolutionary Peninsular lodges of *Communeros, Carbonarios, Cadenarios,* and *Soles.*[16] General John A. Quitman was Grand Master of Mississippi.[17] A modern Cuban writer has said that the revolutionary movement in mid-nineteenth century was entirely controlled by Masons.[18]

Early in 1851, Captain-General Concha became aware of the movement at Puerto Principe and appointed his most ruthless commander, Marshall Lemery, to suppress it. At the same time

15 Cano, *Hombres del '51,* 7.

16 Vilá, *Lopez,* I, 77.

17 James B. Scot, *Outline of the Rise and Progress of Freemasonry in Louisiana* (New Orleans, 1925), 61-5.

18 F. J. Ponte Dominguez, *La Masoneria en la Independencia de Cuba* (Havana, 1944).

he roused the anger of the townspeople by initiating the abolition of their *Audiencia,* the oldest in the island. When arrests began, Agüero and a handful of mounted men escaped to the mountains where they established a camp, *El Buen Refugio,* and set about collecting arms and recruiting an army. Late in May the news arrived of the seizure of the *Cleopatra* and postponement of López's arrival. Agüero, encouraged by evidence that he was widely supported, was unwilling to postpone action in Cuba. He hoped to accelerate the arrival of the expedition by an immediate revolt. The reckless patriots, whose *noms de guerre* were Franklin, Washington and other leaders of the American Revolution, fixed on July 4 as the day for a general rising and a declaration of independence.

A document was accordingly drawn up which stated grievances against Spain and that :

> The Island of Cuba is unanimously declared to be independent of the Government and Peninsula of Spain, in order that she may be recognized before the world as an independent nation, which has spontaneously placed itself under the protection and auspices of the Republic of the United States, whose form of government we have adopted.[19]

The reference to protection by the United States indicated that the Liberating Society of Puerto Principe held a middle position between advocates of independence and the advocates of annexation, and its policy corresponded with López's efforts to postpone the issue until Spain should have been overthrown. Despite this conciliatory program, the annexationists of the Havana Club refused to support Agüero or López, particularly as the chief liaison between them, Cristóbal Madan, had temporarily deserted the cause and was attempting to make his peace with the Spanish authorities in order to recoup his fortune. He was tricked into returning to Cuba and imprisoned

19 Translated copy in Department of State, *Lopez Expeditions to Cuba.*

by the Captain-General in spite of the mediation of Secretary of State Webster.[20]

The Cuban revolution of July 4, 1851, was betrayed before it began. The wife of Agüero and other women of Puerto Principe ordered Masses to be celebrated for the intention of Cuban independence in all the churches of the town on July 2. They had made flags for the revolutionary army. The design was a single star with implications like that of Texas on the ground of a Masonic triangle. It was first flown on the New York *Sun* building in 1850, was carried by López to Cardenas and is now the emblem of the Cuban Republic. The women of Puerto Principe offered their flags to the priests to be placed on the altars and blessed during the Masses. The Señora Agüero told the whole plot to a priest in the confessional, and he informed Marshall Lemery. Lists were taken of male attendants at the Masses and on July 4 arrests and military patrols prevented the revolt from starting in the towns. Agüero and his band at *El Buen Refugio* nevertheless proclaimed independence. They were hunted down and all but the leader and three others were killed in combat with Spanish lancers. The last four were captured and executed in Puerto Principe on August 12.[21]

On that same day, López and over 400 men disembarked from the *Pampero* at Bahia Honda in hope of joining up with the revolutionaries of Puerto Principe. They had heard exaggerated news of the rising but nothing of its betrayal and defeat. The *Herald* on July 22 published the first account. It was rich in detail and pictured 1000 patriots as entrenched in the mountains, holding the Spanish Army at bay and awaiting aid from the United States. A week later, the same newspaper

---

20 Webster to Calderón, Washington, March 6, June 4, 1851. Department of State, *Notes to Legations: Spain*, VI. See also, Madan to Owen, Havana, June 6, 1851; Owen to Webster, Havana, June 7, 1851. Department of State, *Consular Despatches: Havana*, XXIV; and Theodore Sedgwick to Webster, New York, October 4, 1851. Crittenden Papers.

21 Cano, *Hombres del '51*, 7-74.

published the Declaration of Independence.[22] Public excitement in New Orleans ran high when word arrived of the Cubans' revolt. The existence of a revolutionary "government" in the island strengthened the legal position of the filibusters. Supported by strong and general sympathy, López openly and hurriedly organized. Mass meetings were held in Lafayette Square and Bank's Arcade. A member of the expedition described the atmosphere:

> The Cuban flag . . . was to be seen in almost every direction, displayed in ample folds from buildings, or in miniature form in windows. Placards on the walls invited to public meetings, and Cuba, Cuba, Cuba, was the topic of the newspapers, the Exchange, the street corners, and the bar-rooms. It even ascended into the pulpit.[23]

Volunteers swarmed into the city, and a motley crowd was put aboard the only available vessel, the *Pampero,* a small steamer for which L. J. Sigur paid $75,000 out of his own pocket.[24]

Southerners again composed the large majority of the filibusters but this time exiles from the defeated European revolutions of 1848 made up small Hungarian and German "regiments," besides one of Cubans. Speeches and newspaper editorials were almost exclusively focused on doctrines of liberalism, but the southern political leaders who urged on the filibusters had somewhat different motives. John Claiborne, the intimate associate of Quitman, wrote shortly after the Cardenas Expedition:

> The truth is that our people want Cuba free not only because they detest the Despotism of its government, but for reasons of the strongest political necessity. If the Cubans wish to be-

22 New York *Herald,* July 22 and 28, 1851.

23 "Personal Narrative of Louis Schlesinger," *Democratic Review,* XXXI (September, 1852), 212.

24 Anderson C. Quisenberry, "Lopez's Expeditions to Cuba," *Filson Club Publications* (Louisville, 1906), 74.

come free and to be admitted to share our civil rights, very well. If not they must go away from Cuba which must be be ours whether its present inhabitants desire it or not. Such is the reasoning of the great mass of our Southern and Western men.[25]

At the height of the excitement in July, 1851, the son of former President Tyler wrote to Quitman:

I look to the acquisition of Cuba as of great importance to the South. Through its acquisition the question as to the abidance of the North, *honestly* & *fairly,* by the provisions of the Constitution as to slavery, would be tested while yet the South have the *power of resistance* & the privilege of seceding. This point is of consequence looking to the rapid increase of the free soil States & their abolition population.[26]

López seems to have moved closer to the annexationist program of his American supporters. He prepared two proclamations to the people of Cuba. One of them offered them a provisional government until the people of the island should elect a constituent assembly. The second ended with the words:

The star of Cuba, today hidden and closed in by the mists of despotism, will rise beautiful and refulgent perchance to be admitted gloriously into the splendid North American constellation according to its inevitable destiny.[27]

López in his haste to join Agüero left with only a fraction of the volunteers available. Quitman and Gonzalez planned to follow him with reënforcements.[28] Calderón was confused by

---

25 John Claiborne to Thomas Claiborne, New Orleans, June 14, 1850. Thomas Claiborne Papers.

26 John Tyler, Jr., to Quitman, Philadelphia, July 31, 1851. Quitman Papers. Italics in original.

27 Diego Gonzalez, *Historia Documentada de los Movimientos Revolucionarios por la Independencia de Cuba de 1852 a 1867* (Havana, 1939), I, 31-2. Author's translation.

28 Asbury, *The French Quarter*, 182.

false leads. He relayed rumors to Webster that southerners gathering at Buffalo to aid Canadian revolutionaries were actually to invade Cuba and that in New York a " new, insidious plan " was on foot to infiltrate filibusters into Cuba five and ten at a time pretending to look for work as mechanics. Meanwhile, he added, the real expedition was organizing in Mississippi.[29] The Secretary of State left Washington for his vacation. In New Orleans, the Spanish Consul on Friday, August 1, asked Collector Freret to prevent the departure of the *Pampero*. Freret was afraid the owner of the vessel might claim damages. The Consul pointed out that the ship had not been cleared and was openly taking munitions aboard. The Collector answered that he would act on Monday.[30] This information Freret probably passed on to one of the employees of the Customs House, William L. Crittenden, who was also a Colonel in the expeditionary force. Crittenden was a nephew of the Attorney General, John J. Crittenden, and a graduate of West Point. He had served in the Mexican War and then fallen into evil ways, from which his uncle attempted to rescue him by giving him employment in the federal service.[31] The imputation is usually made that the Attorney General betrayed the plan to apprehend the filibusters on Monday, August 4, but Freret's dilatory tactics and close contact with William makes such a charge gratuitous.

Forewarned, López and his men on the overloaded *Pampero* steamed out to the Gulf early Sunday morning, August 3. Freret was subsequently discharged. His defense was illuminating. He had standing orders to use the Army and Navy if necessary to prevent violation of the Neutrality Act, and Major General Twiggs, in command of the military forces of

29 Calderón to Webster, Washington, July 16, 1851. Department of State, *Notes from Legations: Spain*, XIII.

30 Laborde to Calderón, New Orleans, August 6, 1851. *Ibid.*

31 John J. Crittenden to J. A. Crittenden, Frankfort, July 7, 1849. Crittenden Papers, Duke University.

the district, told him on August 1 that he was ready to help.[32] Freret asserted that a command to the Army and Navy from him would have been extra-legal and entailed too much responsibility for a Collector. Twiggs should have been on the scene of his own motion. Freret asked his superior:

> Is it to be supposed that at two o'clock in the morning, the hour at which the *Pampero* departed, the whole levee lined with friends of those departing, that I could have gone on board that vessel single handed, and enforced the law? [33]

Close attention by the administration in Washington and use of the telegraph would have made impossible the evasions of a Freret. As it was, not even a naval vessel interfered as the *Pampero* stopped in the lower channel of the Mississippi to take aboard more guns from a tug, was towed across the bar, and proceeded slowly to Key West, where a celebration with champagne was provided by the enthusiastic townspeople on August 10. Still the federal authorities did nothing.

At Key West, López received word which may have been planted by the Captain-General and led him to change his plans and strike the western end of the island instead of the central area where Agüero had staged his revolt. The western end was sparsely settled, and López's decision precluded aid from Cuban patriots except after conquest of a considerable area. After eluding Spanish vessels on August 11, the *Pampero* discharged its passengers on a deserted shore of Bahia Honda. They fell into a virtual trap. Colonel Crittenden and 120 men were left behind to guard supplies and the arms intended for Cuban volunteers, while López and 300 men marched inland. Both groups were quickly surrounded. Crittenden and about fifty men escaped in small boats only to be picked up by a

32 W. L. Hodge, Acting Secretary of the Treasury, to Freret, Washington, August 23, 1851. William Freret, *Correspondence between the Treasury Department, &c., in Relation to the Cuba Expedition, and William Freret, Late Collector* (New Orleans, 1851), 12-3.

33 Freret to Hodge, New Orleans, September 3, 1851. *Ibid.*, 13-15.

Spanish warship, taken to Havana, and, after a hasty examination, shot in the public square by order of Concha. López and his men fought bravely in desperate rear-guard actions as they retreated into the jungle-covered mountains of the interior. General Enna commanding the Spanish troops was killed. The unequal struggle ended on August 31 when López and 160 wounded and starving survivors were captured and taken to Havana. Concha had meanwhile rescinded the order that all captives be shot, but López was garroted before a pro-Spanish, holiday-making mob. Before he died, the chieftain shouted: " My death will not change the destiny of Cuba !" [34] Four of the 160 were released and the rest sent to Spain.

A profound reaction of sympathy even among those who opposed the expedition was produced in the United States by the news of the summary executions of Crittenden and his men. Terrible and evidently truthful stories were told of the brutalities they suffered before death and of mutilation of their bodies afterwards by the mob seeking horrible trophies.[35] Pathetically brave letters of farewell the condemned men had written to their families and friends in the United States and especially one by Crittenden were widely circulated.[36] In New Orleans, mobs ran wild. The Spanish Consul narrowly escaped from the city, his Consulate was wrecked, its flag and portrait of the Queen were torn to shreds, and shops and a newspaper office owned by Spaniards were demolished as their proprietors fled for safety on the first ship to Cuba. In Mobile, sailors and soldiers from a shipwrecked Spanish warship were mistaken for reënforcements en route to Cuba and were mobbed. Elsewhere in the Union less violent demonstrations took place.

34 Vilá, *Historia de Cuba*, I, 457-61.

35 Reports (four, in Spanish and unidentified). Department of State, *Lopez Expeditions to Cuba*. For an eye-witness account by an American, see William May to Frederick May, *Saranac* off Havana, September 16, 1851. Crittenden Papers, Library of Congress.

36 New York *Daily Tribune*, September 18, 1851.

Calderón was at first less concerned over abuse of the Spanish Consul and nationals than that reënforcements might go to rescue López.[37] Acting Secretary Derrick's first reply to Calderón was a delayed and rather cool statement that officers of the United States would " display the same faithfulness and vigilance in executing the laws of the country, as they have done on former occasions." [38] Repeated warnings by the Spanish Minister were finally heeded on August 30. The departure of López had not been allowed to disturb the mid-summer apathy of Washington. But the public outcry over the execution of Crittenden and his men stirred Fillmore and the administration to action. A flurry of orders issued from Washington to federal officials, one of them in President Fillmore's hand, and another a printed circular ordering attorneys of the Gulf and Atlantic districts to stay at home and do their duty.[39]

President Fillmore wrote to Webster on September 2 that he had returned from White Sulphur Springs, Virginia, " prematurely " and in great haste on August 30 and was occupied with Cuban matters ever since. He felt aggrieved, as he wrote:

> In times like this, the telegraph in the hands of irresponsible and designing men, is a tremendous engine for mischief, aided as it is in many places by a mercenary and prostituted press. Agitation and excitement seem to pervade all the large cities, and this is greatly aggravated by unscrupulous partizans who desire to turn it to political account against the administration. I think the summary execution of the 50 prisoners taken in

37 Calderón to Derrick, New York, August 10, 25, 28, 29, 30, 1851. Department of State, *Notes from Legations: Spain*, XIII.

38 Derrick to Calderón, Washington, August 21, 1851. Department of State, *Notes to Legations: Spain*, VI.

39 Fillmore to United States Marshall Tallmadge, Washington, August 30, 1851; Derrick to Williams, Washington, August 30, 1851; Derrick to Ten District Attorneys, Washington, September 1 1851; Fillmore to District Attorneys, Washington, September 2, 1851; Derrick to District Attorneys of Gulf and Atlantic Districts, Washington, September 2, 1851; Derrick to Hall, Washington, September 4, 1851; Derrick to Hall, Washington, September 23, 1851. Department of State, *Lopez Expeditions to Cuba*.

Cuba, was unfortunate. This wholesale slaughter of officers and men, in so summary a manner, excited the sympathy & indignation of the community. But I still hope to prevent any further violation of our neutrality laws, and to save our young men from a similar fate.[40]

That Democrats did make political capital of the affair is indicated by a letter to William L. Marcy in which Charles Eames, assistant editor of the Washington *Union*. drew attention to articles published against the President: " You see the blows we are dealing him," and observed: " It is general opinion here that Cuba has killed Fillmore." [41]

The administration's worry over further violations of the neutrality laws was relieved when news arrived of López's execution and discouraged would-be filibusters. The second dose of bad news seemed to increase anger at the administration. Fillmore and his cabinet were hard pressed to prevent Cuban affairs from destroying the sectional truce that followed the Compromise of 1850. The presidential-election year in the offing increased the pressure on them to satisfy partisans of Cuba. During the winter, a certain amount of sympathy for Kossuth was shown by administration leaders and helped to placate the enthusiasts of Manifest Destiny, but intervention against Austria could hardly be undertaken and Webster was forced to throw cold water on the public mania for the Hungarian patriot. Many could be satisfied only by annexation of Cuba. But the administration did not even satisfy those who advocated a strong stand in negotiations with Spain on the complex problems precipitated by the Bahia Honda Expedition.

Spain put itself in the wrong when it committed serious offenses against American shipping during August. The United States mail steamer *Falcon* was chased by a Spanish warship near Cuba, stopped by shots dropped over her stern

[40] Fillmore to Webster, Washington, September 2, 1851. Webster Papers.

[41] Eames to Marcy, Washington, September 14, 1851. Marcy Papers.

and bow, and searched. The Spanish commander said he acted
under orders. In answer to the protest of the American Consul, the Captain-General expressed regret and gave assurance
that it would not happen again.[42] Calderón, on the other hand,
justified the Spanish action with a quotation from Vattel that
assumed belligerent rights for Spain.[43] This extraordinary assumption was passed over without objection by the United
States government. And in spite of the Captain-General's assurance, the schooner *Heroine* was stopped, searched, towed
to Havana and detained. The Captain-General blandly asserted
that, lacking a wind, she had been in distress and the Spanish
warship merely gave her aid.[44] The new American Consul,
Allen E. Owen, reported the incident to Washington, where
it was ignored. He evidently ceased to concern himself with
the troubles of Americans in Cuba. Captain Larabee of the
brig *Franklin* was seized on shore on suspicion that he was
involved in the filibuster expedition, dragged by the legs and
tied up in prison until he contracted gangrene. After being
transferred to the hospital of an American doctor in Havana,
he died there. Owen had been notified of the Captain's arrival
in the hospital and he promised to call but, according to the
Doctor's report to Webster, he took no further notice of the
case.[45] No reproof appears to have been given to the Consul
by his superiors for this neglect of duty.

But public clamor made the President anxious to secure
from Owen evidence that something had been done by him in
favor of Colonel Crittenden, the 50 who were executed with
him and the 156 prisoners who survived the filibusters' battles.

42 Owen to Webster, Havana, August 17, 1851. Department of State,
Consular Despatches: Havana, XXIV.

43 Calderón to Derrick, New York, September 29, 1851. Department of
State, *Notes from Legations: Spain*, XIII.

44 Owen to Webster, Havana, August 29, 1851; Owen to Concha, Havana,
August 26, 1851; Concha to Owen, Havana, August 26, 1851. Department of
State, *Consular Despatches: Havana*, XXIV.

45 Wilson to Webster, Havana, October 27, 1851. *Ibid.*

The sympathy of the government and the country were aroused, Acting Secretary Derrick wrote, and the President was embarrassed for lack of information.[46] In regard to Crittenden and his band, Owen admitted that he had made no attempt to interfere or even to see the doomed men, because the Captain-General had given him prior warning that the filibusters would be treated as pirates and citizens of no country and would allow no consul in official or personal capacity to intervene. Besides, Owen wrote, he had had little time and none of the condemned men asked to see him.[47] The Consul showed little more interest in the prisoners. J. M. Rodney, United States Consul at Matanzas, and Consul McLain of Trinidad gave Owen support in an interview with the Captain-General, but the captives had already been sentenced and shipped to prison in Spain. They were treated, however, not as pirates but as prisoners of war.[48] A month later, Owen was removed. The administration had found his efforts to avoid the mistakes of General Campbell all too successful. William L. Sharkey was appointed Consul in Havana.

The question of the prisoners was extremely difficult for the administration. Derrick in a note to Calderón claimed no right of the United States government officially to intervene. But he wrote that the excitement of the public and the danger that harsh treatment of the prisoners would exasperate it constrained him to ask as the " private wishes " of the government that Spain appease American opinion.[49] Calderón made no response to this advance but wrote numerous notes complaining of the injuries suffered by Spain. He worked to create a back-fire of pro-Spanish propaganda in the American press,

[46] Derrick to Owen, Washington, September 1, 29, 1851. Department of State, *Instructions to Consuls*, XIV.

[47] Owen to Webster, Havana, September 17, 18, 1851. Department of State, *Consular Despatches: Havana*, XXIV.

[48] J. M. Rodney to Webster, Havana, October 7, 1851. *Ibid.*

[49] Derrick to Calderón, Washington, September 5, 1851. Department of State, *Notes to Legations: Spain*, VI.

but, aside from the bought pages of *La Cronica,* succeeded only in enlisting the pen of Orestes A. Brownson, the famous Catholic convert and ex-reformer who, according to his biographer, felt a subtle commitment to Cuba because its rulers were Catholic.[50] Calderón helped the American write bitterly denunciatory articles on the filibusters which were published in *Brownson's Quarterly Review.* His letters to Brownson show that he wanted the United States government to pay damages to Spain for the injuries done by the invaders of Cuba. However, he despaired of doing anything with " the demigod," Daniel Webster.[51]

Calderón's superiors were less ambitious. In October he received instructions from his government and demanded satisfaction and indemnities only for the mob violence in the Gulf ports. The demand was coupled with threats that the American Consul and all Americans from the southern states would be expelled from Cuba and of other " fatal complications," and also with a hint that if the United States completely satisfied Castilian honor, the Queen might show clemency towards the prisoners.[52]

At this serious stage, Webster returned to Washington and took charge. In the meantime, Attorney General Crittenden had for some weeks assumed responsibility for the State Department. Personally mourning an expeditionary, he wrote touching pleas in favor of the survivors as youths beguiled by false lures and misguided enthusiasm for liberty. He asked

50 Arthur M. Schlesinger, Jr., *Orestes A. Brownson* (Boston, 1939), 207.

51 Calderón to Brownson, New York, September 4, 1851, Washington, September 19 and November 10, 1851. Henry F. Brownson, *Orestes A. Brownson's Middle Life: from 1845 to 1855* (Detroit, 1899), 299-309.

52 Calderón to Derrick, New York, September 10, 1851; Calderón to Derrick, Washington, September 13, 1851; Calderón to Acting Secretary of State, Washington, September 15, 1851; Calderón to J. J. Crittenden, Washington, October 5, 8, 14, 1851; Calderón to Webster, Washington, October 31, 1851. Department of State, *Notes from Legations: Spain,* XIII.

Calderón for a pardon for all the prisoners.[53] Owen was told to aid families who wished to remove bodies of executed men to the United States. The Acting Secretary expected that Spain would not object: " Their mouldering bones have long since ceased to be fit objects of resentment." [54] Numerous petitions for pardons signed by eminent and obscure citizens were transmitted to Minister Barringer in Madrid. Crittenden wrote that he would not give him official instructions on the " delicate and painful " subject of the prisoners, but requested him " as an American to procure the pardon and release " of his " unfortunate countrymen." The whole American people were interested in their fate and a pardon would have " most salutary consequences " in the United States.[55]

Sentiment appears to have played at least a minor part in the Queen's final decision, but not before Barringer and Miraflores had played out an ill-tempered little comedy. The news of the Bahia Honda Expedition arrived in Madrid at a moment particularly inauspicious for the United States. Late in July opponents in the Cortes attacked the government for not taking stronger measures to protect Cuba from the United States. Statesmen in that country, Deputy Badia said, were ruled by the people, who abandoned legality and invaded the world of Columbus as if it were their exclusive property. The infant giant was felt in all directions and might compromise the peace of the world. Cuba would be the " expiatory victim " of the infamous American slavery system. The Deputy found consolation, however, in his opinion that annexation would precipitate dissolution of the Union. Miraflores shut off debate with statements that he felt the Fillmore administration was more friendly to Spain and that England and France had given

53 Crittenden to Calderón, Washington, September 29, 1851. Department of State, *Notes to Legations: Spain*, VI.

54 Crittenden to Owen, Washington, September 29, 1851. Department of State, *Instructions to Consuls*, XIV.

55 Crittenden to Barringer, Washington, October 6, 1851. Department of State, *Diplomatic Instructions: Spain*, XIV.

orders to their naval forces to oppose invasions of Cuba by
filibusters. Attacks on the government caused it to prorogue
the Cortes *sine die* early in August.[56] Newspapers took up the
campaign when word arrived of Lopez's descent on the island
and they demanded war on the United States. Barringer wrote
to Webster that the war fever was particularly high in coastal
regions of Spain where privateering against American shipping was eagerly planned. The Minister confirmed that English and French naval forces had " stringent " orders to act
against the filibusters.[57]

Excitement in Spain subsided after the news of López's
defeat and execution and Barringer believed that the mother
country felt new security in her dominion because of the victory
over the invaders and demonstration of the Cubans' loyalty.
Nevertheless, the government again addressed a circular to
European governments asking support and proposed to Britain
and France that they guarantee Spanish possession of Cuba.[58]
The results were the same as in 1850: the European governments were uninterested and the project of a guaranty collapsed
on Palmerston's demands for reform in the administration of
Cuba and statement that " it will be impossible for Great Britain
to support Spain in a quarrel thus unnecessarily brought on by
Spain herself." [59] Barringer had information that Britain and
France demanded abolition of slavery, political reforms and
commercial treaties as conditions of a guaranty of the island to
Spain.[60] The British Foreign Minister became interested in a

56 Barringer to Webster, Madrid, August 4, 12, 1851. Department of State,
Diplomatic Despatches: Spain, XXXVI.

57 Barringer to Webster, Madrid, September 18, 22, 25, 1851. *Ibid.*,
XXXVII.

58 Barringer to Webster, Madrid, October 14, 1851. *Ibid.*

59 Palmerston to Howden, London, November 21, 1851. Quoted in Amos
A. Ettinger, *The Mission to Spain of Pierre Soulé: 1853-1855* (New Haven,
1937), 56.

60 Barringer to William C. Rives, Madrid, October 16, 1851. Rives Papers.

different project, a treaty of renunciation in which Britain, France and the United States should declare that none of them would seek to obtain possession of Cuba.[61]

This project developed slowly behind the scenes while Barringer attempted to obtain the release of the condemned filibusters. They arrived in Spain early in October. The American was little conciliatory or appreciative of Spanish feeling that the gravest injuries had been those done to Spanish honor by rioters in the American South. His first request was that American Consuls be allowed to see the prisoners. Miraflores took it for granted that Barringer wanted them pardoned and answered that the United States must first yield satisfaction and indemnities for injuries done by the rioters: let the United States show Spain justice and she would show the United States clemency.[62] Barringer expressed " surprise and regret " to the Spanish Minister that he had not consented to the request but instead took up other questions. Barringer wrote that the " tone and unusual character " of some of Miraflores' observations were objectionable. He had not asked the Spanish Minister to forget the injuries committed by the rioters. The United States had given Spain ample proof of its determination to do its whole duty and left no doubt of its friendship— " a friendship allow me to say certainly as important to Spain and to the peace and integrity of Spanish territory as it is to the welfare of the United States." Miraflores could be assured that the United States would act on a sense of intrinsic justice regarding the riots and independently of what Spain might do in a different matter. He said he could not forbear to remark that " the excellence of the sovereign, sublime & holy

61 Amos A. Ettinger, " The Proposed Anglo-Franco-American Treaty of 1852 to Guarantee Cuba to Spain," *Transactions of the Royal Historical Society* (London, 1930), Fourth Series, XIII, 152-163.

62 Miraflores to Barringer, Madrid, November 1, 1851. Department of State, *Diplomatic Despatches: Spain*, XXXVII.

63 Barringer to Miraflores, Madrid, November 4, 1851. *Ibid.*

attribute of mercy consists in its being entirely free & gracious." [63]

The Spanish Minister answered that he was equally surprised by Barringer's letter and he would therefore refrain from discussing it. At the same time he announced that the Queen, who was about to become a mother herself, had been so moved by a letter from the mother of one of the American prisoners that, without other solicitation, she had pardoned him.[64] Barringer now received Crittenden's request that he work unofficially to secure pardons for all the prisoners. Ill-temper gave way to sentimentality. He wrote an emotional plea in the key of Miraflores' announcement:

> By the grace of a kind Providence H. Majesty is soon to add to Her Royal title of *Queen* that of *Mother* and bring happiness to a great nation. The sincere and ardent prayer of these unhappy prisoners and their distressed kindred is, not only that this propitious event may happily take place . . . but that it may also be signalized by an act of Royal clemency to themselves which will fix an enduring memorial. . . . [65]

The Queen, Miraflores answered, was indeed responsive to such an appeal, but public opinion would not permit a pardon until it was preceded by " an example of friendship and of justice " to Spain by the United States, which the American Minister should use his influence to secure.[66] Barringer gave up. He wrote Miraflores that he would explain the views of the Spanish government to the Secretary of State and that he had no more to say on the subject.[67] On the same day, the Madrid correspondent of the *National Intelligencer* wrote that

64 Miraflores to Barringer, Madrid, November 13, 1851. *Ibid.*

65 Barringer to Miraflores, Madrid, November 28, 1851. *Ibid.*

66 Miraflores to Barringer, Madrid, December 3, 1851. *Ibid.*

67 Barringer to Miraflores, Madrid, December 5, 1851. *Ibid.*

war-risk insurance premiums were demanded for American vessels in Spanish ports.[68]

Before matters had reached this point in Madrid, Webster had returned to his post in Washington. Three days after Calderón wrote to Brownson that he could do nothing with "the demigod," Webster decided to brave the wrath of anti-Spanish Americans by conceding Miraflores' demands. He wrote a masterly letter to Calderón on November 13 that made no mention of the prisoners held by Spain. The actions of the mobs were described carefully to show that no federal or local official could be held responsible. Nevertheless, the President desired the Spanish Minister to tell his government that those events caused him " great pain; & that he thinks a proper acknowledgement is due to Her Catholic Majesty and Government." Calderón thought the enormity of the offense was heightened by insult to the flag of Spain. Webster wrote that he found no wonder that Mr. Calderón was so proud of that flag, which had waved so high and often over fields of valor and floated without stain all over the seas,—and so forth in a practiced apostrophe. The President would recommend to Congress a just indemnity for the Spanish Consul Laborde. And if he or any consul would return to New Orleans, instructions would be given to render a national salute to the flag of his ship, if it was Spanish, to signify the United States government's sense of the " gross injustice " done his predecessor by a lawless mob as well as the indignity and insult offered a foreign state with which the United States wished ever to remain on terms of the most respectful and pacific intercourse. As for other Spaniards whose property had been injured by mobs, they were entitled the same protection as American citizens and they might prosecute for redress in American courts.[69]

68 *National Intelligencer*, January 6, 1852.

69 Webster to Calderón, Washington, November 13, 1851. Department of State, *Notes to Legations: Spain*, VI.

Before Barringer received Webster's instructions to ask again for release of the prisoners, Miraflores told the American Minister that Webster's letter of November 13 to Calderón, with its excellent effect when published in Spain, had induced the Queen to grant a general pardon to the filibusters and a decoration to Calderón for his zeal.[70] After this, all loose ends were cleared up handsomely by both governments. Spain pardoned foreigners among the filibusters as well as American citizens, and even included John S. Thrasher, who had been sentenced to Ceuta for his notorious aid to the filibusters and, as a "domiciled" resident of Cuba, had only doubtful claims to protection as an American citizen.[71] Thrasher's release was grateful to the administration because his many friends among leading Cuban annexationists in the United States had raised a loud clamor that he was innocent and entitled to the full protection of the United States government. Webster had tried to establish that Thrasher had volunarily abandoned his right to American protection,[72] but, as he confessed to Fillmore, the campaign in Congress and "out of doors" to make political capital of the administration's neglect of Thrasher forced him to defend the "domiciled Cuban" as an American citizen. On the letter describing this appeasement, Fillmore wrote: "I concur MF".[73]

After Spain had pardoned Thrasher and all the filibusters, the United States government did more than Webster had promised. In April, 1852, Calderón complained that Spaniards could obtain no redress for injuries by the mobs because juries disagreed in New Orleans and it was impossible to prove who were the instigators of the riots. He was of opinion that lead-

70 Barringer to Webster, Madrid, December 12, 1851. Department of State, *Diplomatic Despatches: Spain*, XXXVII.

71 Barringer to Webster, Madrid, January 14, 1852. *Ibid.*

72 Senate Executive Documents (32:1), 5. *House Executive Documents* (32:1), 10 and 14.

73 Webster to Fillmore, Washington, December 13, 1851. Webster Papers.

ers of the filibuster expedition were the instigators, but juries in New York had equally disagreed in trials of O'Sullivan and others. Therefore he requested that the Federal government indemnify the Spaniards.[74] President Fillmore recommended to Congress that it appropriate money for the purpose as a return courtesy for Spain's magnanimity in pardoning the prisoners.[75] Congress complied, although the amount of $25,-000 which it provided to indemnify Consul Laborde as well as the other Spaniards did not satisfy Calderón.[76]

These conciliatory measures, which Webster initiated with statesmanship that has been contrasted with his Hülsemann Letter, and Spain reciprocated, could be carried no farther. The jury in New York could not agree on a verdict against O'Sullivan and Schlesinger and in New Orleans another batch of filibusters was acquitted.[77] The desire of Americans for Cuba was increasing while the popularity and strength of the administration and the Whig Party waned. Plans for new filibuster expeditions became secondary only to the "Young American" fever to secure in the 1852 elections a new administration that would annex Cuba. Spain anxiously sought aid in preserving her island against the expansionist opponents of the Fillmore administration. Rebuffed in her latest attempts to ally France and Britain to her Cuban interest, she could only await the outcome of British and French efforts to commit the United States, through the anti-expansionist Fillmore administration, to a renunciation of future possession of the island.

This was the last Cuban question faced by that administration and, since it grew out of the events of 1851, it will be

74 Calderón to Webster, Washington, April 22, 1852. *House Executive Documents* (32:1), no. 113, pp. 2-4.

75 *Ibid.*, pp. 1-2.

76 Calderón to Conrad, Washington, October 9, 1852. Department of State, *Notes from Legations: Spain*, XIV.

77 *National Intelligencer*, March 30, April 6, 7, 1852.

treated in this chapter. A hint of the answer to the question was in the President's Message to Congress of December 2, 1851, the first quarter of which was devoted to Cuban affairs. He roundly castigated the filibuster expedition and attributed it to the cupidity of Cuban bond-holders who expected to be paid out of the resources of the island. Nor did anyone have the right to hazard the peace of the country or to violate its laws with vague notions of reforming other governments. But, the Message continued:

> while such are the sentiments of this Government, it may be added that every independent nation must be presumed to be able to defend its possessions against unauthorized individuals banded together to attack them.

The President maintained that the United States had not only enforced the Neutrality Act to the full extent of the power of the government, but had actually led other nations in the policy of neutrality and non-intervention. A standard criticism of Manifest Destiny doctrine followed:

> Our true mission is not to propagate our opinions or impose upon other countries our form of government by artifice or force, but to teach by example and show by our success, moderation, and justice the blessings of self-government and the advantages of free institutions.

Still the United States could not be indifferent to forceful repression by a foreign government of the spirit of freedom in any country. Furthermore, it deplored the French and British naval orders to prevent the landing of hostile adventurers in Cuba, particularly as such orders by the two leading commercial powers might lead to abuses in derogation of the maritime rights of the United States.[78]

This Message gave no ground for hope that the United States might abandon its traditional policies towards Cuba or

78 *Messages and Papers of the Presidents*, comp. Richardson, VI, 2649-53.

Europe. And, in fact, Spain, Britain, and France had little hope of success when the Ministers to the United States of the latter two countries on April 23, 1852, handed to Secretary Webster identical notes containing the text of the proposed tripartite renunciatory agreement. Its essential parts read as follows:

> The High Contracting Parties hereby severally and collectively disclaim, both for now and hereafter, all intention to obtain possession of the Island of Cuba; and they respectively bind themselves to discountenance all attempts to that effect on the part of any powers or individuals whatsoever.
>
> The High Contracting Parties declare, severally and collectively, that they will not obtain or maintain for themselves, any exclusive control over the said island, nor assume nor exercise any dominion over the same.[79]

Webster said that he would send the two Ministers the administration's decision in writing. Meanwhile, they could not state to their governments too strongly " his own entire concurrence in their views with regard to Cuba." [80] The French Minister Sartiges reported to his government that Webster added comments on the difficulties of raising the question in a presidential year while the people of the South demanded that Cuba be annexed. Buchanan's candidacy for the Democratic Presidential nomination was likely to be strengthened by publication at Congress' request of the documents relative to his effort to purchase Cuba in 1848. The American people, furthermore, had " a sort of vulgar reluctance " to make agreements with European monarchs. Sartiges and Crampton, the British Minister, pointed out the purely negative side of the proposed agreement, but Webster only repeated his views, and added

79 Crampton to Webster, Washington, April 23, 1852. Department of State, *Notes from Legations: Great Britain*, XXIX. Sartiges to Webster, Washington, April 23, 1852. *Ibid., France*, XV.

80 Crampton to Malmesbury, Washington, April 25, 1852. Quoted in Ettinger, *Mission to Spain of Pierre Soulé*, 71.

that if the United States rejected the proposal, nothing prevented Britain and France from making a dual agreement. Sartiges, at least, became highly aware of the delicate internal political situation into which the proposal had been dropped.[81]

President Fillmore made this most clear when, Webster being absent, the President told the two Ministers that while the administration was perfectly in accord with their views on Cuba, they must know:

> the moment to negotiate such a convention, which must be forcibly carried before Congress, was inopportune; that this question would fall like a bomb in the midst of the electoral agitation for the presidency and that the passion which the different parties showed in discussing and dissecting it, made its consideration impossible, as it would become a cause of division between the North and the South, and would revive all those dangerous discussions, which had menaced the existence of the Union, concerning Texas, California, and the other territories acquired or annexed.[82]

Later the President specifically explained that the negotiation must be postponed until after the November elections to prevent the use of the Cuban question at the polls. If the convention was negotiated now, he wrote:

> it would enroll half the Country against it, by bringing together the South, who are in favour of the annexation of Cuba, and the party called "Young Americans," who are in favour of all annexations, and thus cause so many Political Men to commit themselves in the matter as to render the ultimate Passage, of the Convention proposed, by the Senate impossible.[83]

It is likely that in encouraging Britain and France to hope that the agreement might be accepted by the United States after

81 Sartiges to Turgot, Washington, April 25, 1852. Quoted, *ibid.*, 72-3.

82 Sartiges to Turgot, Washington, May 7, 1852. Quoted, *ibid.*, 75.

83 Crampton to Malmesbury, Washington, July 12, 1852. Quoted, *ibid.*. 77.

the elections, Fillmore and Webster intended them to understand that they personally favored an agreement against Spanish cession of Cuba to any other *European* nation. This decisive alteration was specified in Webster's written answer in April acknowledging receipt of the proposal,[84] and it lent an air of unreality to the discussions that followed.

Whatever the original intentions of Fillmore and Webster, the latter died in October and the election in November of Franklin Pierce, who was understood to plan the purchase of the island, made the President and his Cabinet agree that the new Secretary of State, Edward Everett, should write a definitive rejection of the Anglo-French proposal. The heart of the celebrated document that Everett prepared was the statement: " The President does not covet the acquisition of Cuba for the United States; at the same time, he considers the condition of Cuba as mainly an American question." The chief objection to American participation in the proposed convention naturally followed, because such an agreement was based on the assumption that the United States had no different or greater interest in Cuba than France or England. The geographic position of the island sufficiently refuted such an assumption, Everett wrote. The island's strategic significance he expounded as follows:

> The island of Cuba lies at our doors. It commands the approach to the Gulf of Mexico, which washes the shores of five of our States. It bars the entrance of that great river which drains half the North American continent, and with its tributaries forms the largest system of international water-communication in the world. It keeps watch at the doorway of our intercourse with California by the Isthmus route. If an island like Cuba, belonging to the Spanish crown, guarded the entrance of the Thames and the Seine, and the United States should propose a convention like this to France and England, those powers would assuredly feel that

84 Webster to Crampton, Washington, April 29, 1852. Department of State, *Notes to Legations: Great Britain*, VII.

the disability assumed by ourselves was far less serious than
that which we asked them to assume.

The Secretary of State described the commercial interest of
the United States in Cuba as being subject to capricious restrictions by the Captain-General with no recourse short of
war available to the United States except through long negotiations at Madrid. The Cuban slave trade he called " an evil
of the first magnitude," and declared that American ownership would be preferable to a Negro republic in the island.

These references to commercial and slavery interests were
of minor importance in Everett's text. He placed main emphasis on generalized national interests and thus affirmed the
political philosophy of the administration and the Whig Party.
Those interests were expressed in terms that coincided with
the more vague rhetoric of expansionists and made the note
attractive to enthusiasts of Manifest Destiny and Young America. In that way Everett treated, besides the geographic question, the history of American expansion and the traditional
opposition of the United States to political alliances with European powers and showed that the proposed agreement ran
counter to deep currents of national policy and feeling. Immediate considerations were that the Senate would reject the
proposed convention and leave the question in a more unsettled
state; it might well be doubted that the Constitution granted
the power to impose a permanent disability on the American
government to do what it had so often done in the past; and
acceptance of the proposal, instead of putting a stop to filibusters, would give a new and powerful impulse to them.

In his conclusion, Everett wrote that the President was per-
suaded Britain and France would not attribute refusal to a
disinterest in harmony among the great maritime states on a
subject of such importance as Cuba, and that Spain would not
draw any unfavorable inference, because the United States concurred with Britain and France in the wish not to disturb
Spanish possession of the island. Everett nevertheless did not

hesitate to write what amounted to the peroration of his eloquent composition in terms which, with the Pierce administration in the offing, must have filled officials of the three European powers with doubt:

> No administration of this Government, however strong in the public confidence in other respects, could stand a day under the odium of having stipulated with the great powers of Europe, that in no future time, under no change of circumstances, by no amicable arrangement with Spain, by no act of lawful war (should that calamity unfortunately occur), by no consent of the inhabitants of the island, should they, like the possessions of Spain on the American continent, succeed in rendering themselves independent; in fine, by no overruling necessity of self-preservation should the United States ever make the acquisition of Cuba.[85]

This note represented the farthest length to which Whigs of the Webster and Clay school could go in appeasing southern expansionists. It was a monument at the end of the Whig Party's history to the failure of its most conciliatory leaders to hold southern support on the program of sectional peace through compromise. The campaign of 1852 had already shown that the South and many of its Democratic friends in the North were determined to bring one or more Cuban slave states into the Union without regard for the spirit of Clay's Compromise, which was to make an end of slavery as a national issue. Seward had been defeated by Clay and Webster first on the Compromise itself, and then by Webster's and Everett's appeasement of southern desires for Cuba. But southerners were not satisfied with appeasement whose fruits were hardly material, and when this was proved by the Pierce administration, northern Whigs finally turned to Seward.

In the meantime, Everett's note effectively closed the Cuban question for the Fillmore administration. Annexationists had

---

[85] Everett to Crampton, Washington, December 1, 1852, *ibid.* Everett to Sartiges, Washington, December 1, 1852. *Ibid., France*, VI.

created a series of difficult situations which constituted the most serious challenge to the administration's domestic policy of sectional compromise and foreign policy of conservative nationalism. If they were dissatisfied by the administration's conception of sectional and national rights and duties, and helped to turn a majority of the electorate against the Whig Party, the political wisdom or cunning of the Fillmore administration may be called in doubt, but not its honorable desire to sustain a just position for the United States in relation to its troublesome island neighbor.

CHAPTER VII
ECONOMIC CONSIDERATIONS

THE climax of American interest in Cuba before the Civil War came in the first two years of the Pierce administration. Economic considerations deepened the current of that interest, and help to explain why the victorious Democrats, despite the glaring failures of Polk and López, renewed the former's attempt to purchase the island and even encouraged the use of force.

At the end of the Mexican War, the United States entered a period of great prosperity. The liquidation of wild-cat banks and the influx of new gold from California created strong foundations for the expansion of agriculture, commerce, transportation and manufactures. In 1850, according to the *Preliminary Report on the Eighth Census*:

> The spirit of enterprise abroad was very strong, and the impression that prices were to rise by reason of the depreciation of gold was prevalent; hence the general desire to operate, in order to avail of the anticipated profits. Industry of all description was very active and productive, and there never was a period when national capital accumulated so fast . . . .[1]

Increased investments and rising commodity prices stimulated production and enlarged purchasing power. A boom in American foreign trade resulted. The value of combined imports and exports more than doubled between 1846 and 1855 when it rose from 235 to 536 millions of dollars. Domestic exports increased from less than 133 millions of dollars in 1849 to more than 253 millions in 1854.[2] Capital poured into the ship-

[1] *Preliminary Report on the Eighth Census, 1860* (Washington, 1862), 76-7.

[2] G. G. Huebner, "The Foreign Trade of the United States since 1789," E. R. Johnson, T. W. Van Metre, G. G. Huebner and D. S. Hanchett, *History of Foreign and Domestic Commerce of the United States* (Washington, 1915) II, 48-50. *Statistical Abstract of the United States: 1878* (Washington, 1879), 27.

building industry. The annual average tonnage built during the ten years before 1852 was 199,000 and it rose to 358,000 during the succeeding decade. The greatest part of the advance occurred between 1851, when 351,000 tons were built, and 1854, when the figure reached 583,000 tons.[3]

The search for new markets and profitable employment of shipping met with considerable success as Great Britain led the way to free trade. Cuba became the most important American market where restrictions still hampered merchants and shippers. In November, 1850, in retaliation against the Cardenas Expedition, Spain raised still higher the Cuban tariffs on products imported chiefly from the United States and imposed onerous new rules on American shippers.[4] Cuba continued third after Britain and France in the value of its combined American imports and exports, but the United States could not overcome its unfavorable balance of trade with Spain and her dependencies, which actually increased from 5 million dollars out of combined imports and exports of 25 million dollars in 1850 to 14 out of 37 millions in 1853.[5] Cuban duties on American corn, ship bread, pork products, dried fish and similar items ranged from 50 to 175 percent. Most burdensome of all was the duty on American flour of $8.50 per barrel when imported in Spanish ships and $9.50 in American ships. In 1852, total duties of $73,000 were paid on $91,000 worth of American flour. This inhibited the sale in Cuba of its most "natural" import from the United States while the latter country lowered its duty on sugar in 1846 and bought the majority of the Cuban sugar crop, amounting to 77 percent

3 *Preliminary Report on the Eighth Census, 1860*, 106-8.

4 *Hunt's Merchants' Magazine*, XXIV (February, 1851), 230-1.

5 James D. B. DeBow, Superintendent of the Census, *Statistical View of the United States* (Washington, 1854), 188. Figures are for trade with Spain and her dependencies, of which Cuba provided by far the largest amount, and Puerto Rico, where the same discriminations against American trade and shipping were enforced, the largest share of the remainder.

of it in 1853.[6] On the other hand, Cuban rates were favorable for the importation of American machinery. Richard H. Dana found that the railroad equipment in the island had been manufactured in Cambridgeport and Troy.[7] Philadelphia, Boston and New York developed a thriving market in Cuba for steam engines to be used in the sugar mills.[8]

The United States in 1848 made a gesture towards ending the tariff war with Spain by suspending all laws that exacted higher duties on Spanish steamships arriving in the United States than were imposed on American steamships arriving in Cuba.[9] A month before he left office, Secretary of State Everett proposed to Spain that a commercial treaty be negotiated to put an end to the tariff war and other vexations that troubled American relations with Cuba.[10] The proposal was renewed by Minister Pierre Soulé in 1854, but nothing came of these efforts because Spain was not interested.[11] Nor would Congress act on the suggestion of Secretary of the Treasury Corwin in 1852 that American retaliations against Spain should all be repealed because they had injured American shipping and reduced exports to Cuba.[12]

Commercial interest had been urged as a leading motive for Cuban annexation by the New York *Sun* when it initiated its campaign in 1847. *La Verdad* took up the argument, declaring as the Gold Rush began that industrial and mercantile

6 *Senate Executive Documents* (34:1), no. 107, pt. 2, pp. 185, 208-9; pt. 3, pp. 122-51; *DeBow's Review*, XVIII (May, 1855), 641-2.

7 R. H. Dana, *To Cuba and Back* (Boston, 1870), 102. Dana's visit to the island was made in 1859.

8 Maturin M. Ballou, *History of Cuba* (Boston, 1854), 145-6.

9 L. W. Maxwell, *Discriminating Duties and the American Merchant Marine* (New York, 1926), 50.

10 Everett to Calderón, Washington, February 5, 1853. Department of State, *Notes to Legations: Spain*, VI.

11 Soulé to Marcy, Madrid, April 7, 1854. Department of State, *Diplomatic Despatches: Spain*, XXXIX.

12 *Senate Executive Documents* (32:1), no. 53, pp. 1-13.

speculations of Americans might better be directed to Cuba than to California's " remote and desert shores." [13] The *Democratic Review* described the great commercial advantages from annexation of Cuba that would follow in the train of Manifest Destiny.[14] Alexander Jones in his book, *Cuba in 1851,* published in New York, eloquently defended the filibusters and offered trade advantages as the chief reason why Americans should support annexation.[15]

The North was less excited by such prospects than the South. *Hunt's Merchants' Magazine* of New York did not advocate annexation and only published objective news of Cuban trade developments.[16] *Niles' National Register,* a Whig publication of Baltimore and Philadelphia, was more interested in annexation as a means of opening up an immense market for American wheat and flour.[17] John S. Thrasher, former editor of *El Faro Industrial* in Havana, member of the Havana Club, and inmate of Spanish prisons, wrote a striking appeal to Americans to support annexation because they would find greatly increased markets in the island for products of every section of the Union. His attempt to stir up national interest in the commercial motive for annexation was made in 1856, after he had thoroughly identified himself with the South as an employee of the New Orleans *Picayune,* a propagandist of southern motives for annexation, and an associate of Quitman in filibuster enterprises. Nevertheless, his essay of 1856 was the best analysis written during the period of national motives, commercial and strategic, for Cuban annexation.[18]

13 *La Verdad*, December 15, 1848.

14 *Democratic Review*, XXV (September, 1849), 193-204.

15 Alexander Jones, *Cuba in 1851* (New York, 1851), 11-6.

16 *Hunt's Merchants' Magazine*, XXI (July, 1849), 36; XXIV (February, 1851), 230-1; XXV (August, 1851), 211.

17 *Niles' National Register*, LXXV (February 28, 1849), 140-1.

18 John S. Thrasher, " Preliminary Essay," in Alexander von Humboldt, *The Island of Cuba* (New York, 1856), 14-49.

The strength of the commercial motive for interest in Cuba is strikingly illustrated by the abolitionist *National Era* of Washington, whose editor wrote longingly of the increased markets for New England manufacturers and western wheat and provisions that would follow annexation. Coffee and sugar prices in the United States would decline, he wrote, American commerce in the Gulf would be safe forever, and American influence would dominate the isthmus of Central America. He admitted that annexation would abolish the slave trade. If only the accession of power by the American slavery system could somehow be eliminated from the measure, the abolitionist editor would find much cause to rejoice in Cuban annexation.[19]

Southern commercial interest in Cuba centered in New Orleans. That city's foreign trade advanced with astonishing rapidity as the cotton, grain and cattle of the Mississippi valley were sent to her wharves for export. The value of receipts of produce increased from 45 million dollars in 1842 to 134 million in 1853.[20] The Crescent City ranked fourth in the Union in value of imports, but in exports it reached first place when they increased from 31 million dollars in 1846 to 67 million in 1853 and surpassed those of New York.[21] James Dunwoody B. DeBow was the leading propagandist of the South's commercial interest in Cuban annexation. He was a native of Charleston, South Carolina, who migrated to New Orleans and there on the advice of Calhoun founded in 1846 *DeBow's Review*. After a severe struggle, his message of economic nationalism as a program for the South awakened interest and was itself stimulated by southern speculation on secession and separate nationality. The pages of the magazine presented a blueprint of economic policy for the South to strengthen it against the North. *DeBow's Review* during the fifties was not only the first successful southern magazine of

19 *National Era*, August 28, 1851. *Cf. ibid.*, July 10, 1851.

20 *DeBow's Review*, XVII (November, 1854), 531.

21 DeBow, *Statistical View*, 186-7.

business and commerce, but acquired the largest circulation of any magazine published in the South.[22]

DeBow began his enterprise with a resolution not to debate the issues which divided the North and South. He abandoned neutrality and advocated secession when sectional lines became more distinct. His contribution to the separatist movement was the conviction, founded on apparently sound reasoning, that the South's economic power could make it a successful nation. He urged that it must develop its commercial, transportation and industrial capacities to balance its agricultural strength. The Southern Commercial Conventions, a southern railroad to the Pacific, and direct trade between the South and Europe and through an isthmian canal to the Orient were promoted in his magazine with the fervor of budding nationalism. The evolution of DeBow's attitude towards Cuba paralleled his evolution from neutrality to partisanship in the sectional dispute as a whole and, since he reflected southern opinion as much as he inspired it, repays study because it clearly illustrates the development and significance of southern interest in the island. In May, 1848, when Polk adopted O'Sullivan's plan to purchase Cuba and the first debate on annexation occurred in Congress, DeBow published a summary of economic and other information on the island. He concluded that Cuba appeared to be " but a part of our own South, unnaturally and arbitrarily separated. In the progress and prospects of Cuba, it is but natural we cherish a deep interest. Alas! the time has not yet come for her regeneration!" [23]

The Cardenas Expedition impressed the editor with the inevitability of American imperialism. Give man power to oppress and he will assuredly do it, DeBow wrote, and he seemed to take satisfaction in the conviction that a government

22 Broadus Mitchell, " James Dunwoody Brownson DeBow," *Dictionary of American Biography*, ed. Allen Johnson and Dumas Malone (New York, 1930), V, 180-2.

23 *DeBow's Review*, V (May and June, 1848), 470.

like that of the United States could conceal but not destroy that propensity. Indeed he rejoiced at signs of the growth of the military spirit: miniature West Points on every hilltop, soldiers in high office, martial games and festivals, and the special favor ladies showed to warriors. Woe to anyone who tried to stay the cry of war! because:

> *We have a destiny to perform,* "a manifest destiny" over all Mexico, over South America, over the West Indies and Canada. The Sandwich Islands are as necessary to our eastern, as the isles of the gulf to our western commerce. The gates of the Chinese empire must be thrown down by the men from the Sacramento and the Oregon, and the haughty Japanese tramplers upon the cross be enlightened in the doctrines of republicanism and the ballot box. The eagle of the republic shall poise itself over the field of Waterloo, after tracing its flight among the gorges of the Himalaya or the Ural mountains, and a successor of Washington ascend the chair of universal empire! . . . The people stand ready to hail tomorrow . . . a collision with the proudest and the mightiest empire upon earth.

However, moderation should be observed in the case of Cuba, and its purchase peacefully negotiated.[24] Such a descent after such a flight was probably inspired by doubts as to the effects of Cuban annexation on the sugar industry of Louisiana. But by 1854, as will appear, those doubts had been resolved and appeals to Manifest Destiny, with their "idealism" and sops to all sections, gave way to a practical program to annex Cuba in order to realize southern economic aims. In the meantime, DeBow decided that the sale of cotton clothing to backward peoples was the second instrument for a civilizing mission whose first was the sword:

> It is by war you conquer an ignorant and barbarian people, and then by commerce and trade with them you introduce the comforts and arts of civilization.

24 *Ibid.,* IX (August, 1850), 167-8.

> In this point of view, the culture of cotton becomes deeply interesting to the statesman and philanthropist. . . . [25]

The commercial aspect of southern interest in Cuba was linked with a program to unite the South and the Amazon River valley as the two poles of an empire of trade and navigation. Lieutenant Matthew Fontaine Maury, the eminent oceanographer and Superintendent of the Naval Observatory, publicized to Congress, the Southern Commercial Conventions, and in the pages of *DeBow's Review* the advantages to the South of free navigation of the Amazon River and a line of mail steamers between New Orleans and Pará. Secretary of State Webster refused to support the project and this perhaps led Maury, himself a southerner, to turn to the South for aid. There the project was taken up with great enthusiasm in the expectation that it would work the " commercial regeneration " of the section.[26] In September, 1854, *DeBow's Review* published two articles on Cuba in which commerce was the dominant theme in a vision of southern empire. The Gulf of Mexico, the second began, was the crossroad of commercial progress where routes met from Europe and the Orient, the Amazon and the Mississippi valleys. The latter two regions could together produce everything known to the civilized world, and:

> The Island of Cuba, from its central position, and its great port of Havana, is the key to all this. The nation that holds Cuba will hold control over the commerce and wealth of this new world.
>
> It is not saying too much to say that if we hold Cuba, we will hold the destiny of the richest and most increased com-

25 " Cotton and Its Prospects," *The Industrial Resources, Etc., of the Southern and Western States*, by J. D. B. DeBow (New Orleans, 1852), I, 174.

26 R. R. Russel, *Economic Aspects of Southern Sectionalism: 1840-1861* (Urbana, 1924), 118-28. Herbert Wender, *Southern Commercial Conventions: 1837-1859* (Baltimore, 1930), 107.

merce that ever dazzled the cupidity of man. And with that commerce we can control the power of the world.

Furthermore, Negro slavery would be perpetuated and expanded in Brazil, the West Indies and the South by this commercial development because these regions could be exploited only by the use of laborers suited to hot climates:

> Think you the Caucasian race can stand to toil and labor under the burning rays of a tropical sun, and sleep in vigor and prosperity under the miasma of its exuberant and mighty plains and swamps? No! its resources are to be finally and fully developed by that race which God in his mercy formed and created for just such regions . . . .
>
> The world will fall back upon African labor, governed and owned in some shape or form by the white man, as it has always been . . . .
>
> We, too, are in the hands of a superintending Providence, to work out the real regeneration of mankind.[27]

In the same issue of the magazine, Doctor A. W. Ely described an immediate threat to slavery everywhere in Spanish plans to emancipate Cuban slaves. The people of the United States, he wrote, were faced in their own country by " free negroism . . . an unsightly, putrifying plague-spot upon the fair face of the nation, that will, some day, be wiped out with a vengeance," and it behooved them to see that it received no further extension in Cuba. But commercial reasons were even more conclusive:

> The annexation of Cuba to the United States would probably quadruple its exports and imports in a very few years, both by vastly augmenting those branches of industry already existing there, and by introducing new branches. The cotton and coffee culture, now almost extinct there, would be revived; the copper mines, by being more effectually wrought, would furnish a more abundant product; and all those

27 *DeBow's Review*, XVII (September, 1854), 280-4.

branches of industry, now almost smothered by the restrictions
and taxation of a despotic and short-sighted government,
would revive with all the vigor and enterprise incident to the
influences of a free government.[28]

DeBow had consistently frowned on " buffalo hunting " as a
method of annexing the island, but in November, 1854, he
opened the pages of his magazine to Samuel R. Walker of New
Orleans, an associate of Quitman, who wrote a justification of
the filibuster expedition the Mississippian was then organizing
and pleaded that the Federal government should respect the
" legality " of the enterprise and not step " beyond what is
pledged to or required of it." [29]

Under the tutelage of DeBow, southerners came to see
Cuban annexation as a measure that would not only protect
their " peculiar institution " but, as the key of a slave empire
which would be bound together by ties of commerce, was essential to the South's economic independence. The *Democratic
Review* in 1850 had sketched such a design and attempted to
make it palatable to the North by offering hegemony over the
slave empire to Britain in exchange for Canada:

> The formation of the cotton states with Cuba, into a great
> cotton, tobacco, sugar and coffee producing union, calling
> forth the boundless fertility of Cuba, and renovating the West
> India Islands with the labor of the blacks of the Southern
> states, in those hands in which their labor and their numbers
> have thriven so well, and this empire annexed to Britain by
> treaties of perfect reciprocity, giving the latter command of
> the Eastern commerce by way of Nicaragua, and all the
> benefits of possession, without the responsibility of slave-
> ownership, would be a magnificent exchange for the useless
> province of Canada.

28 A. W. Ely, " Cuba as It Is in 1854," *DeBow's Review*, XVII (September, 1854), 219-29.

29 Samuel R. Walker, " Cuba and the South," *Ibid*. (November, 1854),
519-25.

If the ingenious author did not expect all the parties to snap up his program, it was at least useful in the sectional struggle of 1850 as a warning to the North of the viability of the South as a nation, granted certain additions to its territory:

> A separation of the Union would involve the immediate connection of the whole South, with Mexico and the West Indies, with England . . . . While the South has now become necessary to every country of Europe, the North has Nothing to offer, being in fact a rival to each and all in manufactures.

But they were few northern partisans of the South who advocated annexation of Cuba as a means of realizing the southern economic nationalism of DeBow.

Shipowners rather than merchants were the chief northern supporters of Cuban annexation for whom economic considerations had personnel bearing. However, the distinction hardly exists, for example, in the case of the New York firm that operated the leading commercial house in Havana, Drake Brothers and Company. It led in the sugar trade, owned steamship lines between the United States and Cuba, and also owned Saratoga, one of the finest sugar plantations in the island. William Cullen Bryant visited this establishment and was much impressed by its " American efficiency." [31] Drake Brothers was the Havana agent of the great, new United States Mail Steamship Company. Cuban slavery, trade and shipping all touched its interests and it was sufficiently sympathetic to annexation to serve as the secret communication agent between revolutionists in Cuba and their friends in the United States.[32]

30 " Stability of the Union," *Democratic Review*, XXVI (January, 1850), 10-14.

31 William C. Bryant, " Letters from Cuba," *Littell's Living Age*, XXII (July, 1849), 11-8. Bryant was also struck by the omnipresence of American engineers in the island.

32 Vilá, *López*, I, 254.

The Havana *Mercantile Report* stated in 1855 that American tonnage in the Cuban trade had increased more than 200 percent during the previous decade. Having had a fair lead in 1846 over the nearest competitor, Great Britain, the United States increased its tonnage until it was in 1855 more than seven times that of Britain and over four times that of Spain. The shipping of the latter country had benefited from discriminations sufficiently to surpass the tonnage of Britain but not that of the United States.[33]

George Law, the President of the United States Mail Steamship Company, was the outstanding representative of shipping interests in the movement to annex Cuba. Starting as a hodcarrier, he had risen to wealth and political influence in the New York Democracy as a contractor who knew how to exploit sound business schemes by combining the methods of the promoter, political intriguer and lobbyist. A contemporary called Law as unpopular a man as could be found in New York because of his ruthless methods.[34] His career set a pattern for the rising generation of " robber barons." With Marshall O. Roberts, he gained control of a government contract in 1847 that gave him mastery of a subsidized line of steamships between New York and Panama by way of Havana and New Orleans. This line and a connecting link between Panama and Oregon, later California, was intended to serve manifold public purposes, all of them indicative of the expansive national mood. The steamships were to be superior to any previous types and built under the supervision of the Navy Department according to designs readily convertible for war purposes. Naval officers served on them as commanding and watch officers to gain experience in steam. As the fastest route to Ore-

33 *Mercantile Report*, August 7, 1855. Quoted in J. Smith Homans, Jr., *An Historical and Statistical Account of the Foreign Commerce of the United States* (New York, 1857), 134.

34 Matthew H. Smith, *Sunshine and Shadow in New York* (Hartford, 1868), 421.

gon and California, the lines carried the mails and provided improved military communications. William H. Aspinwall took the contract for the western line and with Law built the Panama Railroad to improve the isthmian connection between their lines. Up to 1852, Law failed to fulfill his contract, as he bought steamers instead of building them and supplied fewer than the five specified, but, never lacking sympathetic friends in Washington, his United States Mail Steamship Company was nevertheless paid the full subsidy of $290,000 per year.[35] This and the Gold Rush, besides ruthless methods of competition, made Law's venture wonderfully profitable. He became the leader of the " steamboat crowd " and a powerful figure in New York Democratic politics. Prosper M. Wetmore, also influential in New York Democratic circles, was taken into Law's company after being removed for defalcation as Navy Agent charged with supervising construction of Law's ships.[36] The political methods of Law were notorious. He commanded an elaborate and efficient band of lobbyists and the Congressmen who were loyal to his interests included representatives of both parties and all sections. The New York *Evening Post* credited him with controlling the Seward faction of the Whigs as well as the anti-Marcy Democrats.[37]

The United States Mail steamers used Havana as a coaling station and as a transfer point for traffic to and from Chagres. The ships were objects of suspicion to the Spanish authorities. The *Falcon* and others of Law's vessels were frequently subjected to high-handed interference. " Live Oak George " be-

35 George Law, *United States Mail Steam-Ships* (New York, 1850). *House Executive Documents* (31:1), 86. *Senate Reports* (32:1), 267. *House Executive Documents* (32:1), 91.

36 Fessenden N. Otis, *Isthmus of Panama: History of the Panama Railroad; and of the Pacific Mail Steamship Company* (New York, 1867), 50-69. John H. Kemble, *The Panama Route: 1848-1869* (Berkeley and Los Angeles, 1943), 10-188.

37 " The Five Predatory Tribes," *Evening Post Documents* (New York, 1853), Second Series, no. 4, pp. 2-4.

came convinced of the disadvantages of the existing order in the island and looked upon it as one more removable barrier in the way of his line's supremacy in the Gulf. He became a "Young American" with particular reference to Cuba in the Presidential campaign of 1852. Stephen A. Douglas was backed by the Young Americans for the Presidency and jeered at by his opponents as the "Steamboat Candidate." Law's sensational injection of the Cuban issue into the struggle on the eve of the election will be described in the next chapter.

Americans who lived in Cuba, barring a rare exception like John S. Thrasher before he was imprisoned, apparently gave no support to the annexation movement. Certainly they gave no support to López even when he took Cardenas, the "American City," although what their attitude would have been had he made good a beachhead cannot be known. Those with property to protect showed little interest in revolutions later in the century. Many Americans wanted to stay in the island only long enough to make their fortunes and they were not interested in changing its political status.[38] Foreigners enjoyed an advantage over Cubans in exemption from a variety of taxes which they would lose with annexation. But this very advantage, besides abounding economic opportunities, attracted a considerable migration of Americans, whose number increased from 1,256 in 1846 to 1,580 in 1850.[39] The island became a favorite resort of Americans seeking health and pleasure. Its climate attracted particularly sufferers from tuberculosis.[40] American mechanics found profitable seasonal employment in the sugar mills. In 1859, Richard H. Dana found an engineer from Lowell in charge of the machinery at an *ingenio*, "one of a numerous class, whom the sugar culture brings annually to

38 *Danville Quarterly Review*, I (June, 1861), 268-9.

39 Vilá, *Historia de Cuba*, I, 478.

40 William E. Smith, *The Francis Preston Blair Family in Politics* (New York, 1933), I, 143, 183.

Cuba " for the grinding season.[41] Very few Americans abandoned their citizenship, and they created the beginnings of an American economic " sphere of interest " in the island.

Spanish laws were favorable to the introduction of foreign capital and to mining enterprises undertaken by foreigners. Banks were unknown in the island. The agents of American bankers, merchants and shipowners made a lucrative business of extending credit to planters to enable them to harvest, mill and market sugar crops. Twelve percent interest was charged for such notes. Most Americans who became planters in Cuba began with moderate investments of capital. Throughout most of the nineteenth century, Cuba was the chief source of the world's copper, and American as well as English capital was invested in the mines.[42] David Turnbull found the Americans Thomas B. Smith and Hezekiah Bradford operating the *Compañía de Minería Cubana* near Jagua. One of their copper mines employed about 150 men and they had invested $150,-000 in machinery. The product was exported to the United States and England. The abolitionist found praiseworthy the use of free labor instead of slaves in the Company's mines.[43] In 1857, the United States Consul at Santiago reported that the New York Ore Dressing Company owned mines in the village of Cobre and had established works for the cleaning of copper-bearing sand. He also mentioned that an American company had contracted to erect gas works for the lighting of the city of Santiago.[44] Bituminous coal was found near Havana and used by steamships, sugar mills and railroads.[45]

41 Richard H. Dana, *To Cuba and Back*, 129. *Cf.* [Daniel Nason], *Journal of a Tour* (Cambridge, 1849).

42 Leland H. Jenks, *Our Cuban Colony* (New York, 1928), 33 ff.

43 David Turnbull, *Travels in the West: Cuba; with Notices of Porto Rico, and the Slave Trade* (London, 1840), 15-6.

44 *Senate Executive Documents* (35:1), no. 53, pp. 68-9.

45 Amelia M. Murray, *Letters from the United States, Cuba and Canada* (New York, 1856), 248. Maturin M. Ballou, *History of Cuba* (Boston, 1854), 196.

Chrome ores, which were becoming important to the steel industry, were mined in Cuba by American companies.[46] Such enterprises promised that Cuba could become an important market for the surplus capital which the United States began to accumulate after the Mexican War. Pierre Soulé indicated that finance imperialism was an article of his " Young American " faith. In 1852, as Senator from Louisiana, he cried to the upper House: " What! speak you of isolation? Have you not markets to retain for your present excess of production, and markets to secure for the surplus of your future wealth?" [47] Soulé did not need to speak for Wall Street, for his own state was third in the Union in value of stock ownership and second in circulation of money.[48]

The chief economic interest of New Orleans derived from its position as the capital of the cotton and sugar regions of the Southwest. In 1850, the slave-plantation system of this " New South " faced a crisis. A condition of its economic health was continual expansion of the area of land under cultivation with corresponding increments of slave laborers. The one-crop system was almost universal on plantations and that system mined and killed the soil. Reformers struggled manfully to teach planters techniques of restoring the fertility of the soil,[49] but without overcoming their preference for the traditional solution of new and unexhausted tracts of land. The planters' attitude towards land was described in the Patent Office Report of 1860:

> The planter scarcely considers his land as a part of his permanent investment. It is rather a part of his current expenses. He buys a wagon and uses it until it is worn out,

46 John G. Taylor, The United States and Cuba: Eight Years of Change and Travel (London, 1851), 131-2, 165, 176.

47 Congressional Globe (32:1), Appendix, 352.

48 Preliminary Report on the Eighth Census, 1860, 78.

49 Avery O. Craven, " The Agricultural Reformers of the Ante-Bellum South," American Historical Review, XXXIII (January, 1928), 302-14.

and then throws it away. He buys a plow, or hoe, and treats
both in the same way. He buys land, uses it until it is ex-
hausted and then sells it, as he sells scrap iron, for whatever
it will bring. It is with him a perishable or movable commodity.[50]

Land prices indicate that the movement westward in the
South, unlike the North, was not a search for cheap land but
for unexhausted soil. In 1850, occupied land in the southern
Atlantic coast states was valued at an average of only $5.34
per acre, while that of southwestern states was $6.26 per acre.
The poorer planter was likely to remain on old land while his
wealthier neighbor followed the pioneer westward. In such
a "western" state as Alabama, Representative G. C. Clay
said in 1853 that wealthy planters bought out poor men, extended their plantations and added to their slave forces.[51]

Frederick J. Turner and Ulrich B. Phillips arrived at similar conclusions in their studies of the plantation system.
Southwestern frontiersmen moved from fertile lands to the
pine hills and barrens. Large planters engrossed the rich
"buck-shot" soils of the cotton belt. The average size of
farms decreased in the Old South at the same time that it increased in the New. In Georgia, the number of slaves in western
counties increased between 1830 and 1860 more than 300 percent while those in eastern counties increased less than 30
percent. The combined population of Alabama and Mississippi
rose from 40,000 in 1810 to 1,660,000 in 1860, while the proportion of slaves rose from 40 to 47 percent. In the New
South, landlessness increased and tenants became farm laborers
as the large planters took over more and more of the best land.
Sentimental attachment to a piece of land and the patriarchal
relation between master and slaves which featured plantation
life in the Old South were lost as large-scale agriculture became

50 "Patent Office Report 1860," quoted in W. W. Hammond, *The Cotton
Industry* (Ithaca, 1897), I, 83.

51 *Ibid.*, 10, 84.

commercialized and the exploitation of land and slaves a business enterprise like any other.[52]

In their pursuit of quick profits, southwestern planters engaged ever-larger tracts of new land and increased their labor forces not only because they killed the soil, but also because they were engaged in a race against falling cotton prices and rising slave costs. Until the Mexican War, slave prices showed a short-term tendency to rise and fall with cotton prices, but the long-term trends from 1800 to 1845 were for slave prices to rise and cotton prices to fall. The average ratio in 1800 was $300 for a slave compared to 25 cents for a pound of cotton. In 1845, the ratio was $600 to 6 cents. During approximately the same period (1815-1849), the world price level declined about 61 percent, which partially offset the higher cost of slaves and lower money income of the planter. From 1845 to 1860, slave prices rose from $600 to $1500. The world price level went up about 188 percent between 1849 and 1865. With the cost of living and the chief cost of production rapidly rising, the planter required a sharp rise in cotton prices to compensate. But after a quick recovery from the low of 6 cents, they leveled off at approximately 10 cents. Nevertheless, the period 1845-1860 was the first one during which the lows in cotton prices were successively higher (6-8-9-11), and this new experience of rising cotton prices had an exhilarating effect on the planter. It convinced him that a falling price for his cotton was not an inevitable result of increased production and, in spite of the still-widening gap between what he took in and what he paid out, strengthened his faith in the traditional solution of more acres of new soil and more slaves. The increased value of slaves

52 Frederick J. Turner, *The Rise of the New West* (New York, 1906), 91-3. Ulrich B. Phillips, *American Negro Slavery* (New York, 1918), 171-2. James C. Bonner, "Profile of a Late Ante-Bellum Community," *American Historical Review*, XLIX (July, 1944), 663-80. Ralph B. Flanders, *Plantation Slavery in Georgia* (Chapel Hill, 1933), 63, 67. Charles S. Sydnor, *Slavery in Mississippi* (New York, 1933), 187-9.

encouraged plunging on credit and the planters' debts mounted as they expanded their scale of operations.[53]

What were the planters' prospects of increasing their landholdings? Professor C. W. Ramsdell has shown that by 1850 cotton cultivation had been extended westward about as far as possible. Soil and climate limited it on the north at the northern boundary of Arkansas. The struggle for Kansas by the South was defensive and political rather than an attempt to extend the plantation system to that region. The lack of transportation and of wood for fences were barriers to planting the central prairies of Texas, as were the German settlements and the proximity of cheap Mexican labor in the southern part of that state. Southern as well as northern leaders knew that soil and climate made the right won by the South in the Compromise of 1850 to take slaves into New Mexico a hollow victory. The conclusion that Professor Ramsdell set out to prove by these and other considerations is that slavery-extension was a false issue unnecessarily pushed to the point of civil war by agitators on both sides. He discusses the possibility of slavery-extension south of the United States and dismisses it as being remote. But he curiously omits from his long list of "mixed motives" for Cuban annexation the one that bears on his argument: the desire for land suited to the slave-plantation system.[54]

The clearest evidence that Cuba offered a practical answer to the land-hunger of southern planters is the migration of Americans to the island where they prospered as plantation-

[53] Ulrich B. Phillips, *American Negro Slavery*, 370. E. Q. Hawks, *Economic History of the South* (New York, 1934), 241. Cotton prices are for New York "uplands;" slave prices are sectional averages for "prime field hands."

[54] C. W. Ramsdell, "The Natural Limits of Slavery Expansion," *Mississippi Valley Historical Review*, XVI (September, 1929), 151-71. In 1856, when the southern "Grey-eyed Man of Destiny" and filibuster, William Walker, gained control of Nicaragua, his first act was to decree slavery there. He was heartily backed by important southwestern political leaders, but few Americans actually settled in Nicaragua.

owners. Contemporary observers frequently remarked on this migration.[55] A traveler wrote in 1860 of one family that operated a cotton plantation in Mississippi and in Cuba a sugar plantation worth two million dollars.[56] *DeBow's Review* pointed out that the prices of land and slaves were much lower in Cuba than in the American Southwest.[57] Rewards of land were held out to volunteers in the filibuster expeditions. The descent on Cuba in 1851 was made by members of planter families some of whom, according to the spy, Burtnett, had mortgaged their plantations " that the owners might share in the future wealth of broad plantations well stocked with negroes." [58] In 1854, when Senator Slidell of Louisiana proposed to the Senate that the neutrality laws be suspended in favor of the filibuster expedition Quitman was organizing against Cuba, one of the motives he offered for annexation of the island was the attractive calculation that " a plantation, yielding a net revenue of $25,000, can be bought for less than $100,000 " in Cuba.[59] Quitman made plain to the members of the Central Southern Rights Association why he supported annexation of Cuba. Answering their congratulations upon his release from indictment for organizing the Cardenas Expedition, he wrote:

> We have been swindled by [the administration and the anti-slavery states] out of the public domain. Even a portion of Texas, supposed to be secured as slaveholding, has been wrested from us. Every outlet to the extension of our institutions has been firmly closed. The golden shores of the Pacific, open to the adventurers of the wide earth, is denied to Southern labor, though in part acquired with our blood

55 *Danville Quarterly Review*, I (June, 1861), 265. R. R. Madden, *Island of Cuba* (London, 1853), 83. David Turnbull, *Travels in the West*, 133.

56 J. S. C. Abbott *South and North* (New York, 1860), 17.

57 *DeBow's Review*, XVII (July, 1854), 46.

58 Quoted in Caldwell, *López Expeditions*, 84-5.

59 *Congressional Globe* (33:1), 1021-4.

and purchased with our treasures. We are now hemmed in on the west as well as the north. The line once fixed, to save the Union, has been contemptuously disregarded. The area for the employment of our labor has been circumscribed by the fiat, " Thus far shalt thou go, and no farther." [60]

Land hunger had played a part in the Texas movement, and it was even more urgent by 1850. However, differences between Cuba and Texas were obvious, and a leading one was the fact that the island was already fairly extensively cultivated by sugar planters. This caused opposition to annexation in Louisiana.

An important debate on the question was conducted in *DeBow's Review*. Campaigns for tariff protection had pictured the American sugar industry as weak and unable to compete on even terms with sugar grown in Cuba and elsewhere. In 1849, *DeBow's Review* published a letter by Ashbel Smith, former Secretary of State of the Texas Republic, in which he declared that the sugar planters of Louisiana and Texas would be "immediately smitten with ruin" if Cuba was annexed. If they turned to cotton, its price would fall disastrously, and slave property in the border states would be rendered nearly worthless. The loss of slave states there would weigh heavier than the political benefits to the South of Cuban annexation. [61] A few months earlier, the *United States Magazine and Democratic Review* had anticipated the argument and answered it in a statement that the prices of land and slaves in Cuba would be equalized with those in the United States after annexation, whereupon "the sugar plantations of Louisiana would find, in the hitherto untouched soil of Cuba, the means of underselling the world in sugar." [62] But this answer in the New York publication was ignored by DeBow. In January, 1853, under

60 Claiborne, *Quitman*, II, 130.

61 *DeBow's Review*, VII (December, 1849), 538-41.

62 *Democratic Review*, XXV (September, 1849), 203.

a statement that he did not always agree with it, DeBow published an article by W. J. Sykes of Tennessee repeating the warning of Ashbel Smith to sugar planters that annexation would ruin them.[63]

Coincident with the inauguration of President Pierce, the New Orleans magazine published a thorough study of the question by a resident of the city, Dr. Cartwright. He remarked that most sugar planters believed annexation of Cuba would ruin them and he commended their glorious patriotism for nevertheless advocating it " as a public good." Happily, their assumption that the cane was a sickly exotic in Louisiana was without foundation. The yield of Louisiana fields was superior to that of Cuba and the cane juice was richer. Superior mills and machinery in Cuba and its biennial crop as compared with the annual cut in Louisiana, should have made Cuba more productive, but it actually obtained only one hogshead of sugar per laborer while Louisiana obtained five hogsheads. The difference was that slaves in Louisiana were treated so much better that they worked harder.[64]

This tribute to the labor system of the state did not convince Sykes,[65] or an anonymous contributor who claimed to have better figures which proved the superiority of Cuban soil and production. When Cuba was annexed, he wrote:

> the intelligence and skill now displayed here, will be equally remarkable there, and in a short time the cultivation of Sugar in Louisiana would become extinct. (We differ with the writer here. —Editor.) However, the benefits resulting from annexation would more than overbalance the evils which would result from the extinction of the Sugar culture in Louisiana, and it would be well if the Sugar planters would

63 *DeBow's Review*, XIV (January, 1853), 63-6.

64 *Ibid.*, XIV (March, 1853), 197-208. *Cf.* J. S. C. Abbott, *South and North*, 52 ff.

65 *Ibid.*, XIV (May, 1853), 417-22.

begin to consider what kind of cultivation could be most profitably pursued by them in that case.[66]

It remained for John S. Thrasher to have the last word. In May, 1854, he wrote a long letter to his employer, the editor of the New Orleans *Picayune*, which was first published in that newspaper, then was reprinted separately, widely copied by southern newspapers and published by DeBow in July. The reprinted version was introduced by the editor of the *Picayune*, who wrote that Thrasher exposed the fallacies of economic opposition to Cuban annexation and that:

> considerations of large pecuniary, direct interest to New Orleans, Louisiana, and the Southwest, are added to those reasons of state, of public peace, and of national security, which make the Spanish rule in Cuba injurious and offensive to the United States, and which prompt the unanimous desire here, that the island should free herself of the hateful burden.[67]

Thrasher, drawing upon his experience as editor of *El Faro Industrial*, asserted that sugar production per acre and per laborer were very similar in Cuba and the United States. The great elements in Cuba's lower cost of production were the lower prices of land and slaves. The average value of field hands in Cuba was $500 while in Louisiana it was $1200. The mean value of land was also much less in the island. But the first great result of establishment of a free government in Cuba or of its admission to the United States would be the immediate cessation of the slave trade with Africa and an appreciation in the value of slaves consequent upon the cutting off of that source of cheap supply. An economic result attending admission of Cuba to the Union would be the equalization of the value of slaves there and in Louisiana. Thrasher supposed that prices would advance in the island but they might decline in

[66] *Ibid.*, XV (December, 1853), 647-8.

[67] John S. Thrasher, *Cuba and Louisiana: Letter to Samuel J. Peters, Esq.* (New Orleans, 1854).

the United States. He presumed that no one doubted a great increase in the value of Cuban land would follow annexation and pointed out that an increase in the cost of production of Cuban sugar would be:

> a far more permanent and efficient protection to the sugar planter of Louisiana, than the present fiscal impost upon sugar; while so long as Cuba is enabled to produce it at less cost than Louisiana, and the desire in the North to obtain cheap sugar persists, the danger to the sugar planting interest in this country will not only remain, but may continue to increase.

Spain, by trying to introduce the apprentice system in Cuba, intended to reduce the cost of labor to $200 per hand. The present American duty would offer no protection against such competition. Louisiana stood alone against the struggle of the North to obtain sugar and molasses free of duty. On the other hand:

> While the equalization of the cost of production of sugar in Louisiana and Cuba would bring to the Louisiana planter a permanent protection, the admission of Cuba to the Union would make the United States the great sugar grower, as it is the great cotton grower of the world.

Under the increasing power of American moral influence, relaxations of the fiscal regulations of other countries would occur and consumption would increase. Thrasher went on to paint a glowing picture of the monopoly position New Orleans would also enjoy in the provision of food from the Mississippi valley which a liberated Cuba would buy in doubled quantity. In short, annexation was the only measure that would confer stability and conduce to the permanent welfare of the planting community of Louisiana.[68]

68 John S. Thrasher, "Cuba and the United States: How the Interests of Louisiana Would Be Affected by Annexation," DeBow's Review, XVII (July, 1854), 43-9.

After the wide circulation of Thrasher's letter, no more was heard of opposition by the Louisiana sugar planters to Cuban annexation. His argument was reiterated and amplified in subsequent numbers of *DeBow's Review*. Cuban planters used less than one-fifth of the island's arable land. Taxes and wretched government were heavy handicaps on sugar production. If Cuba nevertheless produced one-third of the world's sugar, efficient American planters under a just and helpful government would make it with Louisiana the monopolist of the world's sugar supply.[69] Thrasher's article was admiringly quoted in Congress by Representative E. W. Chastain of Georgia.[70]

During the same years when this debate took place, Louisiana planters sought to increase their profits and improve their position against foreign competitors by the development of superior refining techniques. The leader in this movement was the eminent New Orleans lawyer, Judah P. Benjamin, who later became United States Senator and cabinet officer in the Confederate government. He owned an important cane plantation which he made a model of advanced methods. When Norbert Rillieux, a Negro chemist of New Orleans, improved the multiple vacuum-pan system of refining sugar, Benjamin helped to develop it and installed it in his mill. He wrote in *DeBow's Review* to teach the method to other planters and advocated improved ways of cultivating cane.[71] But this versatile leader of the planters did not look upon increased productivity as a cure-all for Louisiana sugar interests or fear the effects of Cuban annexation. He was a leading advocate of the movement to encompass the rich sugar lands of the island

69 *DeBow's Review*, XVIII (February, 1855), 163-5; see also (March, 1855), 306.

70 *Congressional Globe* (33:2), *Appendix*, 192-5.

71 Judah P. Benjamin, "Louisiana Sugar," *DeBow's Review*, II (November, 1846), 322-45; *ibid.*, V (January, 1848), 44-57 and (April, 1848), 357-64.

in the United States. After he assisted the government prosecutor in the trial of Senator Henderson as a filibuster in 1850 and thereby incurred the wrath of the extremists, the certainty of political ruin if he opposed annexation, apart from any other consideration, made Benjamin proclaim his support of the policy.[72] In May, 1854, he introduced in the Senate resolutions that the federal government should adopt "most decisive and energetic measures" on Cuban annexation.[73]

The demand for slaves in the Southwest and the alarming rise in prices caused many to cast about for new sources of supply. Lewis C. Gray, the leading authority on agriculture in the ante-bellum South, believes that a greater labor supply was more necessary to the lower South than acquisitions of land.[74] DeBow preached that the shortage of labor was a hindrance to the expansion of cotton cultivation.[75] The movement to re-open the slave trade with Africa in reckless defiance of the course of world opinion gained ground steadily during the fifties, until in 1859 the Southern Commercial Convention at Vicksburg recommended repeal of all state and federal laws prohibiting the traffic. DeBow became president of the African Labor Supply Association to create propaganda in favor of repeal.[76] But the half-million slaves of Cuba and their low price were sufficient to provide some relief to American planters if the island's markets were thrown open to them. *DeBow's Review* hinted as early as 1848 that the well-stocked and flourishing condition of the slave markets of Cuba was a reason for the South to take an interest in the island.[77] This was the most

72 Pierce Butler, *Judah P. Benjamin* (Philadelphia, 1906), 180-5.

73 *Congressional Globe* (33:1), 1298.

74 Lewis C. Gray, *History of Agriculture in the Southern United States to 1860* (Washington, 1933), II, 642.

75 "Cotton and Its Prospects," *Industrial Resources, Etc., of the Southern and Western States*, DeBow, I, 175.

76 Gray, *op. cit.*, 668-9.

77 *DeBow's Review*, V (May, 1848), 470.

distasteful of all motives for annexation and it was seldom heard. Rather an appeal was frequently made to humane sentiment by promising that the slave trade between Cuba and Africa would be abolished after annexation. Lieutenant Matthew F. Maury believed that the South would soon suffer from a surplus of slaves, but this did not cool his expansionist ardor. He insisted that Cuba and especially Brazil should serve as profitable markets for " excess " American slaves. Without such markets, he feared emancipation might be resorted to in order to relieve the slave-owners of their predicament, which he likened to that of the man who had a wolf by the ears.[87]

This chapter suggests that economic motives played a part in the movement to annex Cuba. They help to explain why New Orleans was the chief center of annexation sentiment in the Union: it was the headquarters of southern commercial, shipping and financial interests as well as the capital of the cotton and sugar slave-plantation regions. Southern economic nationalism was irradiated from New Orleans by the indefatigable DeBow. The filibusters gravitated to that city. And there the dream of a slave-commercial empire flourished. A frank expression of that vision, free of the " democratic idealism " on which most propagandists concentrated attention, was written by Edward A. Pollard of Virginia, who was to be the first historian of the Confederate States of America. He wanted the slave trade re-opened, partly in order to create an opportunity for poor whites to become planters and acquire a stake in the slavery system. Besides this, he wrote:

> Regarding the magnificent country of tropical America, which lies in the path of our destiny on this continent, we may see an empire as powerful and gorgeous as ever was pictured in our dreams of history. . . . It is an empire founded on military ideas; representing the noble peculiarities of Southern civilization; including within its limits the isthmus of America and the

78 M. F. Maury, " Southern Direct Foreign Trade," *Industrial Resources, Etc., of the Southern and Western States*, DeBow, III, 11-13.

regenerated West Indies; having control of the two dominant
staples of the world's commerce—cotton and sugar; posses-
sing the highways of the world's commerce; surpassing all
empires of the age in the strength of its geographical position;
and, in short, combining the elements of strength, prosperity,
and glory, such as never before in the modern ages have been
placed within reach of a single government.

What a splendid vision of empire! How sublime in its
associations! How noble and inspiriting the idea, that upon
the strange theatre of tropical America, once, if we may
believe the dimmer facts of history, crowned with magnificent
empires . . . the destiny of Southern civilization is to be con-
summated in a glory brighter even than that of old.[79]

Pollard in his rapture saw a new Aztecan empire of militarism
and slavery as the ultimate destiny of the South, and such
dreams, increasingly common towards the end of the fifties,
were increasingly associated with the program of southern
secession from the Union. They contained the ultimate implications of southern interest in Cuba as it was expressed in the
Gulf states and the regional capital, New Orleans.

Trade, shipping and financial interests also help to explain
why New York was the second center of the Cuban movement.
The general tie between northern commerce, banking, and industry and the southern plantation system cemented the alliance
in the Democratic Party of New York business men and southern planters. Even the Whig business men of the Northeast
and their political leaders showed in the sectional struggle of
1850 that in the cause of profitable connection with the South
they could rise above anti-slavery principles. The movement to
annex Cuba expressed the economic community of interests
between northern business and southern slavery. As James
Gordon Bennett, editor of the New York *Herald*, wrote after
Free Soilism had defeated the Democratic Party in 1848, action
on Cuba would unite the South with the northern commercial

79 Edward A. Pollard, *Black Diamonds* (New York, 1859), 52-3, 108-9.

and manufacturing interests and leave only Free Soilers of both parties outside the powerful combination. Cuba, he thought, could in this way decide the 1852 election.[80]

Yet in 1852 the first choice of the annexationists for President was Senator Stephen A. Douglas of Illinois, who represented the section of the Union most remote from the economic interests which have been described. How Douglas and his supporters attempted to organize a grand sectional alliance that was not without relevance to those interests will be observed in the next chapter.

80 New York *Herald*, December 21, 1848.

CHAPTER VIII

CUBA AND THE CAMPAIGN OF 1852

STEPHEN A. DOUGLAS, the "Little Giant" of Illinois, founded his political career on the policy of expansion. He sought territorial expansion for national purposes and, as Chairman of the Committees on Territories of the House and the Senate, fought against sectional obstructions to the extension of government into the West. He ignored the issue of slavery as long as he could and then advocated the "neutral" principle of popular sovereignty in the hope that the sections would unite to allow the people of the territories to determine the question. He found a potent aid to unity in the railroad. When the people of his own state, and even his Democratic supporters, developed a miniature version of the sectional division that threatened the nation after the Mexican War, Douglas worked to obtain a gift of land from Congress to aid in the construction of a central railroad through his state which would draw his northern and southern constituents closer together. Such a gift required votes from more than one state. Douglas won eastern votes by promising that a branch line would connect the Illinois railroad with lines from the east at Chicago. Southerners became interested when the Illinois Central Bill was amended to grant lands to Alabama and Mississippi and continue the railroad to the Gulf. The project had become national and the Bill passed.[1]

In this episode, Douglas made the Northwest the apex of a triangle whose sides would be arteries of commerce binding together the three great sections of the nation. It expressed his vision of the Mississippi valley as the heart and soul of his country which he believed would make disunion impossible. During the same months when he put through the Illinois Central Bill, Douglas played a large part in the successful con-

[1] Allen Johnson, *Stephen A. Douglas: A Study in American Politics* (New York, 1908), 167-75.

clusion of the Compromise of 1850 and he hoped that it would put an end to the slavery controversy forever. In the debate, he declared his conviction that nature, more effectively than any possible laws, would prevent the extension of slavery into the territories of the West. Seventeen free territories would be formed there, but, he asked the Senate:

> where are you to find the slave territory with which to balance these seventeen free territories, or even any one of them?... There is none—none at all.[2]

He had no answer in 1850. Two years later, as a candidate for the Democratic Presidential nomination, he offered one as his only specific platform: Cuba.

Douglas' motives for Cuban annexation were not pro-slavery except as he was willing and even anxious to strengthen slavery and the South in order to satisfy that section and put the slavery issue at rest. The moral obtuseness of the appeaser but not the plot of a friend of slavery is discernible in his policy. To him, expansion southwards would be not a provocation of the North but a means of binding the South to the Union. His optimistic spirit hoped even to bring the North into positive partnership. Again he would use the binding power of great transportation routes to create unity.

The managers of the Illinois Central Railroad planned to carry the sugar of Cuba directly to the Chicago market, and the wheat and pork of the Northwest to the West Indies.[3] Judah P. Benjamin was a leading promoter of the Jackson Railroad that connected the Illinois Central with New Orleans.[4] The United States Mail Steamship Line provided the southern and eastern sides of what would now be a vast quadrilateral with Chicago,

2 *Congressional Globe* (31:1), *Appendix,* 371.

3 Johnson, *Douglas,* 175n.

4 Nathaniel W. Stephenson and H. W. Howard Knott, "Judah Philip Benjamin," *Dictionary of American Biography,* ed. *Allen Johnson* (New York, 1929), II, 182.

New Orleans, Havana and New York at its corners. And beyond the Gulf, isthmian routes being built or planned led to the fabulous trade of the eastern and western Pacific ports. Douglas was a confidential adviser of John L. Stephens, President of the Panama Railroad Company.[5] He also encouraged the promoters of the Tehuantepec route, P. A. Hargous of Philadelphia and J. M. Cazneau.[6] Judah P. Benjamin was President of a New Orleans company, capitalized at $9,000,000, that took over from Hargous his grant from the Mexican government to build a railroad across its territory.[7]

The most important figure in Douglas' alliance was George Law. The Illinois Senator was a practised speculator and promoter. He formed a working combination with the " Steamboat Crowd " in 1850 when, after some bickering, their lobbyists pushed the Illinois Central Bill and the Senator voted for the appropriation to pay the United States Mail Steamship Company's subsidy.[8] Late in 1851, William L. Marcy was trying assiduously to win the support of Law for his ambition to be Democratic nominee. Douglas made his first approach in New York to the shady characters who managed ward primaries for Tammany Hall. The Empire Club declared for him, dinners were given in his honor, and he was initiated into Tammany.[9] Despite the efforts of Marcy and his friends, George Law, Curtiss, Croswell and other " Steamboat Democrats " supported Douglas and placed large amounts of money at his disposal.[10] Marcy then decided that Law's money came

5 Stephens to Douglas, New York, August 6, 1850. Douglas Papers.

6 Cazneau to Douglas, New York, July 15, 1852. *Ibid.*

7 Butler, *Benjamin*, 125-6.

8 Percy M. Wetmore to William L. Marcy, New York, November 28, 1851. Marcy Papers.

9 Roy F. Nichols, *The Democratic Machine: 1850-1854* (New York, 1923), 111.

10 L. B. Shepherd to Marcy, New York, December 15, 1851. Thomas N. Carr to Marcy, New York, February 3, 1852. Marcy Papers. *Cf.* A. C. Flagg to Martin Van Buren, New York, January 26, 1852. Martin Van Buren Papers.

from "flagiciously fraudulent" government contracts and would injure Douglas.[11]

The Law-Douglas alliance was at the center of the Young America movement that tried to sweep Douglas into the Presidency in 1852. That movement was an attempt to organize the nation's Manifest Destiny and make it pay immediate dividends in votes, political offices, intervention in favor of European liberalism, economic benefits and Cuban annexation. Stephen A. Douglas was inevitably the hero of Young America because his youth, his fame as the nation's outstanding expansionist, his " neutrality " on the slavery question, and his energy of a " steam-engine in breeches " in crusading for the universal extension of democratic institutions made him the master-image of the movement. As a stock-jobber, he also illustrated Professor Henry S. Commager's remark that the New England abolitionist preacher Theodore Parker " saw through all the fanfaronade about Manifest Destiny and the bombast about patriotism and the sententious devotion to the Union; what men were really talking about was their balance at the bank." [12]

Douglas adopted Young America as much as the movement adopted him. It offered him a national following and a national platform at a time when he insisted on banishing the slavery issue from politics and had need of a rousing program besides internal improvements and the preservation of the Democratic party.[13] The strident liberalism of Young America promised to drown in noise the doubts of those who found the pro-slavery aspects of Cuban annexation difficult to reconcile with either liberalism or national unity. Douglas did not hide that he wished to annex Cuba, but as the campaign approached he adopted the Young American trick of ignoring troublesome problems attendant upon annexation of that specific territory

11 Marcy to James G. Berret, Albany, February 4, 1852. Marcy Papers.

12 Henry S. Commager, *Theodore Parker* (Boston, 1936), 284.

13 *Congressional Globe* (32:1), *Appendix*, 68.

in a spate of words about the right of self-determination and the need for " an *American policy* in our foreign relations, based upon the principles of our own Government, and adapted to the spirit of the age." [14]

This was the general platform Douglas offered to the electorate in a speech to the Senate supporting Kossuth. Behind the scenes, the chief propagandist of Young America and of Douglas' candidacy, George N. Sanders of Kentucky, made an astonishing offer to the Hungarian patriot. On January 27, 1852, the latter wrote to Sanders that he was trying with the aid of his friends to obtain a declaration by Congress that foreign interference in the domestic affairs of any country was a violation of international law and that the neutrality laws were suspended in respect to the powers claiming interference. He wanted to remove the Russian threat to suppress the Hungarian revolution against Austria. But, he continued:

> I see in your communication a much more important point yet, an offer, *the greatest made to me since I came to the U. S.,* which if realized, would be sufficient in itself to take my visit in America for entirely successful [*sic*]. You write that *you shall be prepared, are in fact ready to purchase the best and fastest-going steamer in the U. S. mercantile marine & place her at my disposal, that you are prepared too to arm her, fit her, & steam her* . . . [15]

Sanders' immediate motive is not far to seek. He had been the agent of George Law and Samuel Colt in 1848 when he went to Europe to sell arms to revolutionary groups.[16] Law's friend, Navy Agent Prosper M. Wetmore, had obtained for

14 *Congressional Globe* (32:1), 70-1.

15 Kossuth to Sanders, Pittsburgh, January 27, 1852. *The Political Correspondence of the Late Hon. George N. Sanders: Confederate Commissioner to Europe during the Civil War*, The American Art Association (New York, 1914), 92.

16 Siert F. Riepma, " *Young America:* " *A Study in American Nationalism before the Civil War*, unpublished doctoral dissertation, Western Reserve University, 1939, 77-9.

him 144,000 new muskets from the War Department at $2 each, a price lower than they were fetching at public auction, and then, when Sanders failed to sell them in Europe, Law neglected to pay the government.[17] These muskets probably figured in the López expeditions, and Law finally offered a free sample of 5,000 to Quitman. After his failure in Europe, Sanders worked for Law to establish the Ebony Line of steamers to Africa. The plan was to settle free American Negroes there and open the continent for exploitation. This effort to make an honest penny out of the unfortunate also failed.[18]

In January, 1852, Sanders had enough money to buy the *Democratic Review,* and in that magazine he published Young America's manifesto in favor of Douglas for President. The source of his funds and of the arms and steamers he offered Kossuth was doubtless George Law. These circumstances have led students to emphasize the dedication of Douglas' candidacy and Sanders' Young American propaganda to the extension of democratic institutions in Europe. Professor Merle E. Curti has portrayed Sanders as a promoter who hoped to profit from governmental intervention in Europe and planned to divert filibusters from Cuba and organize expeditions to free Hungary and Italy; Law as the link between Young America and big business hopes to profit from trade with American protegés abroad; and Douglas as the instrument to win political power for northern capitalist interests.[19] The foreign policy of Douglas would thus acquire an European orientation to the exclusion of Cuba.

Intrinsic flaws in this analysis are that it ignores Sanders' pro-slavery principles and Douglas' sensitivity to southern opposition to crusades for liberty and trade in Europe. This

17 "The Five Predatory Tribes," *Evening Post Documents* (New York, 1853), series 2, no. 4, p. 3.

18 Riepma, *loc. cit.*

19 Merle E. Curti, "George Sanders: Patriot of the Fifties," *South Atlantic Quarterly,* XXVII (January, 1928), 79-87. Curti, "Young America," *American Historical Review,* XXXII (October, 1926), 41 ff.

opposition was made clear when Senator Cass, condemned as an " Old Fogy " in Sanders' manifesto in the *Democratic Review,* spryly hopped aboard the Young America bandwagon with a resolution against repression of liberalism by European autocrats. He was promptly pushed off by the South. It voted solidly against the resolution. Whigs voted against it, although Seward pointed out the trade advantages to be gained from a Hungarian republic. Representatives of the Northwest were almost unanimous in favor of it on idealistic grounds, and eastern Democrats for commercial reasons.[20] This vote showed that the South had abandoned the Jacksonian ideal of the extension of the area of freedom when a specific issue offered no interest to slavery. Southerners had soon found that the European liberal doctrines of 1848 contained a threat to slavery which made them an awkward weapon of expansion. The failure of the Kossuth movement was owing first to the opposition of Democratic leaders of the South.[21] The stand of Cass on Kossuth helped to kill his candidacy for the Democratic nomination.

The Young Americans tried to remove the offense from liberalism by marrying slavery to it. Sanders sought to obtain from Kossuth a commitment in favor of the South's peculiar institution. That section must be reassured that the foreign policy of Young America and its candidate was not exclusive. But Kossuth refused. He later wrote to Sanders that in America he had avoided controversies over slavery because:

> it would be impossible for me not to say that I disapprove of slavery in whatever shape,—it would be impossible not to say, that though I perfectly appreciate the immense practical difficulties of the question, still I know equally well that it is the question which endangers the future of the great Republic . . . . Do not mix me in any other way with the question, *non intervention is my principle* . . . [22]

20 *Congressional Globe* (32:1), 105, 186, 310; *Appendix*, 243-7, 531-2, 542, 551-60.

21 Nichols, *The Democratic Machine*, 50. George S. Boutwell, *Reminiscences of Sixty Years in Public Affairs* (New York, 1902), I, 195 ff.

22 Kossuth to Sanders [London ?], May 8 [1854 ?], *Political Correspondence of . . . Sanders,* III.

Sanders showed no further interest in providing the means of a filibuster expedition for Kossuth. The great liberal patriot was appropriated by Free Soilers and abolitionists.[23] But their enthusiasm also proved to be platonic. In July and December, 1852, and the following February, the Hungarian, disillusioned by the sudden cooling of American ardor, clung to the hopes Sanders had roused and begged him to make good his promises, but without result.[24]

The pro-slavery Young Americans had not quite done with Kossuth. In September, 1852, John T. Pickett, former consul at Turk's Island, filibuster from Kentucky, and an enthusiastic supporter of Douglas for President, wrote a " diplomatic report " to " General C. F. Henningsen, Secretary to His Excellency the Governor of Hungary, Astor House, New York," from the city of Santo Domingo. The Kentuckian was trying to draw Kossuth into the neighborhood of Cuba for mysterious purposes. Unfortunately, President Báez was aware of Pickett's connection with the Cuban movement and, the " Hungarian envoy " wrote, uninterested in concessions to American " immigrants " and steamship lines. Báez was a mulatto and anti-American. The Archbishop, a pure Castilian, favored immigration of Americans to regenerate the Republic. General Santana, the Liberator, feared the Negroes would oppose Americans, but Pickett had a plan drafted by Duff and Benjamin Green to take care of that situation. As for the small fry, " every white, yellow, or black and woolly scamp among them " could be bought, and he would not be niggardly but follow his instructions. And, should all other plans fail :

> I am confident that, if our noble chief, and the others whom we represent should desire to make another effort we might, by addressing ourselves to the amiable enterprise of setting these people together by the ears manage to " divide and

23 Boutwell, *loc. cit.*

24 Kossuth to Sanders, London, July 29, 1852, December 24, 1852; n. p., February 10, 1853. *Political Correspondence of . . . Sanders,* 96-8.

govern," and by subsidizing the stronger party to secure the most advantageous contracts, and a foothold upon this most magnificent Island . . . [25]

The " regeneration " of the Dominican Republic, overthrow of the Negro republic of Haiti, and use of the island as a base for the invasion of Cuba was a favorite scheme of the Cuban annexationists.[26] But Kossuth was not interested in making the West Indies safe for the slave-owners of Cuba and the American South.

The Kossuth affair illustrates the tendency of the Young America movement to hitch liberalism to slavery, intervention in Europe to Cuban annexation. The movement originated [27] in response to Ralph Waldo Emerson's address of 1844 to the Boston Mercantile Library Association on " The Young American." The philosopher expressed mystical faith in the democratic mission of the United States, which he pictured as the leading nation of the world and itself led by young Americans. Untrammeled by decadent feudalism, they marched towards a utopia of self-reliance and individualism by their daring exploitation of free land and free commerce.[28] A small literary school led by the Duyckinck brothers and Parke Godwin adopted Emerson's slogan and called for a nationalist literature free of foreign affectations. The unlikely history of Emerson's notion took form as John L. O'Sullivan made his *Democratic Review* an organ of Young American literary attitudes and twisted the Sage of Concord's meaning in the direction of Manifest Destiny, pro-slavery and Cuban annexation. Edwin

25 Pickett to Henningsen, Santo Domingo, September, 1852. Pickett Papers. See also Theodore O'Hara to Pickett, Frankfort, December 8, 1851. *Ibid.*

26 Editorial of *La Verdad*, quoted in *National Era*, September 4, 1851.

27 The following account, except where other citations are made, is based on Riepma, *Young America*.

28 Ralph W. Emerson, *Nature, Addresses, and Lectures* (Cambridge, 1883), 343-72.

De Leon of Charleston, South Carolina, a southern patriot of the DeBow school, became the leading interpreter of Young America in the South. In his address to the South Carolina College in 1845 on " The Duties and Position of Young America," and for years thereafter, he preached southern unity and expansion as the true creed.

George H. Evans drew reformist implications from the slogan, and applied it to his movement for free homesteads as a cure for unemployment. Parke Godwin supported him, as did a variety of radicals, loco-focos, and westerners in great numbers. This wing of Young America was related to the Free Soil movement and inclined to anti-slavery. It saw the nation's Manifest Destiny through the eyes of the northern pioneer farmer. William M. Corry, a lawyer and editor of Cincinnati, became the spokesman of Young America in the Northwest. For a time, he oriented the movement there towards anti-slavery and free-land agitation.

George Francis Train in his fantastic career and prolific writings tried to fuse Young America, Wall Street, and the Workers' Revolution. Among his exploits were the financing of Donald McKay's clipper ships, a term in an Irish jail as a revolutionist, the promotion of the first street railway in Britain at Liverpool, a campaign for the presidency of the " Australian republic," the organization of Credit Mobilier to finance the Union Pacific Railroad, and leadership of the Marseilles Communards when they marched to Paris in 1870. High finance, socialism, spread-eagle oratory and megalomania made up the eccentric brew of Train's Young Americanism.[29] For good measure, he supported Cuban annexation by filibusters. After all, he wrote, the island was only alluvium washed up by the Mississippi River. " What God has joined together let no man put asunder." Besides, the South wanted Cuba.[30]

29 George F. Train, *My Life in Many States and in Foreign Lands* (New York, 1902).

30 George F. Train, *Young America in Wall Street* (New York, 1857), 322-3.

Foreign immigrants attached themselves to Young America. Herman Kriege tried to give it a socialist cast in his German-American group known as *Jung Amerika*. Other German exiles, disappointed by the defeat of their hopes that the European revolutions of 1848 would establish a liberal international order, turned to the United States and advocated that it create a " republic of the world." Theodore Poesche and Charles Goeppe assured Americans that all the peoples of the world were anxious to be annexed. In Britain, for example, only the Church of England would be found in opposition. As for Cuba, a filibuster expedition would be in order. These desperate dreamers wrote out their plans and dedicated the book: " To Franklin Pierce . . . Being a Guess at the Spirit in Which He Was Elected." [31]

Up to 1850, Young America was Unionist. The sectional struggle of that year, speculation on imperialism, and addiction to states' rights relegated domestic reform to the background and turned many leaders towards the South. This evolution was typified by Corry and the Tammany leader, Mike Walsh. The former abandoned reformist causes, became an intimate associate of George N. Sanders, championed the South, and finally became a secondary Vallandingham in the Civil War. Mike Walsh in the early forties was a radical working-class leader in New York and helped edit the vigorous newspaper, *The Subterranean*. As the popular "poor man's friend" and " Champion of the Young Democracy," Walsh was forced on Tammany for the Assembly in 1845.[32] He became the leader of a Tammany faction of immigrant workers called the " Young Spartans," and rallied it to the cause of free land and Young America in close association with George H. Evans. But after 1850, Free Soil was no longer a going concern in New York politics. Mike Walsh attached himself to Quitman and his

31 Theodore Poesche and Charles Goeppe, *The New Rome, or The United States of the World* (New York, 1852), iii, 74, 90 *et passim.*

32 M. R. Werner, *Tammany Hall* (Garden City, 1932), 44-50.

filibuster enterprises to take Cuba, and boasted of his triumphs in purging from the Democratic leadership of his state the followers of John Van Buren and all those who were tainted with abolitionism under whatever dastardly disguise. In 1853, as he wrote Quitman, he was anxious to take part in an expedition to Cuba, devoted himself almost exclusively to the undertaking and, while most men in New York took a "dollar and cent view" of annexation, he felt it was "pregnant with more to the future of our country—aye of the world than anything now half as likely to take place." [33]

The drift southwards of northern Young Americans fitted into the plans of George N. Sanders. This pro-slavery Kentuckian intended to free Young America of reformist elements unfriendly to the South, unite its factions into a nation-wide movement to revitalize the Democratic Party with a spread-eagle foreign policy, and elect Douglas President to carry it out. The chief appeal would be the one most suited to oratory in all sections: a crusade against the autocrats of Europe. The Manifest Destiny of the United States to expand would be affirmed as a corollary, and southern fears of too much talk about liberty would be quieted by the promise of Cuba.

Sanders' propaganda program was foreshadowed in the resolutions passed by a mass meeting of Cuban sympathizers in Washington when news arrived of the execution of López early in September, 1851. The first resolution expressed sympathy for all oppressed peoples, including those of Europe, India and South Africa, but especially Cuba. The second announced faith that Providence would soon overthrow all tyranny. The third declared it to be the duty of Americans to assist the wretched and establish government by law everywhere. The last resolution was directed against Spanish rule in Cuba.[34] " Young Cuba " was in the vanguard of the groups of exiles the Young Americans organized for the election campaign. " Young Italy,"

33 Walsh to Quitman, New York, October 3, 1853. Quitman Papers.

34 *National Era*, September 11, 1851.

"Young Germany," "Young Ireland," and others gave an authentic flavor of liberalism to the movement.

The ideal of self-determination animated these national groups. Annexation of Cuba to the United States was presented as a practical application of that doctrine. It was the analogue in foreign policy of the "neutral" domestic policy of popular sovereignty as the solution of the slavery-extension problem. Young America would not be guilty of re-opening the sectional struggle. The slavery issue would be shouted down by the revivalists of Jacksonian democracy. Reform on an international scale would shame the petty reformers of domestic institutions. Liberalism and slavery were reconciled. Northern commercial interests would benefit in Europe and Cuba, only Free Soilers and abolitionists would be cast into outer darkness, and the Democratic as the true national Party would triumphantly preserve and expand the Union. This was, after all, Douglas' program, and when Sanders outlined it to him and offered to rally Young America to his standard, the Little Giant happily consented.[35] Pro-slavery filibusters understood the value to their cause of Douglas and Young America, and came to their support. Colonel Theodore O'Hara of Kentucky wrote to Pickett that after he returned from prison in Spain and was lionized in the South, he promptly set about buying a newspaper, the *Yoeman,* to preach Young Americanism and Douglas for President.[36]

But Douglas did not reckon with the explosive methods Sanders considered suitable to blast a place for Young America on the crowded stage of President-makers. In the first, the January, 1852, number of the *Democratic Review* under its new management, Sanders sounded the call to arms. The leading article, "Eighteen-Fifty-Two and the Presidency," expressed disgust with Whig temporizing over Cuba, Spain and expansion in general, and declared that a man must be

35 Douglas to Sanders, Chicago, July 12, 1851. *Correspondence of . . . Sanders,* 42.

36 O'Hara to Pickett, Frankfort, December 8, 1851. Pickett Papers.

nominated by the Democrats who would pursue a foreign policy
of aid to European revolution, protection for filibusters and
expansion. Louis Napoleon's *coup d'etat* was a horrid example
of what President Taylor would have done had he lived and
would be done if the Whigs elected General Scott. The people
of all Europe awaited the unfurling of the American flag to
rise in revolt. The Whigs had thrown away these millions of
" inexpensive " allies. But the year 1852

> beats the roll-call of insurrection. ... He comes, this Brutus
> of years, to restore the will of the people to the rule of the
> United States, and to extinguish under the very dome of the
> capitol the imperial principles of the modern Caesar, even
> through the mantle of the British purple which enfolds them.
> ... The French protected a despotic Pope in Rome—have we
> not maintained a despotic Queen in Cuba?

Gross attacks on the " Old Fogy " candidates for the Democratic nomination were followed by a description of the ideal
candidate, a thin disguise for Douglas:

> The Democratic Party expects from the Baltimore Con-
> vention a new man, a statesman of sound democratic pluck,
> and world-wide ideas to use it on; a State-rights man . . . a
> free-trade man, who will break down the tariffs of every rotten
> monarchy under heaven, and open to the industry and com-
> merce of the United States the trade and exchanges of the
> world; a man of large soul and open heart, who will maintain
> in the teeth of the despots of Europe the democratic doctrines
> upon which his popularity and success are based here; a bold
> man, who can stand the brunt of foreign war, and . . . crush
> the despots of the world in their very dens . . . .   Withal, a
> *practical* statesman, not to be discomfited in argument, or led
> wild by theory, but one who has already, in the councils and
> tribunals of the nation, reared his front to the dismay of the
> shallow " conservative," to the exposure of the humanitarian
> incendiary, and the discomfiture of the antiquated rhetorician.[37]

37 *Democratic Review*, XXX (January, 1852), 1-12.

Whatever might be the wisdom of war upon the Whigs and European despots, Douglas' candidacy was not strong enough to support Sanders' war against other Democratic aspirants. They were bound to unite against Douglas in protection of their own hopes as well as anger at the insults hurled at them in his name. Appalled by Sanders' lack of political acumen, Caleb Cushing, a Douglas supporter of Massachusetts, warned his friend that Sanders antagonized Catholics and was a Red Socialist. Cushing took a dim view of the campaign to capture the vote of reformers. He wrote: " It is not in our power to outdemagogize the Seward men, if we try." [38] This remark by the man who was to be the chief representative of Young America in President Pierce's Cabinet laid bare the political strategy of Sanders: to steal from the anti-slavery men their prestige as radicals. Douglas agreed that Sanders had gone too far.[39] He begged him to desist.[40] Unfortunately, Douglas had at first approved Sanders' article. He and his friends now denied that he had signed a testimonial for the *Democratic Review* after the January number appeared, but their contention was disproved in Congress.[41] The *Southern Quarterly Review* of Charleston did not understand how the southern cause was served by strategy like that of Sanders. It thought Cuban annexation at the cost of rousing so much enthusiasm for liberty would be of dubious value. It preferred to postpone annexation until after the South had seceded from the Union, when it could be achieved without nonsense about liberty.[42]

Sanders nevertheless intensified his campaign. In March, he confessed that Douglas did indeed fulfill his image of the ideal

38 Cushing to Douglas, Newburyport, February 1, 1852. Cushing Papers.

39 Douglas to Cushing, Washington, February 4, 1852. *Ibid.*

40 Douglas to Sanders, Washington, February 10, 1852. *Correspondence of . . . Sanders,* 46.

41 *Congressional Globe* (32:1), 711-4.

42 *Southern Quarterly Review,* XXI (January, 1852), 4 ff.

candidate.[43] Douglas now warned him that his tactics would force him to retire from the field and throw his influence in favor of one of the Old Fogies.[44] Sanders continued to lunge wildly at Cass, Marcy and other elder and ambitious statesmen until the eve of the Baltimore Convention in June.[45] Further indiscretions were blatant articles glorifying Cuban filibusters and associating Douglas with their plans for the future.[46] This contrasted with the tactics of supporters of other candidates. The ardent annexationist Senator Slidell of Louisana counseled Buchanan to keep Cuba in the background.[47] And Senator Robert M. T. Hunter of Virginia, candidate for Vice President on the ticket with Douglas, feared that the Cuban question was one of great danger to the South.[48] Sanders made it easy for Douglas' enemies—who now were mainly his former friends —to kill his candidacy. It was associated with filibusters, jobbers, lobbyists, loafers, and the mad patriots of Young America. In vain, Douglas promised offices to Cass men, Marcy men, Buchanan men. Only Illinois supported him at Baltimore.[49]

Still the nomination of the dark-horse Franklin Pierce of New Hampshire was not a defeat for Young America. He was an expansionist of the Polk school whom the *Herald* called " a discreet representative of Young America." [50] Sanders cheerfully accepted Pierce's nomination as the triumph of the Young

43 *Democratic Review*, XXX (March, 1852), 202-24.

44 Douglas to Sanders, Washington, March 27 and April 15, 1852. *Correspondence of . . . Sanders*, 47, 48.

45 *Democratic Review*, XXX (April, 1852), 366-84; (May, 1852), 425-30.

46 *Ibid.* (January, 1852), 89 ff.; (April, 1852), 307-19.

47 Louis M. Sears, " Slidell and Buchanan," *American Historical Review*, XXVII (July, 1922), 711-2.

48 Hunter to Herschel V. Johnson, Lloyds, Essex County, Virginia, December 2, 1852. *Robert M. T. Hunter Correspondence*, edited by C. H. Ambler, American Historical Association Annual Report, 1916 (Washington, 1918), II, 154.

49 Nichols, *Democratic Machine*, 117-8.

50 New York *Herald*, June 10, 1852.

America movement, and immediately set about propagandizing for his election and the repeal of the neutrality laws by the next —Pierce—administration.[51]

Sanders' assumption was not unfounded. The Southern-rights faction had suggested Pierce to the Convention and the southerners' shift from Buchanan to Pierce at a critical moment had made the latter's nomination possible. On the other hand, many Free Soilers also supported Pierce in the campaign. Pierce was expected to stand on the Compromise and unite all factions. A small group of disunionists nominated George M. Troup of Georgia and John A. Quitman for President and Vice President but they made no headway against the regular ticket. In a desultory campaign, Democratic orators led by Douglas and Senator Pierre Soulé of Louisiana cultivated Young American themes to stir up the electorate. The *Herald* trumpeted:

> National glory—national greatness—the spread of political liberty on this continent, must be the thought by day, and the throbbing dream by night, of the whole American people, or they will sink into oblivion.[52]

Cora Montgomery wrote a book for the campaign that brought to full development the Cuban scheme she had helped launch in 1847. It promoted a comprehensive, pro-southern, imperialist program for the Pierce administration. As sops to the North, she added to the abolition of the Cuban slave trade the freeing of Mexican peons.[53]

Expansionists made capital of an admission by General Scott, the Whig nominee, that he had refused an offer by leading Mexicans when he had conquered their country to take control of it and annex it to the United States.[54] The ease with which

51 *Democratic Review*, XXX (June, 1852), 481-92, 497-512.

52 New York *Herald*, October 11, 1852.

53 Cora Montgomery, *Eagle Pass* (New York, 1852), 97, 137 *et passim*.

54 *Democratic Review*, XXXI (October, 1852), 292.

General Scott offended numerous groups of voters was illustrated when he declared that on racial grounds he favored expansion northwards but not to the south.[55]

Besides publishing a stream of Young American propaganda for Pierce, Sanders sought to tie the candidate firmly to his program. He told Party organizers when they were pressed for funds that if Pierce would come to an understanding with George Law, all the money necessary for the campaign would be furnished. This offer was rejected, but after other efforts to raise money met with little success, August Belmont contributed the amount needed.[56] Belmont was the American agent of the Rothschilds' banking interests and the nephew by marriage of Senator Slidell. Evidently his uncle was not the only politician who drew a sharp distinction between accepting Belmont's money and that of the Steamboat Crowd.[57] The banker's reward was an appointment by President Pierce as Minister to The Hague and an opportunity to work out his scheme for buying Cuba and liquidating Spanish bonds. Thus Cuban interests were served as well as Sanders and Law could have wished and the rectitude of the next administration was preserved.

Sanders' harping in his magazine on his demand for repeal of the neutrality laws suggests that he was interested in the current plans for a filibuster expedition to Cuba. He was particularly interested in obtaining the right of foreign revolutionary groups to buy arms and munitions in the United States.[58] He stoutly maintained the right of exiled revolutionary groups to the assistance of the American government and people in establishing liberty in their homes. Not even free Negroes were safe from these appeals to racial groups. Sanders proposed that they be sent to Africa to conquer it for the United States and

55 *Ibid.* (July, 1852), 65.

56 Nichols, *Democratic Machine*, 161-2.

57 L. M. Sears, *op. cit.*, 714. C. F. Smith, *Sunshine and Shadow in New York*, 666.

58 *Democratic Review*, XXXI (September, 1852), 283.

to " civilize it by the introduction of our system of slavery " as fast as they subdued the natives.[59] This variation on the theme of extending democratic institutions to the oppressed of all lands combined the Ebony Line project with a great market for muskets.

George Law and the filibusters injected some excitement into the Presidential campaign before it closed. After the failure of the Bahia Honda Expedition, Cuban and American filibusters worked to create a new organization in the United States which would give them a wider basis of popular support. The co-operation of Southern Rights Clubs was obtained, and a secret society called the " Order of the Lone Star " was established with locals in southern cities and New York. These functioned in the manner of Masonic lodges. Two representatives from each branch formed the Supreme Council. Quitman was a leading member of the Council. The members of the Order were divided into three grades and were estimated variously to number from fifteen to fifty thousand sworn adherents. The society was founded in New Orleans where the *Delta* office printed its Constitution. This document announced in its Preamble that its authors were " desirous of *Extending the Area of Liberty*," and it was signed by fourteen leaders, including Alexander Walker and Dr. J. V. Wren.[60] Ferencz and Theresa Pulszky, Hungarians who accompanied Kossuth in the United States, wrote that the Order was started principally by " Southern Democrats, with the avowed aim of revolutionizing Cuba, and annexing 'the jewel of the Antilles' to the United States." Those who countenanced such enterprises, this account continued, were denounced by Whigs as pirates, but:

> the success of Texas is a too attractive precedent for the enterprising and adventurous youth of the South, whom the melancholy fate of General López and his companions does not deter. " We failed," said one of the invaders of Cuba to me—a

59 *Ibid.* (August, 1852), 100.

60 *Constitution of the Order of the Lone Star* (New Orleans, 1851).

gentleman who had just returned from his African prison at Ceuta; "therefore we are pirates, had we succeeded, Lopez would have been a second William the Conqueror." [61]

"Division 3" of the Order was called "La Union" and composed of Cuban exiles in New York and John L. O'Sullivan. Another Division in New York was made up of Americans. Ambrosio José Gonzalez succeeded López as military leader of the filibusters. An expedition to Cuba was planned to sail in June, 1852, in conjunction with the Conspiracy of Vuelta Abajo which was organized in the island by Francisco de Frías, the wealthy brother-in-law of López who had bought the title of Count of Pozos Dulces. Its organ was *La Voz del Pueblo,* the first revolutionary newspaper of Cuba, which was printed in the face of frantic efforts by gangs of Spanish agents to suppress it. *La Voz* was printed with type bequeathed to the revolutionaries by John S. Thrasher. The Cubans were said to have been stung into new efforts in their own behalf by a sensational article in which the New York *Herald* turned on them, called them cowards much given to brag and unable to conquer their own liberty. The point was driven home by a cartoon of a Cuban with tongue so large it reached the floor. The Cubans' efforts to live down such insults of their erstwhile friends led only to disaster. One editor of *La Voz* was forced to escape to the United States, another was garrotted, and the Count of Pozos Dulces was sentenced to prison.[62]

The collapse of the Conspiracy of Vuelta Abajo occurred in August and does not explain the failure of the filibusters to sail in June. During the spring, Minister Calderón had information which he transmitted to Secretary Webster that John L. O'Sullivan, Theodore O'Hara and the Cuban exiles were

---

61 Ferencz and Theresa Pulszky, *White, Red, Black* (London, 1853), I, 147-8. See also Alexandre Holinski, *La Californie et les Routes Interocéaniques* (Brussels, 1853), 281.

62 D. Justo Zaragoza, *Las Insurreciones en Cuba* (Madrid, 1872), I, 642-6. Morales, *Iniciadores,* II, 335-7, 359-89.

organizing an expedition to sail from Gulf ports. The leaders of the Order of the Lone Star actively assisted in the project. The Spanish Minister incidentally complained that an attaché of his mission and his footman were beaten up by a respectably dressed young man, and again that Marshall Lemery was attacked on the streets of New York while visiting the city.[63] It is likely that the expedition was postponed when Pierce was nominated in order that the filibusters might help to elect him and claim indulgence towards their enterprise as a reward. Louis Schlesinger, a veteran of the Hungarian revolution and the López expeditions, electioneered for Pierce among foreign groups so effectively that John Van Buren thought he deserved a diplomatic post as a reward.[64] Recruits for the expedition were kept in a state of readiness during the campaign. The leaders expected Quitman to take command once he was assured of a friendly attitude in Washington. They organized a new Cuban Junta in October. Newspapers published rumors of impending events, and Calderón, as he communicated his fears to Webster, assured him that the Spanish government had implicit confidence in the " chivalrous sentiments " of President Fillmore and would shoot all filibusters within three hours of capture.[65]

In September, the Order of the Lone Star began to conduct public meetings in favor of the filibusters. José Ambrosio Gonzalez published in the newspapers a " Manifesto to the American People " describing the sufferings of the Cuban people and asking for aid in like manner as the United States

63 Calderón to Webster, Washington, March 1, 19, May 1, 1852; Calderón to Acting Secretary Hunter, May 7, 14, 1852. Department of State, *Notes from Legations: Spain*, XIV. Webster to Calderón, Washington, June 14, 1852. Department of State, *Notes to Legations: Spain*, VI.

64 John Van Buren to Marcy, New York, April 25, 1853. Marcy Papers. The younger Van Buren abandoned Free Soilism in 1852 and was " regular " during the campaign.

65 Calderón to Webster, Washington, July 1, 1852. Department of State, *Notes from Legations: Spain*, XIV.

during its revolutionary struggles received aid from France. In New York, New Orleans and other cities, " Cuban Guards " companies of filibusters drilled publicly and engaged in target practice. Enoch Camp, Tammany leader and editor of the *Police Gazette,* was Captain of the First New York Company of Cuban Guards.[66] A Mass memorializing López was celebrated on the anniversary of his death in Saint Patrick's Cathedral in New York. Cuban leaders called on Spanish Consuls, read manifestos of their political faith, and then published the documents in the newspapers. Calderón indignantly called attention to the growing boldness of the Cuban movement, but, as the election approached, the administration told him it was not of much importance.[67]

While Cuban Guards marched and countermarched in the streets of American cities, the Captain-General of Cuba created an incident admirably suited to the purposes of annexationists. On September 3, Lieutenant David D. Porter, United States Navy, in command of the United States Mail Steamship Company's *Crescent City,* was told by the Spanish authorities in Havana that his Purser, William Smith, could not go ashore because he had written insultingly of the Captain-General and his government in the New York *Herald.* Eleven days later, the *Crescent City* was forbidden to land at Havana as long as the objectionable Purser was still aboard. Porter left without discharging his mail or passengers and at New Orleans was instructed by George Law to return to Havana with the Purser and attempt to land. He did so, and when the Captain of the Port signalled him to leave, Porter refused, anchored and insisted on his right to discharge and take aboard mail and passengers. The ship was held incommunicado but the resourceful Lieutenant by a trick sent a protest for the Captain-General to

66 New York *Herald,* September 22 and 24, 1852.

67 Calderón to Conrad, Washington, September 30, 1852. Department of State, *Notes from Legations: Spain,* XIV. Conrad to Calderón, Washington, October 7, 1852. Department of State, *Notes to Legations: Spain,* VI. Zaragoza, *op. cit.,* 647-9, Morales, *op. cit.,* 392-404.

the American Consul. In New Orleans, the Company ordered him again to return.

Law and his associates found certain interesting possibilities in the situation. It was an opportunity to challenge both the Spanish authorities and the Whig administration on an issue of American commercial rights. It was even a chance to take action in the spirit of Young America at a moment when voters' enthusiasm needed to be aroused. Marshall O. Roberts wrote to Secretary Webster, then on his deathbed, demanding protection for the Company's ships and redress for the gross insult to the American flag, or alternatively, " to be allowed to redress the grievance and repel the insult to our national flag, with such means and in such manner as we can, and shall deem equal and due to self-protection." [68] The means were apparently Law's plentiful supply of guns, the ships of the Company, and contingents of Cuban Guards. The Order of the Lone Star called public meetings, as one organizer, Francis V. R. Mace, wrote to Quitman, " to impress feelings of resentment for the insult offered to our national colors at Havana." Spain, he continued, did not fear war because she had assurances from Napoleon III. The crisis was at hand. The remainder of this report suggests that Lieutenant Porter had received orders from his Company to do more than merely return to Havana : he would overstay his time limit in Havana and provoke firing on his ship—" which would result in prompt action " by the cohorts of the Lone Star. " A Brigade is now being raised in anticipation of a war with Spain." The grand password had been given out : " *Action! Action!! Action!!!* " [69]

Porter also had orders from the Postmaster General to return to New York with his passengers and mail if he was not

68 Roberts to Webster, New York, October 6, 1852. Department of State, *Consular Despatches: Havana*, XXV.

69 Francis V. R. Mace to Quitman, New Orleans, October 14, 1852. Quitman Papers.

permitted to land them in Havana.[70] In Havana again on October 14, the *Crescent City* was again held incommunicado except for a visit from the American Consul, who took charge of another protest for the Captain-General. The Consul told Porter to leave the port. He did so, but as he passed the Morro he raised the American flag and fired a gun at the fort.[71] Fortunately, the defenders took no notice.

President Fillmore decided that something would have to be done. Newspapers and orators were whipping up patriotic anger at the pusillanimity of an administration that tolerated insults on the country's doorstep from a despotic European monarchy. Many previous incidents as well as the *Crescent City* affair were used to show that the Whigs were in league with autocracy. Acting Secretary Conrad sent a worried inquiry to the Havana Consul as to the truth of public charges that the Spanish authorities customarily rifled American mail bags.[72] Nothing could be accomplished through the Consul, as the new Captain-General Cañedo refused to admit that the *Crescent City* or any such affair involved the commercial and sailors' problems to which the American representative's jurisdiction was confined.[73] The President determined to send Judge Conkling, newly-appointed Minister to Mexico, aboard the frigate *Powhatan* to Havana with an explanation for the Captain-General of the difficult position in which he had placed the administration and a request for concessions. The envoy was provided with an affidavit by Purser Smith declaring his innocence to give to the Captain-General as a basis for leniency. This move was kept secret. The insolent demands of Roberts and Law

70 Acting Consul Morland to Cañedo, Havana, October 14, 1852. Department of State, *Consular Despatches: Havana*, XXV.

71 Porter to Secretary of the Navy Kennedy, n. p., October 24, 1852. *Ibid.*

72 Conrad to Sharkey, Washington, October 11, 1852. Department of State, *Instructions to Consuls*, XIV.

73 Acting Consul Morland to Cañedo, Havana, October 18, 1852. Department of State, *Consular Despatches: Havana*, XXV.

were answered by the removal of Lieutenant Porter from command of the *Crescent City* and a warning to Law on October 25 that the ship might not be permitted to land in Havana if Purser Smith was aboard.[74]

According to Cañedo, a deception was played on him as the Secretary of State sent him a telegram on October 23 assuring him that Smith as well as Porter would be removed from the ship. On that understanding, the Captain-General told Judge Conkling that the *Crescent City* might land at Havana. He did this, as he wrote to Calderón, in order not to increase "the difficulties, which at this moment harass the worthy President Fillmore." [75]

While the Captain-General thus patronized the President, George Law defied them both. He wrote another offensive letter to Conrad [76] and dispatched Purser Smith and his ship to Havana. They arrived on election day, November 2. The Captain-General allowed ship, mail, and passengers to land but not Smith. Law, however, was not satisfied with this or the victory of Pierce at the polls. Cañedo informed the captain of the *Crescent City* that the ship would not again be allowed to land with Smith aboard. Law told Hugh Maxwell, Collector of the Port of New York, that he would nevertheless send the *Crescent City* and the Purser to Havana. If the ship was fired on, she would be surrendered and then he and others would immediately "commence hostilities" against Cuba. Thus tall talk of the election campaign issued in a direct challenge to the defeated administration: Law told Maxwell he would infer he had a "right" to pursue the course described unless Fillmore forbade him. The President in his reply struggled against being cornered. He wrote that he did not admit the right of Law, or

74 Conrad to George Law, Washington, October 25, 1852. Department of State, *Instructions to Consuls*, XIV.

75 Cañedo to Calderón, Havana, October 29, 1852. Department of State, *Notes from Legations: Spain*, XIV.

76 George Law to Conrad, New York, October 27, 1852. Department of State, *Consular Despatches: Havana*, XXV.

any citizen, to threaten a war on his own account and then call on the government to say whether it approved or disapproved such conduct, and assume its approval unless the act was forbidden. Then he wrote a brief exegesis of the Constitutional provision that vested in Congress " *alone* " the power to declare war and added that he presumed Law as a good citizen would not make war on Cuba.[77]

The administration evidently informed the Captain-General that Law was seeking a popular excuse to launch an invasion of the island. Calderón was enlisted to impress this on the Captain-General.[78] On November 16, Cañedo once more lifted the ban on the *Crescent City* and on the 30th he dropped his feud against Purser Smith.[79]

The Fillmore administration could not claim honors in the affair of the *Crescent City* and it had gained no votes for General Scott from that large number of Americans who believed the code duello should be the nation's foreign policy. But it may have prevented an invasion of the island by filibusters that would have embarrassed Everett's attempt in his note of December 1 to Britain and France to give the government's Cuban policy a moral as well as a nationalistic significance.

The whole affair only increased the impatience of the Young Americans. They yearned to smite the despot. They had helped elect Pierce and they were hungry for the fruits. They would wipe out the charge of Free Soilers and abolitionists that the slave power brought shame and dishonor upon the nation in its

77 Fillmore to Maxwell, Washington, November 12, 1852. *Millard Fillmore Papers*, edited by Frank H. Severance (Buffalo, 1907), II, 334-6, *Publications of the Buffalo Historical Society*, XI. See also Henry A. Murray, *Lands of the Slave and the Free* (London, 1857), 153-7.

78 Galliano to Drake & Company, Havana, November 16, 1852. Department of State, *Consular Despatches: Havana*, XXV.

79 Calderón to Everett, Washington, December 10, 1852. Department of State, *Notes from Legations: Spain*, XIV.

foreign policy.[80] The conviction of southerners that slavery for Negroes was the best possible foundation of liberty for whites the Young Americans would now erect into the foreign policy of the United States.

80 This charge was first formally made by the Liberty Party in 1844. K. N. Porter, *National Party Platforms* (New York, 1924), 11.

CHAPTER IX

THE TRIUMPH OF YOUNG AMERICA

FRANKLIN PIERCE won the electoral vote of every state except Massachusetts, Vermont, Kentucky and Tennessee. This great victory was a ratification of the Compromise of 1850 and a mandate to take up expansion where President Polk had left off. But the two policies were incompatible because expansion would re-open the slavery question. Cuba, the Mesilla valley and Central America were looked to for territorial gains, and Nebraska Territory was organized for statehood. Cuba as slavery territory and the Mesilla valley as the route of a transcontinental railroad to link the slave states with the Pacific were desired chiefly by the South. Central America as the site of isthmian connections between the oceans and Nebraska as the route of Douglas' projected railroad to connect Chicago and the Pacific coast were chiefly interesting to northern commercial, shipping, financial and farming groups. Douglas carved Kansas out of Nebraska and offered it to the South for slavery extension in return for votes in favor of his northern transcontinental route. But the repeal of the Missouri Compromise which Douglas' scheme entailed aroused the North and broke the administration before it could win more than the Mesilla valley among its other expansionist goals.

When it took office, the Pierce administration did not intend to throw even the railroad route to the North as a balance for Cuba and the Mesilla valley. Polk had won at least part of the northern program in Oregon. Canada was remote as a field for northern expansion, particularly after the Reciprocity Treaty of 1854 satisfied the Canadian wheat-growers who had pondered annexation to the United States when the Repeal of the Corn Laws destroyed their protected market in Britain. Pierce in his small way had been one of the expansionists of 1844. In 1853, he intended to pursue the southern program that had been formulated originally by the imperialists of Mississippi, Robert J. Walker, Jefferson Davis, John A. Quitman, Albert G. Brown, Henry S. Foote and Jacob Thompson.[1]

Young America had won northern democratic idealists and commercial interests to support Pierce. Douglas' Nebraska program was calculated to make the Northwest safe for slavery extension. Polk had narrowly escaped the Wilmot Proviso when he pursued the dual program of expansion into Oregon as well as Texas and Mexico. After the issue was with so much difficulty settled in 1850. Pierce dared to re-open it on the assumption of southerners that extension of slavery territory would not violate the Compromise. If there was a " plot " by southerners during the decade before the firing on Fort Sumter, this was it: to win an extension of slavery territory in defiance of the Compromises of 1820 and 1850 or secede from the Union.

The unity of the Democratic Party on which the southerners depended for success was more complete in 1853 than at any time since Jackson had left the White House. Yet it rested precariously on a coalition of northern Free Soilers, conservative Unionists, and States'-Rights southerners. The loyalty of the first and last groups was dictated more by expediency than conviction, and immediately after Pierce's election the struggle began in Congress to impose a policy on the next administration. Southerners like Soulé, who had fought the Compromise and called for secession when it passed, had already united on the program of Young America with northerners devoted to the Union like Douglas. Those two had dominated the campaign for Pierce. Their specific aims were not incompatible as Soulé wanted Cuba and Douglas, quite willing that the South should have the island, was chiefly interested in opening the West for a railroad to complete the transportation system that would make Chicago the trade capital of the nation. They

1 William E. Dodd, *Jefferson Davis* (Philadelphia, 1907), 64-7.

hoped now to commit Congress to their program and ensure that Pierce would make the Young American program his own.

During the short session of Congress between Pierce's election and inauguration, the question of Cuba was injected into debates on any subject as representatives of all shades of opinion took position in relation to the Young Americans. In July, 1852, in response to an unconsidered resolution of the House, the Fillmore administration had published confidential correspondence covering relations with Spain over many years, including, most pointedly, the Polk attempt to buy Cuba.[2] To this material for debate, the President in his Message of December added his views on recent events. He admitted that no permanently satisfactory arrangement had emerged from the *Crescent City* affair and announced that he had rejected the tripartite convention because it was " of doubtful constitutionality, impolitic, and unavailing." He warned that annexation would nevertheless be a very hazardous measure:

> It would bring into the Confederacy a population of a different national stock, speaking a different language, and not likely to harmonize with the other members. It would probably effect, in a prejudicial manner, the industrial interests of the South; and it might revive those conflicts of opinion between the different sections of the country, which lately shook the Union to its center, and which have been so happily compromised.

Furthermore, the interventionism preached by Young America would combine all Europe against the United States. Americans should spread their institutions by their example, not by force as proposed by filibusters of low motives.[3]

Immediately after the reading of the Message, Weightman, the delegate in the House of Representatives of New Mexico, declared his resentment of the President's slur against Spanish-speaking people in Cuba and in his own constituency. He

2 *House Executive Documents* (32:1), 121.

3 *Congressional Globe* (32:2), 7-11.

wanted five thousand copies of the Message printed in Spanish. Homogeneity, he said, was the principle of Europe and of centripetal consolidation in the United States. Diversity, on the other hand, preserved the rights of the states. The American government was capable of making more than one race of people happy and he expected it to annex a great deal of territory to the south.[4]

With this for a beginning, the session was with difficulty kept in the course of ordinary business and away from the subject of Cuba. When the tariff was debated, a protectionist, Jones of Pennsylvania, turned the argument that the Treasury was accumulating a dangerous surplus into an appeal to expansionists to maintain the rates because, he said, the government had need of money in the face of European events that threatened Cuba.[5] Johnson of Georgia eagerly agreed that the surplus might be used to buy the island.[6]

Abolitionists forced the Cuban question completely into the open. Joshua R. Giddings of Ohio, the uncompromising veteran of many battles against the apologists of slavery, made a speech on December 14 that ignored all issues involved in the question except the burning one of the South's peculiar institution. He began quietly by defending the President against the assaults of southern newspapers for publishing the Spanish correspondence. The documents proved, the Ohio Representative said, that for thirty years the Executive had worked to maintain slavery in Cuba in order to strengthen it in the United States. He was bitter against Webster for opposing emancipation in the island in 1843. Others might eulogize the dead statesman but it was right and proper that the evil deeds of statesmen be remembered. The evidence of Whig perfidy made Giddings doubt the honesty of Whig promises in the recent election. Abolitionists had been told, he said:

4 *Ibid.*, 12, 19.

5 *Ibid.*, *Appendix*, 29.

6 *Congressional Globe* (32:2), 49.

that unless we voted for the Whig candidate, if we permitted the Democratic candidate to be elected, Cuba would be annexed and slavery extended and strengthened in the United States. Plausibility was given to this argument by a certain distinguished Senator from the West [Douglas], who traveled somewhat extensively, making speeches in favor of Cuban annexation and filibustering expeditions to that Island.

Annexation by purchase would fail, Giddings believed, because the lower House would never appropriate the money. The free states stood only to lose by annexation. The three-fifths rule would give the whites of Cuba a large representation in the House. The Spanish Army in Cuba was twice as big as the whole American Army, and the cost of maintaining such a force to hold the Cuban slaves in check, besides other expenses, would make Cuba a net drain on the national Treasury of twenty million dollars. The great object of southerners was to increase the value of their slaves by creating a demand for them in the island. But annexation would precipitate civil war there, it would spread to the Gulf states, and the fire would rage until slavery was consumed. "Then we will make peace with the Negroes and admit them to the enjoyment of their liberty."

This vision of abolition through annexation did not make the Ohioan want the island. He was willing to let Britain have it, and assured that country that the United States would not fight over it. Since Spain would not sell and would free the slaves rather than allow filibusters to capture Cuba, and abolitionists turned the public against their schemes, " our political fillibusters will now disappear. They will escape the garrote, but will be reserved for political suffocation." [7]

John P. Hale of New Hampshire was Giddings' wittier but no less ardently abolitionist counterpart in the Senate. He had been read out of the Democratic Party for his refusal to support the annexation of Texas, returned to the Senate as the

[7] *Ibid., Appendix,* 39-40.

leader of an independent movement in 1846, and was the candidate for the Presidency of the Free Soil Party in 1852. He had received even less support than Van Buren in 1848. The legislature of his state returned to orthodoxy under the influence of Pierce so that the good-humored and popular idealist was temporarily leaving the Senate. On December 21, he arose to mock the anxieties of Cuban annexationists. A New Hampshire editor had made a semiofficial statement for the President-elect that all former factionalists of the Democratic Party were forgiven and would have an equal chance at offices. That left, Hale said, Young Americans and Old Fogies on " the anxious stool." Nor did the editor make it clear that Pierce thought the Gulf of Mexico was " our basin of water." Worst of all:

> He is also entirely silent about Cuba, the great question—the question of questions—about which all hearts are palpitating. *sic* ... Why, sir, patriotism is impatient under check to go and plant the standard of republican liberty on the shores of Cuba, and to extend the area of freedom over that Island. There are a great many who, with a patriotic devotion and a patriotic desire to outrun the impulses of Democracy, are anxious to be beforehand on this subject. They are left in the most frightful state of uncertainty . . . .

Hale then satirized the fears of sugar planters that they would be injured by annexation. Such doubts by southerners, he said, had more effect on prudent politicians than a dozen condemnations by northerners.[8]

Two days later, Senator James M. Mason of Virginia, Chairman of the Committee on Foreign Relations, resolved to take the lead away from opponents of annexation and give the moderate leaders of the Democratic Party an opportunity to present their views. He offered a resolution asking the President for the correspondence on the rejected tripartite convention and made clear his own position. He did not agree with the President's statement in his Message that annexation now

8 *Congressional Globe* (32:2), 109-10.

was fraught with serious peril. An alliance between Britain and France against acquisition of the island by the United States was to be feared. Speaking " as a Senator from the South," Mason said he was content with Cuba under Spain unless it could be acquired peacefully from that country or at the request of Cubans after they overthrew it. Interference by Europe might hasten annexation but could not prevent it, for it was inevitable and merely a question of time and method.[9]

Mason fairly expressed the attitude of Democrats from the border slave states. Cass of Michigan seconded Mason in a speech that was Young American in all but its regard for legal niceties. He professed faith in Manifest Destiny and wanted the United States to buy Cuba. However, he denied charges in the press that he favored filibusters and he called George Law's behavior in the *Crescent City* affair " presumptuous and unpatriotic." Cass wanted Cuba chiefly for its military position as the " true key to the Mississippi," but he also objected to British abuse of American slavery interests. He did not fear the foreign population of the island: security and prosperity following annexation would create unity.[10]

These speeches elicited a moderate reply from Joseph R. Underwood, a Whig of Kentucky. He favored progress and wanted a Pacific railroad to be built from the mouth of the Ohio River in order to cement the Union and carry the trade of Brazil and the West Indies. But he was against " all efforts to instruct mankind by whipping them with the implements of war into a knowledge of the truth." Filibustering would be fatal to the Union. The annexation of foreigners might produce " the taint of death." The purchase of Cuba would be too expensive. He looked for progress not through revolutions, aggressions or interventions, but through hard work, the spread of the doctrines of the Bible, intelligence, justice and peace.[11]

9 *Ibid.*, 139-40.

10 *Ibid.*, 140-1.

11 *Ibid.*, 142-5.

The extreme and the moderate opponents as well as the moderate supporters of Cuban annexation had now been heard and only the Young Americans remained. Speaking for them, Senator Soulé said they were unprepared for the subject but the turn the debate had taken forced them to meet it, and he asked for a postponement. Senator Gwin of California said that he, too, was interested because his state sent several million dollars in gold by way of Cuba every two weeks. After some wrangling, the Senate agreed to Soulé's motion.[12]

In the lower House, E. C. Cabell of Florida introduced a new theme in a resolution to complete the fortifications at Key West and the Tortugas. He connected the project with the acquisition of Cuba, which was, he said, " by far the most important question pending in this country." But he anticipated trouble with Britain or France if not Spain when the United States " conquered " the island and the fortifications would control the water passage to the Gulf. Indeed they would give the United States strategic control of Cuba with or without annexation, so he claimed the support of all factions.[13]

After the Christmas recess, both Houses debated annexation in earnest. Representative Venable, a Democrat of North Carolina, dissociated himself from his party colleagues of the South. He believed that the American mission was to spread democratic institutions by example rather than expansion. The filibusters made Americans seem to be " the brigands of the world." No one could be ignorant of the true cause that made Cuba desirable, which was slavery. Venable claimed that Calhoun, two days before he died, had charged him to give the world his opinion on Cuba if he was misrepresented. Calhoun had not favored annexation. Venable had been present when Cuban exiles discussed López's plans with Calhoun and the latter said: " ' Gentlemen, you are mistaken; Cuba is not ripe for revolution; her people are not ready for such a state of

12 *Ibid.*, 146-7.

13 *Ibid., Appendix*, 47-52.

things; and if Lopez invades Cuba, the enterprise will be a failure, and I tell you that under no circumstances can this Government be complicated with this revolution.' " And he often said to Venable that nothing but unavoidable necessity could justify force in taking the island.

It was not opposition to slavery that made the North Carolinian oppose annexation. Rather he feared that slaves would be drained to the island from the Atlantic states which were already deficient in that form of labor. And he wished to protect the South from the northern hostility he believed would revive if it acquired more territory. World opinion also dictated caution:

> Can any one from the slaveholding country fail to see that the slave interest in the United States is the focus against which the sympathies, the meddlesome sympathies of the whole world is directed? Can any one fail to see the importance of having as many interested in that institution as possible? Suppose we could absorb Cuba today, we should have the united opposition of all the governments of the earth against us, and against our institution.

As it was, Spain as " stakeholder " of Cuba necessarily befriended the institution in the councils of Europe. The argument that the United States should bestow liberty on the Cubans Venable dismissed with scorn. He had formerly believed sophomoric talk about liberty but he had seen it associated with all kinds of fanaticism and thought that every nation that could take care of its liberty already had it. Underneath the pretext of loving justice, liberty and human rights, lay the real purposes of plunder and robbery.[14]

Alexander H. Stephens of Georgia found one thing objectionable in Venable's speech. Stephens as a Whig had earlier opposed both expansion and the Wilmot Proviso. But in 1852 he had turned against Scott because of his alleged Free Soil tendencies and supported Douglas and Pierce. Now he used

14 *Congressional Globe* (32:2), 189-92.

the Douglas doctrine of popular sovereignty to reprove Venable
for his statement that acquisition of Cuba would violate the
Compromise of 1850. That doctrine he hailed as one of the
greatest triumphs of republicanism since the foundation of the
government because it meant that Cuba could enter the Union
as a slave state without anyone having the right to object. Still
he was against annexation because he saw no benefit to be
gained by it.[15]

Albert G. Brown of Mississippi totally disagreed with
Venable. He broke the silence of the extreme annexationists
because, he said, he was so disturbed to see his former associate
from North Carolina surrounded by admiring Whigs as he
filibustered against the United States. It seemed he had abandoned his old States'-Rights friends and gone over to the
enemy. When they two had stood shoulder to shoulder battling
on the shores of the Pacific, what were they battling for but the
right to carry slavery to California? Brown said he wanted
it distinctly understood now that he wanted Cuba as an outlet
for slavery. In the extension of the area of slavery he saw safety
for the South and no harm to the rest of the Union. The institution was moving south as it had been since New England
emancipated its slaves. When the Deep South found its slaves
too numerous, troublesome and profitless, it, too, wanted a
South to which it could sell them. Venable hastened to assure
Brown that he was not opposed to extending the area of slavery.
He only feared that Spain would emancipate the Cuban slaves
before it would allow the United States to take the island, and
he also objected to filibustering. Brown answered that if Spain
freed the slaves, they would have to be re-enslaved. As for
filibustering,

> I am for no filibustering in the ordinary acceptance of the
> term. But I will tell you what I am for. I am for this: I
> am for demanding and exacting, at all times, and under all
> circumstances, a proper respect for the flag of this country,

15 *Ibid.*, 192-3.

and if in doing that, we should become involved in a war with Spain, or with any other country, I am for fighting it out; and if in the general settlement, we can get nothing but land, I am willing to take land. (Laughter.) Venable: So am I.

The *Crescent City* affair, Brown continued, was a good occasion to speak boldly and act firmly. " If war had come, why let it come; if Cuba was acquired, why let it be acquired; and if the people of North Carolina wanted to carry their slaves there, let them carry them there." Venable now prodded the Mississippian and elicited a statement that he might favor annexation of Canada if northern brethren showed themselves liberal in allowing the South to obtain a little more land; but he admitted that a vast amount of his zeal and enthusiasm would ooze out very suddenly if Cuba came to the United States as a free state. Wilcox of Mississippi said he completely approved Brown's views. He foresaw the possibility that acquisition of Cuba might become a " public necessity " to the South if it seceded from the Union.[16]

William H. Polk, a Young American of Tennessee and brother of the former President, welcomed Brown's suggestion that grievances against Spain be pressed to the point of war. The Thrasher case particularly, he believed, justified a declaration of war. The administration broke down the respectability and honor of the United States by its supine attitude towards Spain. Joseph Lane, who had been appointed Governor of Oregon by President Polk and was now its Delegate, declared that the authorities of Cuba had committed a heavy sin in the massacre of the filibusters that would be wiped out only by their overthrow.[17] A northern Whig, Brooks of New York, defended the administration and Spain against these attacks. The trial Thrasher had received compared favorably, he said, with the drum-head procedure of General Jackson in the similar cases of Arbuthnot and Ambrister. Publication of the

16 *Ibid.*, 193-5.

17 *Ibid.*, 209-13.

Spanish correspondence would make the public pause and think
If the Pierce administration instituted policies of propaganda
and plunder, it would only hurry the return of the Whigs because the public would appreciate conservatism by contrast. He
pleaded:

> The sword, the bayonet, and the cannon ball are not the
> missionaries that are exalting our people among the nations
> of the earth. Every ragged dirty letter from an Irishman,
> or German, sent to the banks of the Shannon, the Liffey, the
> Rhine, the Danube, the Elbe, or the Weser, setting forth the
> rates of wages, the demand for employment, the abundance of ·
> bread, the happiness of himself, his wife, his children, or the
> general glory, peace, and prosperity of this our great country,
> is more of a propagandist, more of a missionary for converting
> the other nations of the world than an army of five hundred
> thousand men, with great parts of artillery.[18]

Representative Howard of Texas threatened Spain with a
quotation from Kent: "A rational fear of an immediate danger
is said to be a justifiable cause of war." The Gulf states,
Howard explained, would never permit Spain to abolish slavery
in Cuba because they could not allow such an example to be
successful so near their shores. The instinct of self-preservation
was too strong. Any attempt of that sort would be followed by
an immediate seizure of Cuba. If the federal government did
not act, the slave states of the Gulf coast would take matters
into their own hands. He was sure that northern commercial
and manufacturing interests would not allow the Union to be
dissolved over annexation of Cuba.[19]

While the Cuban debate in the House led to talk of secession
and war, the Senate with greater restraint struggled to formulate a policy that would serve notice on the new administration
of its members' views. On January 3, 1853, Mason's resolution

18 *Ibid.*, 212-5.

19 *Ibid., Appendix*, 80-1.

was passed, but before the scheduled debate on the tripartite convention could be held, Senator Cass had introduced two resolutions that concentrated attention on positive policy for the future. The first was a general statement that the United States declared the American continents were henceforth not to be considered as subjects for colonization by any European power. Cass showed in his speech that he intended to warn against British expansion in Central America and French projects for colonizing Sonora as well as against designs by both countries on Cuba. But in his second resolution a threat of force was attached only to a warning against efforts on the part of any other power to gain possession of the Spanish island.[20] Even so, the resolution caused animadversion, Cass said, because it did not announce that the United States wanted to purchase Cuba. In a long speech, the Michigan Senator amplified his earlier views. He believed that Britain and France had known the United States would reject the tripartite convention and had wanted it rejected as an excuse for action against Cuba. His resolutions were necessary in order at least to delay them. The declaration that the United States would fight might do some good and even those who opposed the resolutions admitted that they would go to war if Britain or France acted.[21]

Senator Andrew P. Butler of South Carolina agreed with Cass in everything except that he doubted the wisdom of making generalizations before a concrete situation arose. He expected all the Caribbean islands to be " de-Europeanized." " Why, sir, you might as well attempt to stop the progress of the Mississippi with a hundle of hay, as to stop the progress of American influence upon this continent." If a test of title to Cuba came with Britain, he was sure the American people would not be found wanting. They did not require resolutions.[22]

20 *Congressional Globe* (32:2), 199.

21 *Ibid.*, *Appendix*, 90-6.

22 *Ibid.*, 96.

Senator Hale had introduced an amendment to Cass's second resolution that duplicated it except for the word " Canada " instead of " Cuba." He complained that although his amendment was the order of business, Senators contrarily insisted on debating Cuban annexation. The strategic position of Canada he believed was much more important than that of the island. Cass, when he was Presidential candidate of the Democratic Party in 1848, did not go to bed a single night beyond the reach of British shells. This brought a retort from Cass that he nevertheless slept very comfortably. The two Senators then agreed that he had been safe from both the election and gunfire. Hale pointed out that the internal commerce which was in danger from Canada was larger than the total foreign commerce of the United States. Should not the United States tell Britain not to sell Canada to third parties? Britain had never been offered a hundred million dollars, and might accept it. He thought citizens of the northern states, even of Michigan, might extend a little of that vigilance which had been freely extended southwards to the north. " It is a very remarkable fact in our history, whenever we have made a treaty relating to our northern boundary, you always cut off, and when we negotiate a treaty relative to our southern boundary, we have taken on." If control of the Gulf was desired, the Bahamas commanded it strategically even more than Cuba, so why did not the United States tell Britain not to sell them? If the Monroe Doctrine was to be enforced against colonization, the time had come for action, because Britain had colonized the Bay Islands of Honduras. Why pick on Spain? It was weaker than Britain, but, Hale said, he did not want to be invidious.[23]

This devastating assault was only feebly met by Mason, who said that the Monroe Doctrine was confined to Spanish America. Hale's speech laid the basis for a motion by Dixon, Clay's successor from Kentucky, that the Cass resolutions be referred to the Committee on Foreign Relations with instruc-

23 *Ibid.*, 97-9.

tions to examine the Clayton-Bulwer Treaty and ascertain whether Britain, by colonization in Central America or otherwise, had violated it. This motion eventually passed, but not before Soulé secured a postponement [24] and delivered the outstanding speech for Young America on Cuba.

The Louisiana Senator's impressive manner, romantic background as a French revolutionary, and position in the minds of many as a spokesman of the incoming administration made his address of extraordinary interest to Europe as well as America. He began, on January 25, by rejecting the positions of Cass and Mason as too moderate. The Pierce administration was bequeathed "a fearful inheritance of difficulties and dangers" in regard to Cuba. Senators were unwilling to commit theft in taking Cuba but were ready to receive stolen goods by purchase from Spain. The filibusters were no more marauders than had been Lafayette and Kosciusko when they aided the American Revolution. The Fillmore administration had acted on the side of Spain and against American citizens in the López and *Crescent City* affairs. Soulé suspected the Whigs wanted to postpone annexation until Britain freed the slaves in the island. He warned the South against Spain's policy of Africanizing Cuba as the only alternative to Spanish rule. Filibusters could point to earlier British and Spanish governments and men like Alexander Hamilton and the Americans who aided Texas against Mexico as practitioners of their methods. The purchase method was "obsolete" in the face of the pride of Cubans as well as Castilians. The independence of Cuba was just as desirable as annexation but military conquest was well suited to the spirit of the epoch of Young America.[25]

This speech made Soulé, in the opinion of Pierce, not unworthy to be Minister to Spain. Soulé would have preferred appointment as Minister to Russia but its government objected. A prime object of the administration was to get Soulé out of

24 *Congressional Globe* (32:2), 330; *Appendix*, 100-2.

25 *Ibid., Appendix,* 118-23.

Louisiana and leave Slidell in undisputed control of that state. Foreknowledge of his appointment to Spain would not have deterred Soulé from making the speech: he publicly supported the filibusters even more ardently after he was named Minister. Although they were widely regarded then and by later students as mere bombast, the details of Soulé's views were highly significant. As will appear, his opposition to Cuban purchase, favorable word for independence rather than annexation, and advocacy of filibustering coincided with the latest attitudes of the Cuban Junta, and became the policies of the Pierce administration.

Cass was not to be outdone. He assured the Senate that Soulé's program had such respectable sponsors as Jefferson and Monroe.[26] The course of this " Old Fogy " suggests not only his desire to live down the insult of Sanders, but also that he feared northern and conservative Democrats would be left behind the march of their southern colleagues and found " disloyal." Contempt for such cravenness and the realization that southern aims could be achieved only through the assistance of northern allies were evidently the reasons why Senators like Hale and Seward answered Cass rather than the fire-eaters. Seward, the outstanding Whig and Republican expansionist during the fifties and sixties, made significant conditions without which he would oppose annexation of Cuba. Jeering at Cass, he said he was glad the Michigan Senator had at last joined the expansionist John Quincy Adams whom he had formerly calumniated. As for himself, he would vote for Hale's amendment, but he did not see how he could support annexation of Cuba until slavery ceased to counteract the workings of nature in that beautiful island, or even then unless it came with the consent of Spain and without internal dissension in the United States. He did not believe Britain or France wanted Cuba. Their principles would require them to free the slaves and pay the owners. In fact, the Cuban issue was obsolete.

26 *Ibid.*, 123-4.

Commercial expansion was the order of the day and the Pacific Ocean, its isles and continents, was the proper sphere of American interest.[27] Cass was enraged by Seward's speech, which he called the most disingenuous, self-complacent and patronizing he had ever heard in the Senate. Angry interchanges and calls to order followed.[28] But Seward had made clear the position of northern expansionist Whigs: slavery forbade annexation of Cuba.

Senator Stephen R. Mallory of Florida, who had defeated Yulee in an election without opposing his views on Cuba, attacked Seward's argument and defended the strategic and commercial importance of Cuba. He praised Everett for his support of Manifest Destiny. After letting slip the remark that heaven helped those who helped themselves, Mallory denied that he meant it literally in regard to Cuba. He wanted the United States to repeal its trade discriminations in order to speed the Americanization of the island. Then annexation would become a political necessity to the United States.[29] Senator Gwin despaired of a chance to speak on Cuba. He said that everyone was so anxious to be heard on it that the business of the session was being neglected. He moved postponement of the debate on Cuba until after March 4, when it should be continued in executive session. Hale accused him of wanting to postpone until many anti-annexation Senators had left, and suggested that Canada be debated immediately.[30]

To fend off the irrepressible abolitionist, Senators Mason and Jefferson Davis turned to the question of British colonization of the Bay Islands. And on February 1, the former introduced resolutions of the Committee on Foreign Relations in favor of acquiring the isthmus crossing at Tehuantepec.[31]

27 *Ibid.*, 125-7.

28 *Ibid.*, 127-9.

29 *Ibid.*, 130-1.

30 *Ibid.*, 131.

31 *Ibid.*, 132-4.

This successfully diverted southerners, who had a special interest in the Mexican route to the Pacific, but Cuba continued to crop up and on February 14, Douglas, more moderately than in the election campaign, said he expected the island to follow the path of Texas into the Union. Then he bickered with Cass over the respective merits of the titles " Old Fogy " and " Young American." [32]

Thus the Cuban debate ended on the note Sanders had sounded at the opening of the 1852 campaign. It had shown that annexation of the island was the most important specific action expected of the Pierce administration. While Sanders' wild tactics had made many enemies, the popular support he had won by his general strategy of veiling the desire for Cuba in the panoply of a crusade for the extension of liberty made it politically expedient for Old Fogies to give way and, as administration leaders under Pierce, work to carry out the Young American program. Pierce himself, by no means an Old Fogy, was influenced by demonstrations of Young American strength. In the days prior to his inauguration, the inner band of Young American leaders, including Sanders, Law, O'Sullivan, Soulé, Corry and Henningsen, were often seen together and in consultation with the President-elect.[33]

Their work bore fruit in President Pierce's Inaugural Address. Its most striking feature was his famous statement that, since expansion had in the past strengthened the nation:

> With an experience thus suggestive and cheering, the policy of my administration will not be controlled by any timid forebodings of evil from expansion. Indeed, it is not to be disguised that our attitude as a nation, and our position on the globe, render the acquisition of certain possessions not within our jurisidiction, eminently important for our protection, if not, in the future, essential for the preservation of the rights of commerce and the peace of the world.

32 *Ibid.*, 173-5.

33 Riepma, *Young America*, 271 *et passim.*

Acquisitions would be made, the new President said, in no grasping spirit, " but with a view to obvious national interest and security," and by the strictest legal methods. This placed Cuban annexation first on the agenda of Pierce's foreign policy. He allowed himself a brief flight in the spirit of Young American oratory: The history of the American people was short, he said, " but if your past is limited, your future is boundless. Its obligations throng the unexplored pathway of advancement, and will be limitless as duration." And he granted recognition to the Young American desire for intervention in Europe as he said that the appeal to Americans' sympathy of the cause of liberty was their only interest abroad. On the Monroe Doctrine, he spoke plainly although he did not name it: " The rights, security, and repose of this Confederacy reject the idea of interference or colonization on this side of the ocean by any foreign power beyond present jurisdiction, as utterly inadmissible." The new President's conception of the relation between Cuban annexation and the slavery issue was implied in his eloquent plea to abide by the Compromise of 1850 and intense hope that the question of slavery would be finally removed from politics.[34]

In other words, Pierce's view was that faithful adherence to the Compromise required that no objection be made by the North if Cuba became one or more slave states in the Union. The belief he stated in his Inaugural, that slavery stood like any other right recognized by the Constitution, included belief in the right to expand slavery territory. Obviously, he did not expect such expansion to light those sectional fires that he wished more than anything to quell. A more profound misjudgment was seldom made by an American President. Merely the attempt to grant slave-owners permissive rights in Kansas wrecked his administration and tore apart the Union. But this misjudgment was the common coin of the day and Pierce was little else than an agent of its creators, willing to act on it in

34 *Congressional Globe* (32:2), *Appendix*, 244.

the case of Cuba until his equally passive acceptance of the Kansas-Nebraska Bill revealed the tragic error.

The event was also ironic because Pierce's chief aim when he launched his administration was unity of the sections in the nation and of the factions in the Democratic Party. If he could achieve the latter, the former would naturally follow, and he set out to do it by the seemingly practical route of the patronage. Indeed he worked so assiduously to placate the States'-Rights faction that conservative Unionists complained their loyalty was being made its own reward. The lack of a higher motive of unity than the patronage and the inability of leaders to recognize the force of a moral issue have been said to explain the failure of the Pierce administration.[35] Young American idealism was intended to be a higher motive but it was even less effective than the patronage as a principle of Democratic cohesion because Free Soilers, at least, found Cuban slavery as gross an ingredient in it as the slavery in Kansas which finally revealed the moral bankruptcy of the Democratic Party.

Still Cuban annexationism did unite States'-Rights and Union Democrats, many Old Fogies were sporting the habiliments of Young America, and no other foreign policy united as many members of Pierce's Cabinet and diplomatic corps. This was the end result of the President's attempts to satisfy everybody. In the headlong jockeying for spoils and influence, only Douglas among the expansionist leaders failed to win offices for friends who would strengthen annexationism in the administration. In the opinion of some, he had recently " sold out " to anti-slavery men and recommended them for office.[36] However, the appointment of Soulé to Madrid was considered a compliment to Douglas. Young America of the Northwest was consoled by the appointment of Robert McClelland, former Governor of Michigan, as Secretary of the Interior. The outstanding Young American in the Cabinet was Caleb Cushing of

35 Nichols, *Democratic Machine*, 221-6.

36 *Ibid.*, 198-200.

Massachusetts as Attorney General. A renegade Whig and Cuban annexationist,[37] he was anathema to Free Soilers. For Pierce, he was a New Englander who would please the South. Cushing was second in Cabinet influence to Jefferson Davis, the Secretary of War. The latter represented the extreme States'-Rights faction. He had counseled resistance to the Compromise until just prior to the campaign of 1852. Although he did not indulge in Young American postures, he impressed on the administration's expansion policy a strictly southern orientation. He worked in close harmony with Cushing and the two men secured the appointment of Soulé and other Young American diplomats despite the opposition of Secretary of State William L. Marcy.[38]

The Young Americans fought hard against the appointment of Marcy, whom they considered the worst of all the Old Fogies.[39] But such southern expansionists as Davis and Quitman had favored Marcy for the Presidency,[40] and the greater influence in the Cabinet of Davis and Cushing as well as Marcy's own assumption that an expansionist record would help him at the next Democratic Convention reduced the unfavorable effects of having an opponent of Young America as " premier " in the Cabinet. And the Assistant Secretary of State, A. Dudley Mann, a Young American hero ever since his mission to Hungary during its revolt against Austria in 1849, was expected to, and did, create a favorable atmosphere in the Department of State. On the other hand, the appointments of the Old Fogies Buchanan as Minister to Britain and John Y. Mason of Virginia as Minister to France were pleasing to Young Americans because they were accus-

37 Claude M. Fuess, *The Life of Caleb Cushing* (New York, 1923), II, 159-61.

38 Dodd, *Jefferson Davis*, 131-7.

39 Riepma, *Young America*, 270.

40 J. Addison Thomas to Marcy, New York, February 9, 1852. Marcy Papers.

tomed to favor the South, had supported Cuban annexation in Polk's Cabinet and were ready to co-operate heartily with their juniors in Europe.

Another such "honorary" Young American was August Belmont. The banker's proposition asking for the diplomatic post at Naples in return for past and future financial aid, and outlining his weird plan for Cuban annexation was apparently first made to Marcy, through the latter's political friend, W. J. Staples, shortly after the November elections. As Belmont's scheme was adopted by the administration, it is reproduced in Staples' words:

> It was only a few days previous to [publication of the Spanish correspondence] that Mr. Belmont stated a proposition to me in reference to this Cuba question which it then struck me was entitled to some consideration. He is desirous of the appointment of Chargé des Affaires at Naples, and thinks that he might render important services at that Post, from his connection with the Rothschilds, their various & extended influence, his familiarity with the European languages, his knowledge of the private history, and character, of some of the individuals, who would, most probably, possess a personal interest, & exercise a direct influence, in such a negociation as he contemplates.
>
> It seems that one of Belmont's oldest, & closest personal friends, is in high favor at the Court of Madrid—in fact the same individual who was principally influential in successfully negociating the Montpensier Marriage—as it was called —an affair you will doubtless recollect as having caused such a commotion amongst the politicians of Europe, excited the ire of England and ultimately, as one of its consequences, gave us the diplomatic presence of Sir Henry Bulwer. This friend of Belmont, is said to possess immense wealth, & is also endowed with *attractive personal* recommendations, and either quite recently, or at no remote date, held a delicate position of a peculiar nature in relation to a certain exalted personage, as the phrase goes, who is by the way not remarkable for either chastity or patriotism. This exalted personage is

also a member of the Royal family at Naples and as neither purity nor patriotism are supposed to be more in fashion there than at Madrid, and as at both points, bankruptcy and venality are not terms without meaning, entirely, our friend calculates, with no little confidence, upon the use to which he might put his *financial* knowledge. Belmont does not lack ability, and his patriotism and zeal may be relied upon I think. He also suggests, that, as the salary attached to the appointment is no object, he might, by the offer of pecuniary inducements, relieve the Administration from another postulant.[41]

Belmont's "*financial* knowledge," it developed, concerned the defaulted Spanish bonds which he intended to have paid with money the United States would give Spain for Cuba. Apparently the Rothschilds had sufficient interest in the bonds to bribe the Spanish royal family into selling Cuba. This precious scheme Belmont revealed with varying degrees of frankness to Buchanan,[42] who advised Pierce [43] and Marcy,[44] to appoint Belmont, and to Sanders, who also wrote and spoke to Pierce for him.[45] Even Prosper M. Wetmore of the "Steamboat Crowd" urged Marcy to appoint Belmont.[46] Thus the rivalry of Law and Belmont to provide campaign funds for Pierce was liquidated in the interest of Cuba.

The President ultimately gave Belmont the post at the Netherlands. John Slidell was offered the mission to Central America but preferred to compete for the Senatorship vacated by Soulé, which he won after a brief interlude in London selling railroad bonds with the aid of his protegé, Minister

41 Staples to Marcy, New York, November 26, 1852. Marcy Papers.

42 Belmont to Buchanan, New York, November 22, 1852. Cited in Ettinger, *Mission of Pierre Soulé to Spain*, 339.

43 Buchanan to Pierce, Wheatland, December 11, 1852. *Ibid.*, 144.

44 Buchanan to Marcy, Wheatland, March 8, 1853. Marcy Papers.

45 Belmont to Sanders, New York, March 21, 1853. *Political Correspondence of ... Sanders*, 4.

46 Wetmore to Marcy, New York, April 6, 1853. Marcy Papers.

Buchanan.[47] In their long-standing rivalry for the favor of Louisiana voters, Slidell and Soulé outdid each other in support of the filibusters. Slidell tried to get a job for Ambrosio José Gonzalez in the State Department [48] and in the Senate he became the filibusters' official spokesman. Pierce appointed James D. B. DeBow, the outstanding exponent of southern economic imperialism, as Superintendent of the Census.

A handful of diplomatic posts was distributed among the Young Americans. Sanders wanted and received the London consulate. John L. O'Sullivan was made Chargé des Affaires at Lisbon and Edwin DeLeon received a similar post at Alexandria, Egypt, where he made the despot Mehemet Ali feel the disapproval of right-thinking Americans. Solon Borland took the Central American office Slidell had rejected. E. F. Foresti, who had led the Italian exiles of New York into the Young American camp, was sent to Sardinia as Chargé. Robert Dale Owen, the Socialist and Young American of Indiana, was favored for some reason over Belmont for the post at Naples as Minister to the Two Sicilies. John Moncure Daniel of the Richmond *Examiner* went to Turin as Minister Resident. Daniel E. Sickles became Secretary of Legation at London.

Soulé in the key post at Madrid was of course the captain of this squad of Young American diplomats and his appointment made clear that, whatever their antics favoring European liberalism, Cuban annexation was the core of the administration's foreign policy. From the domestic political point of view, the appointment to Madrid of an outstanding opponent of the Compromise of 1850 signified that Cuba was the bait the Pierce administration offered to secessionists to reconcile them to the

47 Sears, "Slidell and Buchanan," *American Historical Review*, XXVII, 719.

48 A. G. Pent to Marcy, Washington, March 24, 1853. Marcy Papers.

Union.[49] If, after Soulé's Senate speech, any doubt remained of the administration's relaxed views as to suitable methods of annexation, the appointment of Belmont signified their error to those in the know and that of the celebrated filibuster, O'Sullivan, and of Sanders, the opponent of the neutrality laws, proclaimed it to the wide world.

A new day was expected to dawn when these pro-slavery imperialists in the guise of democratic revolutionaries moved to the courts of the Old World as the envoys of the great western republic. To save them the humiliation of even a seeming submission to the autocrats, the Dress Circular permitted them to appear at state functions in the simple garb of American citizens so that their mere presence would reproach crowned heads and gilded European diplomats. And they fully intended to make their achievements as startling as their dress.

49 M. J. White, "Louisiana and the Secession Movement of the Early Fifties," *Proceedings of the Mississippi Valley Historical Association for the Year 1914-15* (Cedar Rapids, Iowa, 1916), VIII, 281.

CHAPTER X
CUBA AND THE PIERCE ADMINISTRATION

SEVERAL circumstances suggest the possibility that the Pierce administration during its first year expected Cuba to be freed by a filibuster expedition. Any other assumption makes Marcy's first instructions to Soulé, which were dated July 23, 1853, and governed the Minister until April, 1854, inexplicable, and an anti-climax that could not have been acceptable to an envoy in Soulé's position, for they forbade him to make any attempt to secure annexation of Cuba. August Belmont was expected to obtain banker pressure in Amsterdam, Paris, Brussels and London for the sale of Cuba, but Marcy was undoubtedly right that a proposal to purchase the island would be untimely and offensive to Spain.

Marcy instructed Soulé that the administration hoped Cuba would "release itself or be released" from Spanish control. This was standard phraseology of the time for procedure on the Texas model of internal revolt combined with filibuster expeditions. Previous writers have failed to remark that this hope for an independent Cuba is actually the main theme of Marcy's instructions or to consider the significance of the words quoted. Amos A. Ettinger, the foremost authority on Soulé's mission, found eight "cardinal expressions" in the document: (1) Spanish sovereignty of Cuba must remain undisturbed by the United States; (2) American security forbade that Cuba be transferred to any other power; (3) the United States would not even tolerate any "protectorate" over Cuba by another nation; (4) American proposals to purchase Cuba were "inopportune;" (5) Marcy desired to see a free Cuba; (6) Soulé should watch constantly for any changes in the Anglo-French attitude; (7) Soulé should procure a commercial convention whereby the Captain-General of Cuba might deal directly with the American administration; (8) he should also uphold the honor of the United States and obtain prompt redress for past damages to American ships and citizens.[1] Items (7) and (8) responded to the clamor caused by the *Crescent City* and Thrasher affairs, besides a long list of earlier grievances, gave the new Minister a chance to exercise talents for strong diplomacy, and placed the United States in a powerful bargaining position. It could hardly have been expected that any results would be obtained sufficient to satisfy hatred for the rule of Spain in Cuba. Under item (3), Marcy pointed to the danger of the protectorate device as used by Britain in Central America. Did he fear that at a certain stage Cuba, like Texas, free of the mother country but not yet securely moored in the Union, would tempt Great Britain? This and all the remaining items receive special meaning from (5): the desire for Cuba to " release itself or be released " from Spain.[2]

Ettinger writes that in spite of these instructions Soulé " of course " considered from the beginning that his objective was the acquisition of Cuba.[3] Yet he shows that the rumors of Soulé's attempts to negotiate a purchase were false.[4] " Something more definite " than rumors, the same author writes, was Pierce's statement in his Annual Message to Congress of December 5, 1853, that filibuster expeditions to Cuba might well be apprehended.[5] Actual evidence that Soulé was edging towards an attempt to acquire the island does not appear until late in March, 1854, when he offered the Spanish government a loan on the revenues of Cuba, later on the island itself, as collateral and discussed with the Queen Mother projects more or

1 Ettinger, *Mission to Spain of Pierre Soulé*, 171-2.

2 Marcy to Soulé, Washington, July 23, 1853. Department of State, *Diplomatic Instructions: Spain*, XV.

3 Ettinger, *op. cit.*, 221.

4 *Ibid.*, 242-5.

5 *Ibid.*, 243.

less related to the Belmont scheme.[6] By that time, he was cognizant of the violent changes in the situation which quickly produced instructions from Marcy to buy Cuba. No evidence has turned up that Soulé violated his initial instructions.

On the other hand, prospects were excellent in the latter half of 1853 that Cuba would indeed " release itself or be released " from Spain. After hesitating for three years, John A. Quitman decided that the situation was ripe and assumed personal command of a filibuster expedition to invade the island. His decision depended partly on the large resources the Cuban exiles made available to him and the widespread popular support of the Order of the Lone Star. The Cuban leaders had taken heart from the excitement stirred up by Cuban Guards and manifestations of support of their cause during the election campaign and organized a new Junta to make another effort to free their homeland. Voting by delegates from the Cuban departments resulted in the election of Gaspar Betancourt Cisneros as President, Manuel de Jésus Arango, Vice President, Porfirio Valiente, Secretary, José Elias Hernandez, Vice Secretary, and Domingo Goicouria, Treasurer. Former comrades of López such as Ambrosio José Gonzalez, Cirilo Villaverde and Juan Manuel Macías, the editor of La Verdad, Miguel Teurbe Tolón, and John L. O'Sullivan were also influential in these proceedings. They took place in New York and a solemn installation of officers was held in Apollo Hall at 410 Broadway on October 19, 1852. The new organization marked a further step in the political evolution of the Cuban revolutionary movement in that it rejected annexationism. In election parades, " Young Cuba " took its place in the line of march with Young Italy, Young Germany, and the other exile groups that Sanders encouraged to hope for the freeing of their countries with the aid of Young America. At the Apollo Hall meeting, a manifesto was read that held out the ideal of unqualified independence for Cuba. Soulé reflected its policy in his Senate speech.

6 Ibid., 245-6.

Rumors that the Pierce administration would try to buy Cuba led the Junta to send a protest to the President. This document stated that the civilization of Cubans did not permit them to be bought like barbarians and slaves. The United States could not buy Spanish seignorial privileges in Cuba because they were incompatible with American law. White Cubans intended to fight for their liberty and for control over their own destiny. Since the United States was a free federation, it could not force the Cubans into it against their will. In conclusion, the protest called purchase of Cuba an infamous and disgraceful way of establishing liberty that would not recompense the blood shed by Cuban martyrs.[7] It was sent to the President on July 10, 1853,[8] less than two weeks before Marcy drew up his initial instructions to Soulé.

The attitude of the Cuban Junta probably acquired importance for Soulé, Pierce and administration leaders in the light of Quitman's formidable plans. A few documents published by Claiborne in his biography of Quitman were formerly the only source of exact knowledge of the latter's enterprise. Its scope and ramifications are clarified by the Quitman Papers recently acquired by the Widener Library of Harvard University.[9] Quitman's political career had collapsed after the failure of the Nashville Convention and of his efforts to commit Mississippi to secession. According to Claiborne, the General then decided that the best temporary substitute for secession was a filibuster expedition to Cuba. He dreamed of a southern slavery empire that would include Cuba and Mexico under a "military Government."[10] The latter phrase was recurrent in the plans of

7 Vilá, *Historia*, II, 84-5.

8 G. Castellanos, *Panorama Historica* (Havana, 1934), 494. *Cf.* Morales, *Iniciadores*, II, 354-7.

9 Made available to the author by the courtesy of Professor Samuel Eliot Morison.

10 Alexander M. Clayton to J. F. H. Claiborne, Woodcote, Benton County, Mississippi, July 27, 1879. J. F. H. Claiborne Papers.

southern imperialists and indicates the length to which they
would go to defend slavery against the reformist tendencies of
democracy. Quitman saw himself as the chief architect of the
southern empire. He planned to become dictator of Cuba.
Senator William N. Gwin, who had been Quitman's friend in
Mississippi before he migrated to California, and had helped
him obtain his commission as Brigadier-General during the
Mexican War, later wrote privately of him: " He was one of
the most bigoted egotists I ever met, and all his life eaten up
with ambition." [11]

The first indication of Quitman's decision to head personally
an expedition to Cuba appears in a letter to him of May 18,
1853, from Major Louis Schlesinger. He had failed to obtain
an office in the new administration and wanted to return to his
trade. In his letter, he congratulated the Cuban cause on the
General's " noble decision " to take the lead in emancipating
the unhappy island. It would add one more to the many laurels
he had won. Schlesinger wrote that nothing would exceed his
joy if he was permitted to serve under Quitman's command.
Furthermore, he thought he could raise a regiment in New
York. " Indeed Genl. I have a private account to settle with old
Spain, and I could not lett pass such a oportunity, without
availing myself of it [sic]." Quitman was asked to communicate with him through John L. O'Sullivan.[12] The date of this
letter suggests that the General made his decision shortly after
Pierce took office. He did so on the understanding that he had
the administration's approval. Pierce, Quitman felt, was in his
debt because during the campaign, when charges were made
that Pierce had shown cowardice in military action before
Mexico City, Quitman, his superior officer, " kindly " gave the
public a favorable representation of his bearing.[13] Quitman's

11 Gwin to Claiborne, San Francisco, November 5, 1878. *Ibid.*

12 Schlesinger to Quitman, New York, May 18, 1853. Quitman Papers.

13 Alexander Walker to A. G. Haley, New Orleans, June 15, 1854. Ex-
tracts in Jefferson Davis Papers.

particular friend in the Cabinet was his comrade in Mexican campaigns, Attorney General Cushing, who advocated strong measures towards Cuba immediately after taking office.[14] Davis wanted to get Cuba by purchase if possible, by force if necessary. Lord Howden, British Ambassador in Madrid, later wrote to Lord Clarendon that he had seen a private letter of Soulé in which he said he had the "out and out support" of Cushing and Jefferson Davis for his "great scheme." [15]

O'Sullivan enjoyed Pierce's favor and acted as Quitman's agent until he left for Portugal, when John S. Thrasher took his place in the filibuster organization. In April, O'Sullivan warned Marcy that British warships were searching American vessels on the pretense of looking for slavers, but actually to establish a precedent in order to prevent American aid from being sent to Cuban revolutionaries. An uprising of Cubans, he wrote, would certainly break out in earnest before long, "unless anticipated by you & Mr. Soulé, as I pray to God may be the case." [16] Significantly, O'Sullivan in August no longer expected Marcy and Soulé to anticipate the Cuban revolution by buying the island. Rather, he worked through his relatives in Cuba to encourage a *pronunciamiento* that would coincide with Quitman's invasion.[17] This change of front by O'Sullivan emphasizes the meaning of Marcy's instructions to Soulé.

The new administration could find information about developments in Cuba in a letter from Consul Sharkey, who was not given to enthusiasm in these matters:

> The signs of revolution seem to be growing more and more decided in character, and aid from the people of the United States is looked for. I think it is confidently expected here,

14 Fuess, *Cushing*, II, 159-61, 176.

15 Howden to Clarendon, Madrid, October 23, 1854. "Southern Designs on Cuba, 1854-1857, and Some European Opinions," edited by Gavin B. Henderson, *The Journal of Southern History*, V (August, 1939), 376-7.

16 O'Sullivan to Marcy, New York, April 22, 1853. Marcy Papers.

17 O'Sullivan to Quitman, New York, August 29, 1853. Quitman Papers.

amongst all parties, that expeditions are being organized in the United States and that they may be expected here during the winter or spring . . . .

Sharkey, who was guilty in the opinion of Young Americans of abject submission to the Captain-General, was removed and Alexander M. Clayton, former Judge of the Mississippi High Court of Errors and Appeals and a friend of Quitman, was appointed Consul at Havana. He was intimately acquainted with Quitman's plans. On the steamer trip down the Mississippi en route to Havana, he wrote to Quitman that he expected a crisis in Cuban affairs. He agreed that an independent government " after the fashion of Texas " would be " at first advisable." Then Cuba should come into the Union by treaty or not as circumstances directed. He urged speedy action : " In such a movement, if our Northern brethren take the start, & get ahead of us, shall we not have California over again." Clayton wanted the federal government to act at once to help Quitman if Britain and France had a treaty agreement on Cuba. He knew that the Cubans, of whom he did not expect much, looked to Quitman for aid. The latter should not write to the Consul because the Spanish Post Office was not trustworthy, but should he pay a visit to the island, " for your health," Clayton would welcome him.[19]

Late in July, 1853, Quitman was at the Astor House in New York, receiving offers of service in the expedition which came to him in increasing numbers.[20] He conferred with leaders of the Cuban Guards and obtained their support.[21] On this trip, he sounded the attitude of the Pierce administration towards his

18 Sharkey to Secretary of State, Havana, November 8, 1852. Department of State, *Consular Despatches: Havana*, XXV.

19 A. M. Clayton to Quitman, Steamer *Sultana* near Vicksburg, November 10, 1853. Quitman Papers.

20 I. S. McWicken to Quitman, New York, July 20, 1853, *et passim*, Quitman Papers.

21 Mike Walsh to Quitman, New York, October 3, 1853. *Ibid.*

enterprise, and the circumstances strongly suggest that Marcy's initial instructions to Soulé were written in the hope that Quitman would soon invade Cuba. With such an understanding, Soulé's behavior after he received his instructions and before he left for Madrid becomes explicable if not sensible. Previously, on July 4, Soulé had been serenaded at his hotel in New York by the Order of the Lone Star and Cuban exiles, but on that occasion he gave no sign of approval.[22] After he received his instructions, Soulé evidently felt free to abandon all discretion. A. G. Haley, one of Quitman's agents in Washington, organized a parade of Young Americans headed by the United States Marine Band and a farewell serenade at the Minister's Washington home. Soulé responded to Haley's florid address with generalizations in the Young American vein. A few days later, in New York, Soulé went further. This time the Cuban Junta took the lead in a celebration. " Cuba must and shall be be free " was the theme of transparencies carried in the parade. The last one was sufficiently pointed :

LOPEZ—CRITTENDEN—AGUERO—ARMENTERO,
They and their companions are not forgotten.

A crowd of nearly five thousand people gathered at the Minister's hotel. Soulé, George Sanders, and other Young Americans appeared on the balcony. Teurbe Tolón, speaking for the Junta, adulated the Minister in an address that declared the latter's mission to be the protection of American rights and interests. He hoped that when Soulé returned home, " a new star shining in the sky of Young America may shed its dawning rays upon your noble brow." The Minister responded enthusiastically that his faith in Manifest Destiny was firm and promised he would show that " American sentiments weigh in the scale of the destinies of the nations more than all others that can be wielded by czars, emperors, or kings." If, in Madrid,

22 New Orleans *Commercial Bulletin*, July 18, 1853. Quoted in Ettinger, *Mission*, 169.

American rights were to be vindicated, "they shall be vindicated with the freedom and energy that becomes a freeman." [23]

This demonstration gave to many the impression that the Cuban Junta expected Soulé to buy Cuba and that the latter fed their hope. But, after sending a bitter protest against purchase to Pierce, the Junta would hardly have given his Minister so rousing a send-off had it not received assurance that Soulé would *not* try to buy the island. And careful attention to the speeches of Tolón and Soulé would have revealed their actual plan: liberation of Cuba by revolution and assertion to Spain of Americans' right to aid the revolution. The question remains, did the Pierce administration give positive approval of the filibuster expedition to the Junta and Quitman?

Circumstantial evidence points to an affirmative answer. The decision was probably made in the middle of July when Soulé was in Washington and his instructions were under consideration. Quitman was then on his way to New York and nothing would have been more natural than for administration leaders to consult him. Claiborne wrote that on Quitman's trip east he frankly communicated his designs to "distinguished persons" in Washington, and received the distinct impression "not only that he had their sympathies, but that there could be no pretext for the intervention of the federal authorities. He left the capital buoyant with hope...." [24] O'Sullivan's change of plans from hope in April that Soulé would buy Cuba to activity in favor of revolution and the Quitman expedition in August has been noted. Soulé's change from aloofness towards the July 4 demonstration of the Order of the Lone Star to approval of the Cuban Junta's demonstration on August 5 argues that he had been made confident of a benevolent attitude by the administration towards the Junta. The emphasis

23 *Harper's Monthly Magazine*, VII (October, 1853), 692-3. New York *Evening Post*, August 6, 1853. *New York Herald*, August 6, 1853. *National Intelligencer*, August 9, 1853. Ettinger, *Mission*, 172-6.

24 Claiborne, *Quitman*, II, 195.

in the speeches of Tolón and Soulé on defense of American rights as the object of the latter's mission to Spain recalls the view that Sanders seems to have originated in the *Democratic Review* during the 1852 campaign and Soulé asserted in his speech to the Senate, namely, filibustering was a right of American citizens, and suggests that the Pierce administration adopted their view as the " legal " basis of its support of the Quitman Expedition. Furthermore, Soulé's remark in his Senate speech that purchase was " obsolete " makes him the originator of his own instructions.

Quitman was very evidently satisfied by what he had learned of administration policy. He must have been pleased by the appointment of Alexander M. Clayton as Consul in Havana, and acted as if he knew the key of Marcy's instructions to Soulé was the hope that Cuba would " release itself or be released " from Spain. While Soulé, a day after his public manifestation of accord with the Junta, embarked for Spain, Quitman remained in New York and there on August 18 signed a formal agreement with the same organization. On April 29, 1853, the Junta had addressed a letter to Quitman that described the motives for its organization, the widespread support it enjoyed in the island and its first duty as putting " in the hands of some experienced general of known probity the mission of liberating our country, and that general was yourself in first instance, marked by the public voice of all the Cubans within and without the island." Quitman's sympathy for their cause, the letter continued, his sufferings for it, the gifts which adorned him as an American General, and all the antecedents of his public life inspired the Cubans' unlimited confidence. The Junta therefore begged him to accept nomination as " exclusive chief of our revolution, not only in its military, but also in its civil sense," until such time during or after the revolution " as in your judgment it shall be proper or possible to constitute the island a sovereign and independent nation" and form a regular government.[25] But Quitman answered that he could not finally accept until "the details can be placed upon such footing as to insure success, and *not to compromit my own character and reputation.*" As to the details, he stipulated that all the Cuban patriots in the United States who represented portions of the Cuban people be united in the enterprise, sufficient powers be delegated to himself and adequate means provided. Granted these, he would assume the "distinguished but very responsible position" to which the people of Cuba called him.[26]

Now in August Quitman was satisfied not only on the details but that his own character and reputation would not be compromised. His knowledge of administration policy is the best explanation of his satisfaction on the latter point. The Articles he signed with the Junta first of all transferred the powers of the Junta to him "as civil and military chief of the revolution, with all the powers and attributes of dictatorship as recognized by civilized nations, to be used and exercised by him for the purpose of overthrowing the Spanish government in the island of Cuba and its dependencies, and substituting in the place thereof a free and independent government." For these purposes, he was given absolute control of all funds and means in the hands of the revolutionary party, the power to issue bonds, grant commissions, raise military and naval forces, purchase and charter vessels and all the prerogatives of a dictator. The second Article pledged the obedience of the Junta to its new chieftain, and specified that he should retain and preserve slavery in Cuba:

> . . . establishing therein a free and liberal government which shall retain and preserve the domestic institutions of the country.

25 Cuban Junta to Quitman, Natchez, April 29, 1853. Claiborne, *Quitman,* II, 386-8.

26 Quitman to Junta, Monmouth, near Natchez, April 30, 1853. *Ibid.*, 388. Italics added.

Other Articles provided for the succession to Quitman and minor matters. An annex engaged the people of Cuba to pay the General one million dollars if and when Cuba was freed.[27] Quitman's friend Claiborne is authority for his intention to accept no compensation but devote the money to the establishment of a great military and naval college at Havana. On the question of the ultimate fate of Cuba, Claiborne wrote that Quitman said it ought, once free of the Spanish yoke, " either to ask annexation to the United States, or to establish a formidable navy for self-protection." [28] Quitman's attitude, Marcy's instructions to Soulé, and the propaganda of the Junta indicate an agreement to concentrate on freeing the island and to postpone the question of annexation until an independent government was established. This would improve the legal position of the filibusters. The Pierce administration had doubtless also calculated that a purchase treaty stood little chance of gaining the support of two-thirds of the Senate, while a request for annexation from an independent Cuban government might well lead simple majorities of the two Houses to pass a joint resolution. In short, the Texas model would be imitated in detail, including, perhaps, a navy for the projected republic.

The enterprise moved slowly. Some young Cubans who were to go to Trinidad de Cuba as advance couriers of a " powerful expedition " became impatient and in September O'Sullivan advised Quitman to prevent them from trying prematurely to do " something bold for their country." [29] Chatham R. Wheat, veteran filibuster, volunteered for the new expedition. He wrote Quitman that he dreamed of fighting soon " beside an Apostle of Liberty." In December, Mike Walsh of New York wrote that his whole soul was wrapped up in the enterprise but,

27 Articles signed by the Cuban Junta and Quitman, New York, August 18, 1853. *Ibid.*, 389-90.

28 *Ibid.*, 390n.

29 O'Sullivan to Quitman, New York, September 8, 1853. Quitman Papers.

he complained, Quitman did not answer his letters.[30] Later in the same month, the General wrote to " J.M.M.," probably Juan Manuel Macías, a member of the Junta, that he had not lost confidence in him. His own inaction was rather explained by two months of disease and death in his family. However, he had explained in New York and he still required that the necessary resources be raised before he would act. He would not commit himself publicly to the enterprise before all the means necessary were obtained. He thought the prospects were now fair that his requirements would be met as one-half the amount had been raised. Money had been placed to his order in New York.[31] This letter evidently followed meetings of the Junta and of the Order of the Lone Star in New Orleans. News of them appeared in the press, as well as reports that an expedition of 4,000 filibusters was being organized in New Orleans under " a general who gained laurels in Mexico." The recruiting was conducted by the Order.[32]

All was not well between Quitman and his followers. Early in February, 1854, Samuel R. Walker wrote to him from New Orleans that his inactivity crippled the work of organization. It was not contemplated for a moment that he should depart from the stand he had taken. " But in doing what our mature deliberations point as best in the premises to impel a Southern agitation of the subject we cannot start unless you be here to aid privately in establishing a point round which to rally." [33] Not until November would Walker publish his article in De-Bow's Review calling the South to support an expedition to Cuba.[34] Quitman evidently hesitated to accelerate the activities of his supporters. Felix Huston, former General of the Texas

30 Walsh to Quitman, Washington, December 18, 1853. *Ibid.*

31 Quitman to J. M. M., New Orleans, December 28, 1853. *Ibid.*

32 *National Intelligencer*, December 17, 1853.

33 Samuel R. Walker to Quitman, New Orleans, February 7, 1854. Quitman Papers.

34 Samuel R. Walker, "Cuba and the South," *DeBow's Review*, XVII (November, 1854), 519-25.

Republic, wrote Quitman on March 4 that he had arrived in New Orleans that day and found " nothing done or doing." He had written a letter to planters in which he spoke plainly, and had already tried to stir up influential Whigs in Baton Rouge. But things were " just at a dead halt." [35] Some days later, Huston wrote that he was satisfied the men Quitman relied on would not do. Departure of the expedition would not be possible until the next July, if then. He had signed his own name to the letter to planters according to an agreement with Thrasher, but was worried about committing himself so widely.[36]

Events in the island of a momentous character now stirred Quitman to action and brought the Cuban situation in all its ramifications to a crisis. Spain seemed to begin to carry out its threat to " Africanize " Cuba. The purpose of this policy was to make the island undesirable to southern annexationists. A new Spanish government took power in December, 1852, and imposed a reactionary constitution. The Foreign Minister, De Lis, told Barringer that the new government approved the Captain-General's conduct in the *Crescent City* affair and gave the American to understand that policy towards the United States was stiffening. Barringer heard reports that secret orders had been sent to Cañedo to arm the slaves and let them take power if necessary to prevent the island from falling into the hands of the United States. The controlled press said Cuba must be " Spanish or African." British and French naval forces in the Gulf were increased.[37] The victory of Pierce in the election and Everett's rejection of the proposed tripartite convention made Spain fearful of the future.

Spain's treaties with Britain provided that Negroes who were unlawfully sold as slaves in Cuba should be freed. This pro-

35 Huston to Quitman, New Orleans, March 4, 1854. Quitman Papers.

36 Huston to Quitman, New Orleans, March 10, 1854. *Ibid.*

37 Barringer to Everett, Madrid, December 14, 1852. Department of State, *Diplomatic Despatches: Spain*, XXXVII.

vision, never enforced, was made a complete farce by a Spanish law of 1845 that forbade the island authorities to search the plantations for *emancipados*. In the spring of 1853, Cañedo violated that law. If he acted under orders from Spain, he was repudiated because the outcry by the planters led the government to recall him. Yet this event gave substance to the fear of Africanization, which Soulé was convinced Britain inspired, and on his way to Madrid he made a vain effort to divorce France from Britain. He denied to the French Foreign Minister, Drouyn de Lhuys, that he or his government sanctioned filibustering, but made the significant qualifications: " the Southern States of the Union would not permit, at any cost, that [Cuba] should be Africanized." [38]

As if to take up this challenge, Spain on September 23, 1853, appointed the Marques de la Pezuela, well known for his opposition to slavery, as Captain-General of Cuba. News of his appointment provoked a manifesto by Cuban patriots on October 3 calling for immediate revolution. They despaired of American aid reaching them before a Negro rebellion broke out. England, they believed, was determined to destroy the Cuban sugar industry and had forced Spain to concede emancipation of the slaves.[39] These patriots were planters and conservatives who had been inactive for some time. They had lost faith in filibustering, but their leader, Cristóbal Madan, freed from prison, decided to appeal to the American government to intervene. On October 4, he wrote a letter to President Pierce claiming that, as a naturalized citizen of the United States, he saw no other means to save his valuable property in Cuba than to ask for intervention by his adopted government. Under the dictation of the British Cabinet, he wrote, Spain adopted a course which would not merely suppress the slave trade but destroy slavery. This amounted to British intervention and the

38 De Lhuys to Turgot, Paris, September 10, 1853. Quoted in Ettinger, *Mission*, 184.

39 Morales, *Iniciadores*, II, 405-10.

Monroe Doctrine required the United States to prevent it. The President dared not delay without risking success or " showing unjustifiable indifference to the dearest interests of our Southern States." The Acting American Consul, William H. Robertson, forwarded this communication to Pierce.[40] The new Consul, Alexander M. Clayton, was instructed to investigate. He reported that he doubted Britain had an agreement with Spain regarding slavery in Cuba and furthermore assured Marcy that he had not the slightest knowledge of any filibuster expedition preparing in the United States.[41] After a quarrel with Robertson over fees, Clayton resigned in January, 1854, and left the former, who was in intimate contact with Madan and his friends, in charge of the consulate.[42]

That fears of Africanization were not entirely unfounded became clear shortly after Pezuela arrived in Havana. Leading authorities regard Pezuela's policy as an honest attempt to carry out liberal ideals.[43] Pezuela's personal motives may have been above reproach, but the current Spanish government would hardly bear the charge of liberal idealism.[44] Rather, the time chosen to appoint him Captain-General and the methods outlined in his instructions indicate that the Spanish government, impressed by the imminent danger to Cuba from the new administration in Washington, decided to demonstrate its determination to Africanize the island as a last measure of defense. The plan was ingenious as it seemed to satisfy perennial British demands to enforce the treaties against the slave trade, provided for a new labor supply made necessary especially

40 Madan to Pierce, Havana, October 4, 1853. Department of State, *Consular Despatches: Havana*, XVII.

41 Clayton to Marcy, Havana, December 5, 1853. *Ibid.*, XXVI.

42 Clayton to Marcy, Marshall County, Mississippi, January 18, 1854. *Ibid.*, XXVII.

43 Zaragoza, *Insurreciones*, I, 654. Vilá, *Historia*, II, 75-6.

44 Mathieson, *op. cit.*, 143-4.

after epidemics swept away 70,000 slaves in the summer of 1853, and, if carried out, would make Cuban annexation anathema to the American South. On the other hand, it entailed a risk that it would provoke intervention by the American government or a filibuster expedition and revolution. The fact that preoccupation of Britain and France with the Near Eastern crisis reduced their ability to support Spain in Cuba gave Spanish daring the quality of desperation.

Late in December, 1853, Pezuela decreed severe measures to suppress the slave trade. Free importation of Indians, Asiatics and Spaniards would supply the shortage of labor. *Emancipados* brought into the island before 1835 would be freed and, for the first time, such additions to the free Negro population would be allowed to remain permanently in the island. Furthermore, inter-marriage between Negroes and other races was encouraged. These measures were attributed to the Queen's benevolence. But the inner purpose of the new policy seemed to be the encouragement of immigration from Africa to make the population of the island overwhelmingly Negro. *Emancipados* were taken in charge by the government and hired out to planters as apprentices in return for one-fourth of their wages. Soon after Pezuela announced the new system, slave traders sailed to Africa and brought back cargoes which they represented as " apprentices " to British cruisers. In Cuba, they became, however, *emancipados* and as such were reconverted into apprentices. Such immigrants greatly outnumbered those of other races who were imported. On January 1, 1854, a decree that liberated all slaves imported since 1835 was issued in time for the reception of the first cargoes from Africa. A fleet of Spanish warships assembled at Havana to fend off the expected filibuster invasion, but did nothing to disturb the slave traders. When Marcy indicated to Robertson that he doubted the truth of reports on Pezuela's activities, the latter sent him ample proof in the form of the official decrees besides another letter from Madan expressing the despair of planters who believed that their need for labor was being played upon to destroy slavery and make the Negro population uncontrollable.[45]

Pezuela held further measures of a more transcendent nature in reserve while, with seeming deliberation, he tested the reaction of the United States to provocation of another kind. On February 28, 1854, he confiscated the *Black Warrior*, owned by the New York and Alabama Steamship Company, and arrested her commander, Captain James D. Bulloch, an American naval officer, on the excuse that the ship's manifest declared her to be in ballast when she arrived at Havana that day, whereas she actually carried a large cargo in transit. The *Black Warrior* on seventeen previous voyages and other vessels that touched at Havana without discharging or taking on cargo, by oral agreement with the port authorities, always made out their manifests as in ballast and, while this technically violated regulations, no difficulty had ever arisen. The conclusion is inescapable that Pezuela wished to demonstrate his authority to the United States in an unmistakable manner. He refused to deal with Robertson in the matter, although it clearly concerned the commercial affairs which were within the American Consul's jurisdiction by consent of the Spanish government. The vessel was released on March 16 with a fine of $6,000.[46] The fine was later remitted, but as a challenge to the United States the affair was a complete success.

Public excitement led the House of Representatives unanimously to ask the President for the facts in the case.[47] The Louisiana legislature sent resolutions to Congress calling for "decisive and energetic measures to thwart and defeat" the policy of Pezuela, which had been " conceived in hatred to this

45 Robertson to Marcy, Havana, December 26, 1853, January 5, 12, 27, February 14, 1854. Madan to Robertson, Havana, December 25, 1853. Department of State, *Consular Despatches: Havana*, XXVII.

46 Robertson to Marcy, Havana, March 1, 3, 21, April 7, 1854. Department of State, *ibid*.

47 *Congressional Globe* (33:1), 601.

republic, and calculated to retard her progress and prosperity." [48] These resolutions were directed not only against
abuse of the *Black Warrior* but also against Africanization.
On March 15, the President sent Congress the correspondence
and a message that declared the *Black Warrior* case to be so
clear an instance of wrong that it would be reasonable to expect
" full indemnity " as soon as Her Catholic Majesty's government heard of Pezuela's " unjustifiable and offensive conduct."
But such acts could not long " consist with peaceful relations."
If redress failed, the President promised to take whatever
action Congress authorized. He suggested it should take " provisional measures " immediately.[49] On the same day, Marcy sent
Charles W. Davis on a secret mission to Cuba to investigate
the Captain-General's Africanization program.[50] Even before
the *Black Warrior* affair, Soulé in Madrid asked Marcy for
larger powers in relation to Cuba, hinting that he might have
an opportunity to play a bold card. He believed that an internal
crisis in Spain was at hand.[51]

All aspects of the Cuban situation now pressed on the Pierce
administration of solution. From the broadest political view-
point, Cuba could not be dissociated from the Kansas-Nebraska
Bill with which it competed for attention in and out of Congress. Both issues presented the South with opportunities for
the expansion of slave territory. While Douglas took the
lead in fighting for his Bill in Congress, Slidell clamored for
drastic action on Cuba. The latter demand was presented in the
Cabinet by Cushing.[52] The Senate passed the Kansas-Nebraska
Bill on March 3. Party pressure was exerted to the fullest to

48 *Senate Miscellaneous Documents* (33:1), 63.

49 *Messages and Papers of the Presidents*, comp. Richardson, VI, 2767-8.

50 Marcy to Davis, Washington, March 15, 1854. Department of State,
Special Missions, III.

51 Soulé to Marcy, Madrid, February 23, March 8, 1854. Department of
State, *Diplomatic Despatches: Spain*, XIL.

52 Fuess, *Cushing*, II, 163.

put it through the House. Still that Bill offered the shadow rather than the substance of a victory to the South and Cuba was of vastly more practical importance especially as mere inaction threatened to make it—" Africanized "—a positive danger to the security of the South's peculiar institution. And Quitman was strangely dilatory in launching his much-publicized expedition. Pierce decided to open the door wider for Cuban annexation.

On March 17, Marcy sent instructions to Soulé to demand of the Spanish government an indemnity of $300,000 for injuries sustained by the owners of the *Black Warrior*. But little was expected to come of this for, as Marcy wrote, Spain would doubtless procrastinate as usual, and he did not instruct the envoy to present anything like an ultimatum.[53] Sufficient unity in the Cabinet was obtained by April 3 to send entirely new instructions to Soulé. Marcy told him that the Africanization policy of Pezuela made annexation by purchase possible and desirable. The confusion and backtracking of the Pierce administration in its Cuban policy from this time until 1855 begins with these instructions. Marcy possibly believed that Pezuela had effectively countered the threat of Quitmtan's expedition. Revolution in the island would very likely ensure the completion of Pezuela's Africanization program, and the spectre of a Negro republic hovered over administration leaders. They cast about for a solution and gradually turned against the plans of Quitman. Soulé was now authorized to offer as much as $130,000,000 for Cuba and to make a treaty effecting " the object so much desired by the United States."

Marcy's discussion of the difficulties surrounding such a task indicated little faith in success. Assuming that the Spanish government would be unwilling to sell, he told Soulé to direct his efforts to " the next most desirable object which is to detach that island from the Spanish dominion and from all dependence

53 Marcy to Soulé, Washington, March 17, 1854. Department of State, *Diplomatic Instructions: Spain*, XV.

on any European power." This peculiar expression, "to detach," has puzzled historians and led Henry Barrett Learned, the foremost authority on Marcy's diplomacy, to question whether the "elderly Secretary of State" was "nodding" when he wrote it. Learned furthermore is doubtful that the President could have been satisfied with the letter, although it was sent in his name, or that the ambiguous word "detach" would have escaped the eye of so shrewd an observer as Attorney-General Cushing if the letter was considered by the Cabinet. The mystery, Learned finds, is increased by the fact that the whole passage directing Soulé to detach Cuba from Spain and Europe was withheld from publication, and he suggests that it influenced Buchanan, Mason and Soulé when they signed the "strange" Ostend Manifesto.[54] Yet the next sentence after Marcy's instructions "to detach" Cuba makes fairly clear the object the Secretary of State had in mind:

> If Cuba were relieved from all transatlantic connection and *at liberty to dispose of herself* as her present interest and prospective welfare would dictate, she would undoubtedly relieve this government from all anxiety in regard to her future condition.[55]

Soulé was to exert himself to secure the independence of Cuba, not annexation, although, to be sure, wisdom dictated that free Cuba apply for admission to the Union. But for the present, the United States government would be satisfied with independence.

By what possible means was Soulé intended to "detach" Cuba and set it free? Marcy's silence on this score suggests that his Spanish Minister understood what he was expected to do without instructions. The Belmont scheme was only a special plan for obtaining Spanish consent to sell the island to the

54 Henry B. Learned, "William Learned Marcy," *The American Secretaries of State and Their Diplomacy*, ed. Bemis, VI, 193-5.

55 Marcy to Soulé, Washington, April 3, 1854. Department of State, *Diplomatic Instructions: Spain*, XV. Italics added.

United States. The most likely answer is that Marcy on April 3, 1854, intended Soulé to understand that if he could not buy Cuba, his initial instructions of July 23, 1853, still held and he was urged to exert himself more actively in performing his part of the plan whereby Cuba would "release itself or be released" from Spain. If Quitman's expedition was to do the main work, what was Soulé's part in this plan? His conduct after he received the letter of April 3 leaves little doubt that the administration intended him to foment revolutionary outbreaks in Spain which would, first of all, prevent the government from sending aid to defend Cuba against Quitman. The Crimean War, which began late in March, would prevent Britain and France from using naval forces against the filibusters. Even if the filibusters failed to set forth or to overthrow Spain, revolution in the mother country would present chances to Soulé to make a deal for Cuba with one or another faction which no one expected a well-established Spanish government to consider.

When Soulé, Sanders, Sickles and O'Sullivan first arrived in Europe, they entered into intimate relations with revolutionary exiles from many European countries to canvass the prospects of a general rising on the continent which would be aided by the United States. In London, Consul Sanders held his famous dinner-party on February 21, 1854, and Mazzini, Kossuth, Ledru-Rollin, Garibaldi, Orsini, Ruge, the German, and Herzen, the Russian, as well as Buchanan and lesser lights drank healths to "a future alliance of America with a federation of the free peoples of Europe." [56] But Kossuth and Mazzini lost interest in the Young American dream when Sanders required that they support slavery because annexation of Cuba to the United States to strengthen slavery there was an integral part of the plan.[57] Soulé's next hope was that war between the

[56] Ettinger, *Mission*, 317.

[57] Kossuth to Sanders, London, May 8, 1854. *Cf.* Hawthorne to Sanders, Liverpool, March 14, 1854; Kossuth to Sanders, London, June 2, 1854; and Ledru-Rollin to Sanders. London, August 1, 1854. *Correspondence of . . . Sanders*, iii, 71, 112, 132.

United States and Spain would solve everything, and to that end he turned his instructions of March 17, 1854, to obtain an indemnity for the *Black Warrior* affair, into a forty-eight hour ultimatum.[58] The Washington administration, after disagreement in the Cabinet, refused to take advantage of an unsatisfactory response by the Spanish government, and, in effect, repudiated the Minister to Spain.[59] But the instructions " to detach " Cuba had already been sent, they were not withdrawn, and Soulé proceeded to concentrate his own efforts and those of a motley crowd of European revolutionaries on the overthrow of the Spanish government. Lord Howden later wrote Clarendon that he had very great reason to believe Soulé had made a contract with the heads of the Spanish Republican Party " for the sale of the Island whenever, through Mr. Soulé's assistance and the money supplied by the United States, that party came into power." [60]

The first results appeared in the July uprising in Madrid. In the meantime, further events had raised the Cuban crisis to a new pitch. On May 1, Senator Slidell made a sensational speech in the Senate in support of his resolution to suspend the neutrality laws in relation to Cuba and thereby " legalize " the Quitman expedition.[61] Nothing came of this effort,[62] but A. G. Haley reported to Quitman that " Cuba stock " was now at par in Washington and that Slidell's speech was " endorsed by the Democracy, and was, I apprehend, prompted by the administration." [63] On April 16, Quitman had notified the Cuban

58 Soulé to Marcy, Madrid, April 13, 1854. Department of State, *Diplomatic Despatches: Spain*, XIL.

59 Marcy to Soulé, Washington, May 24, June 22, 1854. Department of State, *Diplomatic Instructions: Spain*, XV.

60 Howden to Clarendon, Madrid, November 12, 1854. Henderson, *op. cit.*, 379.

61 *Congressional Globe* (33:1), 1021 ff.

62 *Senate Journal* (33:1), 354.

63 Haley to Quitman, Washington, May 11, 1854. Quitman Papers.

Junta that he was ready to depart when he could count on 3,000 men, one "moderately-armed" steamer, and a fund of $220,000.[64] And in Cuba, Pezuela, emboldened no doubt by his impunity in the *Black Warrior* affair, began to expand the Africanization program in ways that alarmed the South and multiplied Quitman's support.

The law of 1845 that forbade the Cuban authorities to search plantations for *emancipados* was now canceled by Pezuela. The great majority of slaves in Cuba had been imported after the first anti-slave trade treaty of 1817, no proper papers could be shown for them to prove legitimate ownership, and a registration of slaves decreed by Pezuela was bound to put an end to slavery in the island. The government began to organize apprentices thus freed into a large Negro militia. Free schools were organized for liberated Negro children, although none had ever been provided for whites. Measures were taken to raise the birth-rate of Negroes. Whites were forbidden to possess arms. Sporadic violence broke out. Acting Consul Robertson began to attend meetings of Creole revolutionaries and sent their pleas for intervention to Marcy.[65] Marcy's secret agent, Charles W. Davis, returned from Cuba with complete information which he reported to the Secretary of State with his conclusion that " the emancipation of the slaves and consequent Africanization of the Island is the true object had in view, and to which the march is a rapid as circumstances will allow." He expected a bloody race war.[66] Pezuela presently lost his ardor, and in September he was ordered back to Spain.

But the South was thoroughly frightened. Late in May, Thrasher negotiated for steamers to carry the Quitman expedi-

64 Quitman to Cuban Junta, New Orleans, April 16, 1854. Claiborne, *Quitman*, II, 391.

65 Robertson to Marcy, Havana, April 26, May 7, 10, 11, 14, 15, 16, 18, 23, 27, June 1, 11, 21, 27, 1854; and enclosures. Department of State, *Consular Despatches: Havana*, XXVII.

66 Charles W. Davis to Marcy, Washington, May 22, 1854. *Ibid.*, XXIX.

tion to the island.[67] Then on May 31 the President issued a Proclamation that seemed to demolish Quitman's hopes that the administration approved his plans. This document warned all persons that the government would prosecute violations of the neutrality laws and treaty obligations.[68] The President had signed the Kansas-Nebraska Bill the day before. The two actions might signify that the administration considered Kansas a sufficient gain for the South and feared that Cuba in addition would completely alienate northern sentiment. And Charles W. Davis' report may have confirmed fears that the reckless fili-busters would only ensure Pezuela's success.

But it is not certain that Pierce intended his Proclamation, couched in terms very perfunctory compared with those of Taylor and Fillmore, to inhibit Quitman, or that he stood by his intention if he ever had it. Alexander Walker, acting as Quitman's spokesman, wrote on June 15 to A. G. Haley a letter intended for Jefferson Davis' eyes. He said Quitman believed Davis was behind the Proclamation. The expedition had been organized with the approval of the administration. The District Attorney of New Orleans had declared very publicly that the Neutrality Act rested upon comity and amity between the United States and Spain, and as long as they did not exist, it would not be enforced. Now the Proclamation, Walker continued, violated the understanding on which Quit-man had acted. War between the filibusters and the adminis-tration threatened. " At present, it is like holding in a mettled racer after the drum is tapped, to prevent an open declaration of the great mass of the Southern Democracy against the Administration." Walker was concerned to prevent an open rupture. The South had been " Filibusterized," and wanted to pass Cuba through the process by which Texas entered the Union. However, if he had reasonable assurance that Cuba would be taken, and that Davis fully appreciated the importance

67 Lesesne to Thrasher, Mobile, May 26, 1854. Quitman Papers.

68 *Messages and Papers of the Presidents*, comp. Richardson, VI, 2805-6.

of the measure to the South, the situation would improve. Haley passed on a copy of this letter to the Secretary of War.[69]

Davis' reaction to this threat of political reprisals may be inferred from the fact that a conference was called with President Pierce in which Davis and Senators Slidell, James M. Mason and Douglas induced the President to instruct Marcy to tell the District Attorney of New Orleans that the administration would take "immediate and decisive" measures to annex Cuba. Pierce did this on the assumption that Quitman, believing the administration would pursue an aggressive policy, would not attempt an expedition.[70] Secretary of the Navy Dobbin led Representative A. G. Brown of Mississippi to understand that "if the Filibusters do not spoil things the Island will be ours in twelve months." Brown saw it as the crisis of the administration, but he expected little, because the President wanted "*back bone*" and was no Jackson.[71]

The Grand Jury forced action against Quitman, Thrasher, and Dr. A. L. Saunders. Quitman himself believed it was not the administration but an officious and anti-southern Judge, John A. Campbell of the Circuit Court at New Orleans, who was at the bottom of the Grand Jury action. The upshot was that Quitman, Thrasher and Saunders were each required to enter into a recognizance in the penal sum of $3000 to observe the laws and especially the Neutrality Act of 1818 for a period of nine months. The incident increased public enthusiasm for the expedition. The tone was set by Federal Marshal J. M. Kennedy, when he had the three in custody, attended a public dinner in their honor, and offered the toast: [72]

69 Alexander Walker to A. G. Haley, New Orleans, June 15, 1854. Jefferson Davis Papers.

70 Sears, "Slidell and Buchanan," *American Historical Review*, XXVII (July, 1922), 721.

71 A. G. Brown to "My dear Sir," Washington, June 29, 1854. Claiborne Papers, Mississippi State Archives.

72 Claiborne, *Quitman*, II, 195-209.

Cuba:
We'll buy or fight, but to our shore we'll lash her;
If Spain won't sell, we'll then turn in and *thrash-her*.

Quitman saw no necessity to abandon the expedition. He sent a circular to its adherents in July to explain that Thrasher, Saunders and he had thought to contest the action of the Grand Jury but did not want to stigmatize the cause. Only a portion of Pierce's Cabinet opposed the expedition. The work of organization would proceed, only a little more money was needed, and everyone should go prudently to work, as it would be criminal to neglect an undertaking which was the " only safeguard for the future security and welfare of the sound, political and industrial interests of the Southern and South Western States." [73] Offers of aid and expressions of approval came to Quitman now in great numbers. Samuel R. Walker went to Washington late in July to sound out the situation. He reported to Quitman that " the administration trembles before filibusterism," and that he was told in the presence of the President and the Secretary of War that if the expedition went to Cuba, " the government would not see them sacrificed, that was certain." [74]

Preparations continued. Judge Lesesne recruited William Walker, who had led a filibuster expedition into northern Mexico and by the same means would make himself President of Nicaragua in 1856.[75] And, to complete the roster of expansionists of that name, Robert J. Walker, Secretary of the Treasury under Polk and advocate of annexation by purchase, sent word to Quitman that he now favored an expedition and wanted to help with money.[76] The Memphis *Whig* reported that

73 Circular, July, 1854. Quitman Papers.

74 Walker to Quitman, New York, July 31, 1854. *Ibid.*

75 Lesesne to Quitman, Mobile, June 10, 1854. *Ibid.*

76 John Marshall to Quitman, Galveston, July 18, 1854. *Ibid.*

Quitman commanded $1,000,000, 12 vessels, 85,000 arms, 90 field pieces and up to 50,000 men.[77]

Inspection of his correspondence indicates that late in the summer of 1854 Quitman postponed the departure of his expedition to the spring of 1855. An Ohio correspondent of Lord Palmerston wrote him in September that February, 1855 had been set for the descent on Cuba.[78] Possibly Quitman wanted to wait out the nine-month term of his recognizance. He always hoped that a revolution in the island would break out and make his departure more defensible from the legal standpoint.[79] In September, Samuel R. Walker went to Cuba and made contact with Cristóbal Madan, whom he advised Quitman to cultivate. George Law now offered Quitman 5000 muskets.[80] These or other arms were smuggled to Cuba beginning in October to encourage a promising revolutionary group at Nuevitas, but the gun-runners were soon caught by agents of the new Captain-General, Concha, and their leader, Francisco Estrampes of the Junta, was executed.[81]

The propaganda activities of the filibusters increased during the fall and winter. A worshipful biography was written in Spanish to acquaint the Cubans with their liberator, Juan Antonio Quitman.[82] The third anniversary of the martyrs of the Bahia Honda Expedition was celebrated in New Orleans with a mass meeting at which Thrasher and Betancourt Cisneros spoke. The latter re-affirmed the opposition of the fili-

77 *National Intelligencer*, June 22, 1854.

78 W. H. Holderness to Palmerston, Adams County, Ohio, September 22, 1854. Henderson, *op. cit.*, 375-6.

79 *MS.* by A. M. Clayton in J. F. H. Claiborne Papers, University of North Carolina.

80 Samuel R. Walker to Quitman, New Orleans, September 21, 1854. Quitman Papers.

81 Vilá, *Historia*, II, 96-8.

82 J. A. Quintero, *Apuntes Biograficos del Major General Juan Antonio Quitman* (New Orleans, 1855).

busters to annexation by purchase.[83] The pages of *DeBow's Review* were opened to an article by Samuel R. Walker which presented the official justification of the Quitman expedition. Africanization, Walker wrote, made everyone admit the necessity of action on the Cuban question, and only the best manner of action was in doubt. War between the United States and Spain would be unwise because it would lead the Captain-General to confiscate the Creoles' property and the island would be " a crown robbed of its jewels." Once the slaves were freed, the United States could never return the Negroes to slavery, if for no other reason because " the fanaticism of the North would rear the banner of civil war to prevent such a consummation." On the other hand, if the island were purchased from Spain, it would come into the Union burdened with the decrees already ordained by Pezuela. Spain in any case would not sell.

Therefore, Walker argued, only one road was open. If the federal government would hold off, Cuba would free herself in a short time, and the United States could acquire the island as it acquired Texas. The filibusters would merely aid a people already in a state of " moral " revolution. They would scrupulously avoid infringement of the Neutrality Act—" a law which is a libel on our free institutions." The filibuster movement was a crusade of the people of the Mississippi valley against the sacrilege of divine right claimed by imbecile kingcraft. The South's institution of slavery made Spanish rule in Cuba " an anomaly too monstrous to be borne." Commercial interests also dictated the overthrow of Spanish rule. But it was chiefly a southern question. The idea of northerners who regarded the Negro as a white man was a fatal cancer at the heart of the Union. " The safety of the South is to be found only in the extension of its peculiar institutions, and the security of the Union in the safety of the South—towards the equator." Let the superfluous sympathies of the northern

---

[83] Gaspar Betancourt Cisneros and John S. Thrasher, *Addresses Delivered at the Celebration of the Third Anniversary in Honor of the Martyrs for Cuban Freedom* (New Orleans, 1854), 6.

brethren be absorbed in an unlimited commerce. Cuba would cement the bonds of Union:

> What wealth will float upon our waters! What a bright gem will she, " the Queen of the Antilles," be in the coronet of the South, and how proudly will she wear it!

The South was ready to pay in blood for Cuba's liberty. The Crimean War now distracted Europe and the way was open. Walker ended with a plea that the federal government should not take action against the expedition.[84] This was one of the most frank public utterances of the southern imperialists and expressed the views of a wide section of the public in the Southwest.

Senator Slidell continued to busy himself with Cuban affairs. In October, he was engaged in mysterious negotiations between Cubans and Marcy on which he reported to Thrasher. A certain Cuban harbor, he wrote, would be unmarked.[85] Slidell also advised the administration and its diplomats abroad in the decisions that led to the Ostend Conference. His particular contribution was to urge action on the Belmont scheme.[86]

Soulé's efforts to fish for Cuba in the waters of revolution which he helped stir up in Madrid during July and August, 1854, were a failure, even though he attached himself to the Queen as well as her enemies. Significantly, Soulé frankly reported to Marcy his revolutionary activities, going so far as to state that with three hundred thousand dollars he could make a deal for Cuba with a republican faction.[87] This despatch was sent by special messenger and arrived in time to influence

84 Samuel R. Walker, "Cuba and the South," *DeBow's Review*, XVII (November, 1854), 519-25.

85 Slidell to Thrasher, Washington, October 5, 1854. Quitman Papers.

86 Slidell to Buchanan, Washington, June 17, August 6, 1854. Quoted in Ettinger, *Mission*, 340, 343.

87 Soulé to Marcy, Madrid, July 15, 1854. Department of State, *Diplomatic Despatches: Spain*, XXXIX.

President Pierce's special message to Congress of August 1 in which he again urged it to take "provisional measures" in regard to Cuba and Spain. A proposal was made to place ten million dollars in the President's hands, but Congress adjourned on August 7 without acting on it.[88] The administration then decided to put Soulé in charge of a conference with John Y. Mason and Buchanan to concert measures in aid of the Minister to Spain's attempts to acquire Cuba.[89]

These instructions reached Soulé in the French Pyrenees where he had gone to rest and perhaps for safety after his futile revolutionary labors in Madrid, and they served to revive his hopes. He considered them a renewal and an extension of his authority "to detach" Cuba from Spain. Ettinger has shown in his masterly analysis of the Ostend Conference that plans for violence were the contribution of Soulé to the Conference report known to history as the Ostend Manifesto. Buchanan, on the other hand, favored peaceful methods and the use of the Belmont scheme to bring pressure on the Spanish government. Mason favored both plans without particular enthusiasm for either one. Officially, all three diplomats assumed full responsibility for the document that Ettinger aptly calls "the *Magnum Opus* of the school of 'Manifest Destiny' and Southern Imperialism." [90]

From October 9 to 18 the conferees met, first in Ostend and then in Aix-la-Chapelle, and on the last day signed the joint production and dispatched it to Marcy. The Ostend Manifesto represents the high-water mark of the movement to annex Cuba before the Civil War. It restated the standard commercial and strategic arguments for annexation which had been urged by many Americans of all sections for half a century. To these

88 *Messages and Papers of the Presidents*, comp. Richardson, VI, 2778-9. Ettinger, *Mission*, 341.

89 Marcy to Soulé, Washington, August 16, 1854. Department of State, *Diplomatic Instructions: Spain*, XV.

90 Ettinger, *Mission*, 357-68.

were added the pro-slavery motives which, since Polk's administration, had made the South take the lead in advocating annexation and the North turn increasingly against it. The Belmont scheme was introduced in a reference to the beneficial effect on Spanish bonds should that government consent to sell the island to the United States. But the Africanization of Cuba was likened to a neighbor's burning house that justified tearing it down to prevent its flames from destroying one's own home. In such a situation, the key statement of the Manifesto read, " by every law human and Divine, we shall be justified in wresting it from Spain, if we possess the power." [91] The document thus presents a review of the history of motives for annexation and at the same time a resumé of sectional attitudes in 1854. Buchanan represented the older national view and the element in the North that sympathized with the South, Mason represented the border slave states' willingness to follow the leadership of friends of slavery in both sections, and Soulé represented the latest and most extreme views of the Gulf states. Emphasizing these aspects, Soulé wrote to Marcy favoring war with Spain to obtain Cuba,[92] and Buchanan wrote to him that he had no intention of favoring anything but peaceful acquisition. Yet he could not, and did not, deny that he had supported stronger action if Cuba was Africanized.[93]

The Ostend Manifesto arrived in Washington on November 4, the same day that New York voted every Democrat in the preceding Congress from that state out of office. This completed the disasters the Pierce administration had been meeting at the polls since spring. Its great victory of 1852 was wiped out as Anti-Nebraska men, Whigs and Know-Nothings swept every northern state but two. Democrats in the next House would be in a minority of seventy-five. Opposition to the

91 *Works of James Buchanan*, ed. Moore, IX, 260-6.

92 Soulé to Marcy, London, October 20, 1854. Department of State, *Diplomatic Despatches: Spain*, XXXIX.

93 Buchanan to Marcy, London, December 8, 1854. Marcy Papers.

Kansas-Nebraska Act was the chief cause of this upset. Only seven out of forty-two northern Democrats who had voted for it were re-elected.[94] Know-Nothings were particularly offended by the appointments of many Young American diplomats who, like Soulé, Belmont and O'Sullivan, were neither American-born nor Protestant.[95]

The Cuban-annexation policy of the administration, which had emerged as the main preoccupation of the flamboyant Young American diplomats in the scandalous rumors and facts with which newspapers regaled their readers, helped to create the electoral revolution. Pro-slavery was seen as the essential meaning of that policy as of the Kansas-Nebraska Act, and it was concealed by Young American oratory about extending free institutions to Cuba no more than by the extension of popular sovereignty to Kansas. The grandiose conception of Douglas of a vast network of transportation to bind the Atlantic, Pacific and Gulf coasts to Chicago, with annexation of Cuba and repeal of the Missouri Compromise as inducements to the South, had begun to collapse around his head and wreck the administration and party that adopted it, because the North would not admit that the doctrine of neutrality on slavery was more than a mockery hiding the actual extension of slavery. And Cuba proved the hollowness of Douglas' fundamental doctrine more conclusively than Kansas.

94 Johnson, *Douglas*, 269-80. Ettinger, *Mission*, 378.

95 Anna E. Carroll, *A Review of Pierce's Administration* (Boston, 1856), 24-6.

CHAPTER XI

RETREAT

THE Pierce administration could not retreat from its commitment to the Kansas-Nebraska Act, indeed the South demanded ever more militantly pro-slavery interpretation and enforcement of it. But the administration could and did heed the warning of the elections to retreat from its Cuban policy. On November 13, Marcy wrote to Soulé that, while he did not believe the Ostend Conference report advocated seizure of Cuba, President Pierce was in any case strongly opposed to such a policy. Furthermore, Soulé should refrain from attempts to purchase the island.[1] A masterpiece of evasion, Marcy's letter assumed no responsibility for the results of its author's instructions on April 3 to buy or " detach " Cuba. Soulé was told to busy himself with the *Black Warrior* case, and to observe moderation in his demands. Copies of the letter were sent to Buchanan and Mason.[2] This was repudiation, and Soulé promptly resigned.[3] Buchanan, as has been mentioned, was content to disclaim responsibility for the seizure clause in the Manifesto, and Mason suffered a stroke when he heard of Soulé's October 20 letter to Marcy interpreting the Manifesto to mean war.[4]

1 Marcy's instructions on this point are so ambiguous that Learned interprets them as directing Soulé to enter upon the accomplishment of the purchase (Learned, "William Learned Marcy," *op. cit.*, 209), whereas Ettinger finds that they enjoined the Minister not to press Spain any further (Ettinger, *Mission*, 379). The present author inclines to the latter view because the ambiguity itself was indicative of a change in policy and Soulé so interpreted it.

2 Marcy to Soulé, Washington, November 13, 1854. Department of State, *Diplomatic Instructions: Spain*, XV. Marcy to Buchanan, Washington, November 14, 1854. *Diplomatic Instructions: Great Britain*, XVI. Marcy to Mason, Washington, November 14, 1854. *Diplomatic Instructions: France*, XV.

3 Soulé to Marcy, Madrid, December 17, 1854. Department of State, *Diplomatic Despatches: Spain*, XXXIX.

4 Ettinger, *Mission*, 383.

When Soulé, a pitiable failure, returned to the United States, the heart was gone from the Young American adventure in diplomacy. George N. Sanders, after such exploits as his letter to the London *Times* calling for the assassination of Napoleon III, failed of confirmation by the Senate. He clung to the hope that his friend Pierce would submit his name again, and appealed to John J. Crittenden to rally Whig votes for him. The two former Secretaries of State, Clayton and Everett, he thought, were likely to appreciate his worth. Reports that his interest in the post was the revolutionizing of Europe he denied with a cynical description of his true interest: the opportunity it gave him for speculations " with little or no risk." The height of his ambition was merely to amass a fortune and retire to " a good farm in Ky." [5] But Pierce was in no position to press Sanders on the Senate, and he, too, returned home. He learned nothing from his failure. In 1860, he tried again to " outdemagogize " the opponents of slavery. He appealed to Republicans to abandon Abraham Lincoln and expend their humanitarian impulses in a war for Cuba: " Why not begin with the blood of the foreigner. . . ? Why must our fellow-citizen's blood be poured out to appease the Congo fetich? " [6] Sanders did not hestitate to support the firing on Fort Sumter, and the Confederate government opened new fields to his supposed talent for diplomatic intrigue in defense of slavery.

John L. O'Sullivan, the third of the great triumvirate of Young American diplomats, clung to his post the longest. But he had passed his best days as an international firebrand. He seems genuinely to have interested himself in relatively harmless speculations. His friend, Nathaniel Hawthorne, while serving as United States Consul at Liverpool unwisely loaned O'Sullivan ten thousand dollars to invest in copper mines in

5 Sanders to Crittenden, London, April 7, 1854. Crittenden Papers, Library of Congress.

6 George N. Sanders, *G. N. Sanders on the Sequences of Southern Secession* (New York, 1860), 1.

Spain. He was never repaid.[7] In their personal as well as official conduct, the Young American diplomats reflected no credit on the United States government. Their posturings as the carriers of American democracy to the Old World were exposed as a fraud before Pierce's administration was two years old. And even as agents of pro-slavery imperialism, they had to be written off as liabilities by the most pro-southern leaders of their party. The attempt to dress the cause of slavery in the garments of liberalism for a diplomatic campaign failed, as it would fail again during the Civil War.

After the collapse of Soulé's mission, the Quitman expedition might still have freed Cuba. Southern leaders were not satisfied with their victory in the passage of the Kansas-Nebraska Act. Alexander H. Stephens of Georgia well expressed their view when he wrote to W. W. Burwell in May, 1854, that while the victory was important, he doubted whether it would yield any positive advantages by way of the " actual extension of slavery." He believed Cuba offered a much greater issue.[8] Later in the same month, Stephens wrote to J. W. Duncan that in spite of Presidential proclamations his sympathies would be with the filibusters, and so would the sympathies of the southern people.[9] Then in February, 1855, Stephens personally encouraged Quitman to launch the expedition forthwith. He wrote to him that for nearly twelve months people had been " deceived and bamboozled " by the Pierce administration on the question of Cuban acquisition. He was for rousing the public mind and acting: " You are right sir—now is the time to act ...now is the time to move—while England and France have

7 Julian Hawthorne, *Hawthorne and His Circle* (New York, 1903), 135, 360.

8 Stephens to Burwell, Washington, May 7, 1854. *Correspondence of Toombs, Stephens and Cobb*, edited by Ulrich B. Phillips, Annual Report of the American Historical Association, 1911 (Washington, 1913), II, 344.

9 Stephens to Duncan, Washington, May 26, 1854. *Ibid.*, 345.

their hands full in the East." [10] Stephens' evolution since the time when he had opposed annexation was now complete and it reflected the development of public opinion in the South.

Desperate efforts were made to raise money for the expedition. Quitman apparently demanded a million dollars. In December, 1854, Gaspar Betancourt Cisneros mortgaged his house for $25,000 and contributed it to the fund.[11] On January 5, 1855, Quitman wrote to his agent in Savannah, C. A. L. Lamar, that the expedition must move in sixty days or forfeit a half million dollars already invested. He still needed about $50,000. He now required that men who volunteered each contribute fifty dollars. To avoid breach of the neutrality laws, organizing and arming would not take place in the United States.[12] Letters among the Quitman Papers show that during the winter of 1854-5 volunteers, chiefly from the Gulf states, flocked to Quitman's standard in numbers totaling approximately ten thousand. Colonel Theodore O'Hara and others in Kentucky organized a contingent of one thousand men. Letters in code passed back and forth among the leaders. The motives of volunteers, so far as they are discernible in their letters, were on the whole political and pro-slavery with some admixture of interest in the Cuban bonds which many of them had bought.[13] In February, Quitman was at last satisfied that money and men were sufficient and that revolution in Cuba, currently led by Ramon de Pinta, was ripe. He gave orders which were promptly carried out to obtain plantations on the Gulf coast as *rendezvous* and points of embarkation. Detachments of volunteers began to slip out of New Orleans in the guise of " woodchoppers." [14]

10 Stephens to Quitman, Crawfordsville, Georgia, February 24, 1855. Quitman Papers.

11 R. W. Estlin to Quitman, New Orleans, December 21, 1854. *Ibid.*

12 Quitman to Lamar, New Orleans, January 5, 1855. *Ibid.*

13 *Passim*, September, 1854 to April, 1855. *Ibid.*

14 H. Forno to Quitman, New Orleans, February 6, 1855. *Ibid.*

Had this expedition sailed, it would have been by much the most formidable of the period. To liquidate its Cuban policy completely, the Pierce administration had to prevail upon Quitman to abandon his enterprise, and this it did. A convincing argument was provided by the Spanish authorities in Cuba who, at the end of January, discovered the conspiracy of de Pinta and full information on the expedition from the United States. The Cubans had planned to begin the revolt on February 12 with the assassination of Concha and the leading Spanish officials while they attended the theatre. Then 4,000 filibusters were to have landed at several points. Over a hundred leaders were arrested and de Pinta and others were executed. The *National Intelligencer* reported that business and commerce in Havana were at a standstill because so large a proportion of the city's leading men of wealth were suddenly thrown into prison.[15] Captain-General Concha wrathfully told Consul Robertson that if the Quitman expedition sailed, he would arm the Negroes. For the present, he declared a state of siege and blockaded the coast with the aid of four British warships. Robertson sent full reports to Marcy.[16] Admiral Fanshawe agreed to Concha's request that the British sloop-of-war *Medea* should aid him by transporting Spanish troops.[17]

Marcy now rebuked Robertson for his intimacy with the Cuban revolutionists, but the Consul tartly answered that he had often told the Secretary of State of his activities and had never before been criticized.[18] And the situation was in fact embarrassing for the American government. Concha instructed the Spanish Minister in Washington to

15 *National Intelligencer*, February 17, 1855.

16 Robertson to Marcy, Havana, January 29, February 14, 1855. Department of State, *Consular Despatches: Havana*, XXIX.

17 Crawford to Clarendon, Havana, February 14, 1855. Henderson, *op. cit.,* 382.

18 Robertson to Marcy, Havana, May 9, 1855. Department of State, *Consular Despatches: Havana*, XXIX.

demand that the administration proceed vigorously against the expedition.[19] But public action at this time, when Pierce was no longer able to fend off publication of the Ostend Manifesto and other revealing documents,[20] would have been a damaging admission that the Proclamation of May 31, 1854, had been ignored by Quitman and many another eminent friend of the administration.

Pierce decided to appeal privately to Quitman to save the administration from a crowning scandal. He called the filibuster to Washington and, although what passed between them can only be conjectured, the effect of the interview was soon evident. When Quitman returned to New Orleans, the Cuban Junta found he had lost his enthusiasm and turned dilatory. They learned that he had interviewed Pierce, Marcy and the Spanish Minister Cueta. The latter showed him convincing evidence supplied by Concha of the island's formidable defenses against invasion. The opposition of the American government, which had never before concerned him, Quitman now offered as an excuse for procrastination.[21] Finally on April 30, his decision made, Quitman in a formal instrument surrendered to the Junta his authority over it and the expedition, and Thrasher witnessed his signature and seal.[22]

Without its renowned leader, the expedition disbanded. As no accounting was ever made of funds said to amount to over a million dollars, and nothing was paid to holders of Cuban bonds or other creditors, in spite of insistent demands upon Quitman from the Junta, the whole enterprise was presently in

19 Concha to Cueta, Havana, January 25, February 8, 23, 1855. Morales, *Iniciadores*, III, 63-9.

20 *House Executive Documents* (33:2), no. 64.

21 Morales, *Iniciadores*, III, 26, 54-5. Vilá, *Historia*, II, 100-1. Guillaume Lobé, *Cuba et les Grandes Puissances Occidentales de l'Europe* (Paris, 1856), 21-3. Lobé was the extremely well-informed Consul-General of the Netherlands in Havana in 1855, and claimed to have "positive knowledge" of Quitman's trip to Washington.

22 Claiborne, *Quitman*, II, 392.

extremely bad odor among its former adherents.[23] Disillusioned
and disheartened, the Junta also disbanded, this time not to re-
appear until after the Civil War, when the character of American support for Cuban independence had greatly changed. The
experience with Quitman finally destroyed annexationism
among Cuban patriots and the abolition of slavery in the United
States removed the most potent motive for annexation among
Americans.

For his part, Quitman returned to active political life, was
elected to Congress later in 1855, and in the next year gained
notoriety for his attempts to repeal the neutrality laws. But he
was interested then not in Cuba but Nicaragua. The filibuster
Henry L. Kinney, after gaining a foothold on its coast,
promised Quitman that he would establish "a constitution
suited to the interest of the Southern States." [24] The exploit of
William Walker in seizing the government of Nicaragua, after
which his first act was the repeal of anti-slavery laws, made
Quitman look upon him, he told the House of Representatives,
as "one of those instruments which, in the hands of Providence, are used to facilitate the march of civilization and im-
provement, and the spread of liberal political principle. . . ." [25]
Goicouria, Schlesinger and others of Quitman's followers took
up the burden and fought for Walker in Nicaragua.[26]

The Pierce administration's action in securing the disband-
ment of the Quitman expedition was the logical counterpart of
its repudiation of Soulé. The two actions marked the close of
an epoch in the history of American interest in Cuba. The

23 Vilá, *Historia*, II, 101.

24 Kinney to Quitman, San Juan del Norte, Nicaragua, November 3,
1855. Quitman Papers.

25 *Congressional Globe* (34:3), *Appendix*, 118-9. *Cf*. William Walker to
Quitman, Montgomery, Alabama, January 19, 1858. Quitman Papers.

26 Appleton Oaksmith, "Nicaraguan Minister to the United States," to
Quitman, Nicaraguan Legation, New York, September 4, 1856. Walker's
attempt to set up a military despotism disillusioned Schlesinger. Schlesinger
to Quitman. Rivas, Nicaragua, September 3, 1857. Quitman Papers.

elections of 1854 proved to have been the turning point. Enthusiasm for the annexation of Cuba to the United States declined as the sectional crisis deepened. The Order of the Lone Star went underground and merged with the new secret order of the " Knights of the Golden Circle," who plotted in favor of secession and a slavery empire to contain all the lands of the "golden circle" around the Gulf of Mexico and Caribbean Sea. When the Civil War began, the Knights turned to seduce the Northwest from its allegiance to the Union.[27]

President Buchanan tried several times to revive enthusiasm for Cuba by proposing purchase to Congress. With this and other expansionist projects, he hoped to distract attention from the domestic issue of slavery by conducting an imperialist foreign policy. In 1859, when a bill to place thirty million dollars at the disposal of the President was before Congress, Robert B. Letcher, former Minister to Mexico, wrote to his fellow Kentuckian and Whig, John J. Crittenden, that the money was intended to bribe Spanish officials, and added:

> The great desire to acquire Cuba and to throw before the country a new and exciting topic, one which will override all others, and cover up the errors of this administration, is the policy of the Democratic Party.[28]

But Cuban annexation too obviously strengthened slavery for northerners to allow Buchanan's schemes to succeed.

During his administration, Central America was the chief object of southern expansionists. Northern interests were more apparent there than in Cuba, and slavery was potential rather than actual even after William Walker repealed the antislavery laws of the largest republic. Nevertheless, the North refused to fall in with the program.

27 A Member of the Order, *An Authentic Exposition of the 'K.G.C.'* (Indianapolis, 1861), 5-11.

28 Letcher to Crittenden, Frankfort, January 26, 1859. Crittenden Papers, Library of Congress. See also S. S. Nicholas to Crittenden, Louisville, January 30, 1859. *Ibid.*

The demand of Jefferson Davis and John Slidell for an open door to southern expansion, besides the refusal of the fire-eaters led by the same two men to accept Douglas' proposal of a fair trial of popular sovereignty in Kansas, caused the final split in the Democratic Party.[29] The two issues were clearly seen by northerners as involving the one question of slavery-extension. The southern demands that the federal government intervene in the free states to return alleged fugitive slaves without trial, in the territories to protect slavery even against the will of the majority, and in Spanish America to annex new slave states made northerners regard the cries of southerners for liberty, states' rights and the extension of democratic institutions as noises that concealed the purposes of enemies of those ideals.

When the southern leaders finally left Washington, after ensuring the election of Lincoln by refusing to compromise with the Douglas Democrats, they planned to carry out the scheme for a slavery empire outside the Union.[30] At the last moment, President-elect Abraham Lincoln had prevented such a dénouement inside the Union when Republican leaders hesitated over the Crittenden Compromise. He wrote to Senator Hale of New Hampshire:

> If we surrender [to those we defeated in the 1860 election], it is the end of us and of the government. They will repeat the experiment upon us *ad libitum*. A year will not pass till we shall have to take Cuba as a condition upon which they will stay in the Union . . . . There is in my judgment but one compromise which would really settle the slavery question, and that would be a prohibition against acquiring any more territory.[31]

29 Dodd, *Jefferson Davis*, 184-7.

30 *Ibid.*, 211, 298.

31 Lincoln to Hale, Springfield, Illinois, January 11, 1861. *Complete Works of Abraham Lincoln*, edited by John G. Nicolay and John Hay (New York, 1905), VI, 93-4.

The nation had at last found in Lincoln a leader who beheld a moral issue in slavery. At Jonesboro, Illinois, in his debate with Lincoln, Stephen A. Douglas had said:

> When we get Cuba we must take it as we find it, leaving the people to decide the question of slavery for themselves, without interference on the part of the Federal Government, or of any State of this Union.[32]

To this specious kind of moral neutrality on slavery, Abraham Lincoln's was the final answer because it was ultimately the answer of the American people.

Yet strategic and commercial interests in Cuba survived abolition of slavery in the United States and in the island, where it required the even more prolonged civil war that began in 1868. Those interests grew strong to the pitch of war for Cuban freedom before the century ended. This time the ideal of extending democratic institutions to the Cuban people, while it concealed much that was discreditable, did not conceal denial of freedom to half of them. Relieved of the incubus of slavery, the United States kept its promise not to annex the island and has contributed to the considerable success of Cuba as an independent, democratic community today.

32 September 15, 1858. *Ibid.*, IV, 28.

BIBLIOGRAPHY

UNPUBLISHED MANUSCRIPT COLLECTIONS

James Buchanan Papers, Historical Society of Pennsylvania
John F. H. Claiborne Papers, Mississippi State Archives
————, University of North Carolina
Thomas Claiborne Papers, University of North Carolina
John M. Clayton Papers, Library of Congress
John J. Crittenden Papers, Library of Congress
————, Duke University
Caleb Cushing Papers, Library of Congress
Jefferson Davis Papers, Library of Congress
Stephen A. Douglas Papers, University of Chicago
Thomas Jefferson Papers, Library of Congress
William L. Marcy Papers, Library of Congress
James Monroe Papers, Library of Congress
John T. Pickett Papers, Library of Congress
Franklin Pierce Papers, Library of Congress
James K. Polk Papers, Library of Congress
John A. Quitman Papers, Harvard University
William C. Rives Papers, Library of Congress
United States Trade and Commerce, Library of Congress
Martin Van Buren Papers, Library of Congress
Daniel Webster Papers, Library of Congress

UNPUBLISHED OFFICIAL CORRESPONDENCE: NATIONAL ARCHIVES

DEPARTMENT OF STATE

Consular Despatches: Havana
Diplomatic Despatches: France
————: Great Britain
————: Russia
————: Spain
Diplomatic Instructions: France
————: Great Britain
————: Spain
Instructions: United States Ministers
Instructions to Consuls
López Expedition: 1849-1851: Cuba
Miscellaneous Letters
Notes from Legations: France
————: Great Britain
————: Spain
Notes to Legations: France
————: Great Britain
————: Spain

Panama Congress
Special Agents
Special Missions

NAVY DEPARTMENT

Commanders' Letters
Confidential Letters

PUBLISHED COLLECTIONS AND DIARIES

*Memoirs of John Quincy Adams Comprising Portions of His Diary from
1795 to 1848*, edited by Charles Francis Adams (Philadelphia, 1874-
1877). 12 vols.
The Works of James Buchanan, edited by John B. Moore (Philadelphia,
1909). 12 vols.
Calhoun Correspondence, edited by J. Franklin Jameson, Annual Report of
the American Historical Association, 1899 (Washington, 1900).
Millard Fillmore Papers, edited by Frank H. Severance, Publications of the
Buffalo Historical Society, XI (Buffalo, 1907).
Robert M. T. Hunter Correspondence, edited by Charles E. Ambler, Annual
Report of the American Historical Association, 1916 (Washington,
1917), II.
Complete Works of Abraham Lincoln, edited by John G. Nicolay and John
Hay (New York, 1905). 12 vols.
The Diary of James K. Polk, edited by Milo M. Quaife (Chicago, 1910).
4 vols.
The Political Correspondence of the Late Hon. George N. Sanders, The
American Art Association (New York, 1914).
"Southern Designs on Cuba, 1854-1857, and Some European Opinions,"
edited by Gavin B. Henderson. *The Journal of Southern History*, V
(August, 1939), 371-385.
Correspondence of Robert Toombs, Alexander H. Stephens and Howell Cobb,
edited by Ulrich B. Phillips, Annual Report of the American Historical
Association, 1911 (Washington, 1914).

OFFICIAL DOCUMENTS

Boletin del Archivo Nacional, Havana, III (1909), XVI (1917).
Congressional Globe.
House Executive Documents (31 Congress: 1 Session), 86; (32:1), 2, 10,
14, 64, 83, 91, 113, 121; (34:1), 98.
Messages and Papers of the Presidents, compiled by James D. Richardson
(Washington, 1911), IV.
Preliminary Report on the Eighth Census, 1860 (Washington, 1862).
Senate Executive Documents (31:1), 1; (31:2), 1, 41; (32:1), 5, 53, 86;
(33:2), 93; (34:1), 107; (35:1), 53.
Senate Journal (33:1).
Senate Miscellaneous Documents (32:1), 10; (32:2), 18; (33:1), 63.
Senate Reports (32:1), 267, 318.

Statistical Abstract of the United States: 1878 (Washington, 1879).
Statistical View of the United States, James D. B. DeBow, Superintendent of the Census (Washington, 1854).

CONTEMPORARY PERIODICALS

La Cronica
Danville Quarterly Review
DeBow's Review
Democratic Review
Harper's Monthly Magazine
Hunt's Merchants' Magazine
Littell's Living Age
National Era
National Intelligencer
New Orleans *Bee*
New Orleans *Delta*
New York *Evening Post*
New York *Herald*
New York *Sun*
Niles' Weekly Register
Southern Quarterly Review
La Verdad

CONTEMPORARY BOOKS AND PAMPHLETS

Abbott, John S. C., *South and North* (New York, 1860).
Abduction of Juan Francisco Rey, compiled and edited by Daniel Scully (New Orleans, 1849).
Ashworth, Henry, *A Tour of the United States, Cuba and Canada* (London, 1861).
Ballou, Maturin M., *History of Cuba* (Boston, 1854).
Betancourt Cisneros, Gaspar, and Thrasher, John S., *Addresses Delivered at the Celebration of the Third Anniversary in Honor of the Martyrs for Cuban Freedom* (New Orleans, 1854).
Bigelow, John, *Retrospections of an Active Life* (New York, 1909), I.
Boggess, F. C. M., *A Veteran of Four Wars* (Arcadia, Florida, 1900).
Boutwell, George S., *Reminiscences of Sixty Years in Public Affairs* (New York, 1902).
Bridge, Horatio, *Personal Recollections of Nathaniel Hawthorne* (New York, 1893).
Carroll, Anna E., *A Review of Pierce's Administration* (Boston, 1856).
Claiborne, John F. H., *Life and Correspondence of John A. Quitman* (New York, 1860). 2 vols.
Coleccion de los Partes y otros Documentos publicados en la Gaceta Oficial de la gavilla de pirates capitaneada por el traidor Narciso Lopez (Havana, 1851).
Constitution of the Order of the Lone Star (New Orleans, 1851).
Dana, Richard H., *To Cuba and Back* (Boston, 1870).

DeBow, James D. B., *The Industrial Resources, Etc., of the Southern and Western States* (New Orleans, 1852-1853). 3 vols.

Delaplain, Sophia, *A Thrilling and Exciting Account of the Sufferings and Horrible Tortures Inflicted on Mortimer Bowers and Miss Sophia Delaplain, by the Spanish Authorities, for a Supposed Participation with Gen. Lopez in the Invasion of Cuba; together with the Plan of Campaign of Lopez* (Charleston, 1851).

Editors of *La Verdad*, *A Series of Articles on the Cuban Question* (New York, 1849).

A Filibustero, *Life of General Narciso Lopez* (New York, 1851).

Fiscal de la Superintendencia General Delegado de Real Hacienda, *Informe Fiscal sobre Fomento de la Poblacion Blanca en la Isla de Cuba y Emancipacion Progressiva de la Esclava* (Madrid, 1845).

"The Five Predatory Tribes," *Evening Post Documents* (New York, 1853), Series 2, No. 4.

Freret, William, *Correspondence between the Treasury Department, Etc., in Relation to the Cuba Expedition, and William Freret, Late Collector* (New Orleans, 1851).

Gonzalez, Ambrosio J., *Manifesto on Cuban Affairs Addressed to the People of the United States* (New Orleans, 1853).

Hardy, Richardson, *The History and Adventures of the Cuban Expedition* (Cincinnati, 1850).

Holinski, Alexandre, *La Californie et les Routes Interocéaniques* (Brussels, 1853).

Jones, Alexander, *Cuba in 1851* (New York, 1851).

Kimball, Richard B., *Cuba* (New York, 1850).

Law, George, *United States Mail Steamships* (New York, 1850).

Lobé, Guillaume, *Cuba et les Grandes Puissances Occidentales de l'Europe* (Paris, 1856).

Madden, Richard R., *Island of Cuba* (London, 1853).

Marmier, Xavier, *Lettres sur L'Amérique* (Paris, 1851), II.

A Member of the Order, *An Authentic Exposition of the 'K. G. C.,' 'Knights of the Golden Circle'* (Indianapolis, 1861).

Montgomery, Cora [Mrs. William L. Cazneau], *Eagle Pass* (New York, 1852).

Montgomery, Cora, *The Queen of Islands and the King of Rivers* (New York, 1850).

Murray, Amelia M., *Letters from the United States, Cuba and Canada* (New York, 1856).

Murray, Henry A., *Lands of the Slave and the Free* (London, 1857).

[Nason, Daniel], Journal of a Tour (Cambridge, Mass., 1849).

O.D.D.O. [J. C. Davis], *The History of the Late Expedition to Cuba* (New Orleans, 1850).

Poesche, Theodore, and Goeppe, Charles, *The New Rome* (New York, 1852.

Pollard, Edward A., *Black Diamonds* (New York, 1859).

Pulszky, Ferencz and Theresa, *White, Red, and Black* (London, 1853).

Quintero, José A., *Apuntes Biograficos del Major General Juan Antonio Quitman* (New Orleans, 1855).

Saco, José Antonio, *Coleccion de Papeles* (Paris, 1859), III.

———, *Contra la Anexion, Coleccion de Libros Cubanos*, compiled by Fernando Ortiz (Havana, 1928), V.

Sanders, George N., *G. N. Sanders on the Sequences of Southern Secession* (New York, 1860).

Smith, Duncan, "Narrative of Events Connected with the Late Intended Invasion of Cuba," edited by L. M. Perez, *Publications of the Southern History Association* (November, 1906), X.

Smith, Matthew H., *Sunshine and Shadow in New York* (Hartford, 1869).

Taylor, John G., *The United States and Cuba: Eight Years of Change and Travel* (London, 1851).

Thrasher, John S., *Cuba and Louisiana: Letter to Samuel J. Peters, Esq.* (New Orleans, 1854).

———, "Preliminary Essay," Alexander Humboldt, *The Island of Cuba* (New York, 1856).

Train, George F., *My Life in Many States and in Foreign Lands* (New York, 1902).

———, *Young America in Wall Street* (New York, 1857).

Trescot, William H., *A Few Thoughts on the Foreign Policy of the United States* (Charleston, 1849).

Turnbull, David, *Travels in the West: Cuba; with Notice of Porto Rico, and the Slave Trade* (London, 1840).

SECONDARY WORKS

Adams, Henry, *History of the United States during the Second Administration of Thomas Jefferson* (New York, 1890), II.

Aimes, Hubert H. S., *A History of Slavery in Cuba* (New York, 1907).

Asbury, Herbert, *The French Quarter* (New York, 1936).

Becker, Jerónimo, *Historia de las Relaciones Esteriores de España durante el Siglo XIX: Apuntes para una Historia Diplomatica* (Madrid, 1924), II.

Bonner, James C., "Profile of a Late Ante-Bellum Community," *American Historical Review*, XLIX (July, 1944), 663-80.

Brownson, Henry F., *Orestes A. Brownson's Middle Life: from 1845 to 1855* (Detroit, 1899).

Burton, Theodore E., "Henry Clay," *The American Secretaries of State and Their Diplomacy*, edited by Samuel F. Bemis (New York, 1928), IV.

Butler, Pierce, *Judah P. Benjamin* (Philadelphia, 1907).

Caldwell, Robert G., *The López Expeditions to Cuba: 1848-1851* (Princeton. 1915).

Callahan, James M., *Cuba and Anglo-American Relations*, Annual Report of the American Historical Association, 1897 (Washington, 1898).

———, *Cuba and International Relations* (Baltimore, 1899).

Castellanos, G., *Panorama Historica* (Havana, 1934).

Chadwick, French E., *The Relations of the United States and Spain* (New York, 1909).

Cole, Arthur C., *The Whig Party in the South*, Prize Essays of the American Historical Association, 1912 (Washington, 1913).

Commager, Henry S., *Theodore Parker* (Boston, 1936).

Craven, Avery O., "The Agricultural Reformers of the Ante-Bellum South," *American Historical Review*, XXXIII (January, 1928), 302-14.

Curti, Merle E., *The American Peace Crusade: 1815-1860* (Durham, 1929).

——, "George Sanders: Patriot of the Fifties," *South Atlantic Quarterly*, XXVII (January, 1928), 79-87.

——, "Young America," *American Historical Review*, XXXII (October, 1926), 34-55.

Dictionary of American Biography, edited by Allen Johnson and Dumas Malone (New York, 1928-1936). 20 vols.

Dodd, William E., *Jefferson Davis* (Philadelphia, 1907).

——, *Robert James Walker, Imperialist* (Chicago, 1914).

Donovan, Herbert D. A., *The Barnburners* (New York, 1925).

Ettinger, Amos A., *The Mission to Spain of Pierre Soulé: 1853-1855* (New Haven, 1937).

——, "The Proposed Anglo-Franco-American Treaty of 1852 to Guarantee Cuba to Spain," *Transactions of the Royal Historical Society* (London, 1930), Fourth Series, Volume XIII, 149-185.

Flanders, Ralph B., *Plantation Slavery in Georgia* (Chapel Hill, 1933).

Fuess, Claude M., *The Life of Caleb Cushing* (New York, 1923), II.

Gonzalez, Diego, *Historia Documentada de los Movimientos Revolucionarios por la Independencia de Cuba de 1852 a 1867* (Havana, 1939), I.

Gray, Lewis C., *History of Agriculture in the Southern United States to 1860* (Washington, 1933). 2 vols.

Hammond, W. W., *The Cotton Industry* (Ithaca, 1897), I.

Hawks, E. Q., *Economic History of the South* (New York, 1934).

Hawthorne, Julian, *Hawthorne and His Circle* (New York, 1903).

——, *Nathaniel Hawthorne and His Wife* (Cambridge, 1884), I.

Hesseltine, William B., *A History of the South, 1607-1936* (New York, 1936).

Homans, J. Smith, Jr., *An Historical and Statistical Account of the Foreign Commerce of the United States* (New York, 1857).

Huebner, G. G., "The Foreign Trade of the United States since 1789," *History of Domestic and Foreign Commerce of the United States*, by E. R. Johnson, T. W. Van Metre, G. G. Huebner and D. S. Hanchett (Washington, 1915), II.

Janes, Henry L., "The Black Warrior Affair," *American Historical Review*, XII (January, 1907), 280-98.

Jenks, Leland H., *Our Cuban Colony* (New York, 1929).

Johnson, Allen, *Stephen A. Douglas: A Study in American Politics* (New York, 1908).

Johnson, Willis F., *The History of Cuba* (New York, 1920).

Jordan, H. Donaldson, "A Politician of Expansion: Robert J. Walker," *Mississippi Valley Historical Review*, XIX (December, 1932), 362-81.

Juárez Cano, Jorge, *Hombres del '51* (Havana, 1930).

Kemble, John H., *The Panama Route: 1848-1869* (Berkeley and Los Angeles, 1943).

King, Bolton, *Mazzini* (London, 1902).

Latané, John H., *Diplomacy of the United States in Regard to Cuba*, Annual Report of the American Historical Association, 1897 (Washington, 1898).

Learned, Henry B., "William Learned Marcy," *The American Secretaries of State and Their Diplomacy*, edited by Samuel F. Bemis (New York, 1928), VI.

Macy, Jesse, *Political Parties in the United States: 1841-1861* (New York, 1900).

Mathieson, William L., *Great Britain and the Slave Trade: 1839-1865* (London, 1929).

Maxwell, L. W., *Discriminating Duties and the American Merchant Marine* (New York, 1926).

McCormac, Eugene I., *James K. Polk: A Political Biography* (Berkeley, 1922).

Morales y Morales, Vidal, *Iniciadores y Primeros Martires de la Revolucion Cubana* (Havana, 1931), 3 vols.

Nichols, Roy F., *The Democratic Machine: 1850-1854* (New York, 1923).

——, *Franklin Pierce, Young Hickory of the Granite Hills* (Philadelphia, 1931).

O'Brien, Frank M., *The Story of the Sun* (New York, 1918).

Oliphant, Laurence, *Patriots and Filibusters* (London, 1860).

Otis, Fessenden N., *Isthmus of Panama: History of the Panama Railroad; and of the Pacific Mail Steamship Company* (New York, 1867).

Perkins, Dexter, *The Monroe Doctrine: 1823-1826* (Cambridge, 1932).

Phillips, Ulrich B., *American Negro Slavery* (New York, 1918).

Poage, George R., *Henry Clay and the Whig Party* (Chapel Hill, 1936).

Ponte Dominguez, Francisco J., *La Masoneria en la Independencia de Cuba* (Havana, 1944).

Porter, Kenneth N., *National Party Platforms* (New York, 1924).

Pratt, Julius W., "The Ideology of American Expansion," *Essays in Honor of William E. Dodd*, edited by Avery Craven (Chicago, 1935).

——, "John L. O'Sullivan and Manifest Destiny," *New York History*, XIV (July, 1933), 213-34.

——, "Origin of Manifest Destiny," *American Historical Review*, XXXII (July, 1927), 795-8.

Pulgarón, Luis O., *Apuntes Históricos Sobre la Masonería Cubana* (Guanábacoa, Cuba, 1933).

Quisenberry, Anderson C., *Lopez's Expeditions to Cuba*, Filson Club Publications (Louisville, 1906).

Ramsdell, Charles W., "The Natural Limits of Slavery Expansion," *Mississippi Valley Historical Review*, XVI (September, 1929), 151-71.

Riepma, Siert F., "*Young America:*" *A Study in American Nationalism before the Civil War* (unpublished doctoral dissertation, Western Reserve University, 1939).

Rippy, J. Fred, *Joel R. Poinsett, Versatile American* (Durham, North Carolina, 1935).

———, *Rivalry of the United States and Great Britain over Latin America: 1808-1830* (Baltimore, 1929).

Russel, Robert R., *Economic Aspects of Southern Sectionalism: 1840-1861* (Urbana, 1924).

Santovenia, Emeterio S., *El Presidente Polk y Cuba* (Havana, 1936).

Schlesinger, Arthur M., Jr., *Orestes A. Brownson* (Boston, 1939).

Scot, James B., *Outline of the Rise and Progress of Freemasonry in Louisiana* (New Orleans, 1925).

Sears, Louis M., "Slidell and Buchanan," *American Historical Review*, XXVII (July, 1922).

Sioussat, St. George L., "John Caldwell Calhoun," *The American Secretaries of State and Their Diplomacy*, edited by Samuel F. Bemis (New York, 1928), V.

Smith, Justin H., *The War with Mexico* (New York, 1919). 2 vols.

Smith, William E., *The Francis Preston Blair Family in Politics* (New York, 1933).

Stephenson, Nathaniel W., "California and the Compromise of 1850," *Pacific Historical Review*, IV (June, 1935), 114-22.

Sydnor, Charles S., *Slavery in Mississippi* (New York, 1933).

Turner, Frederick J., *The Rise of the New West* (New York, 1906).

Urban, Chester S., "New Orleans and the Cuban Question during the Lopez Expeditions of 1849-1851," *Louisiana Historical Quarterly*, XXII (October, 1939), 1095-167.

Vilá, Herminio Portell, *Historia de Cuba: En Sus Relaciones con los Estados Unidos y España* (Havana, 1938-1941). 4 vols.

———, *Narciso López y Su Época* (Havana, 1930), I.

Weinberg, Albert K., *Manifest Destiny: A Study of Nationalist Expansionism in American History* (Baltimore, 1935).

Wender, Herbert, *Southern Commercial Conventions: 1837-1859* (Baltimore, 1930).

Werner, M. R., *Tammany Hall* (Garden City, 1932).

Williams, Mary W., "John Middleton Clayton," *The American Secretaries of State and Their Diplomacy*, edited by Samuel F. Bemis (New York, 1928), VI.

Zaragoza, D. Justo, *Las Insurreciones en Cuba* (Madrid, 1872), I.

INDEX